GEOPOETRY

Recencies Series: Research and Recovery in Twentieth-Century American Poetics
Matthew Hofer, Series Editor

Also available in the Recencies Series:

Ingenious Pleasures: An Anthology of Punk, Trash, and Camp in Twentieth-Century Poetry
 edited by Drew Gardner
A Description of Acquaintance: The Letters of Laura Riding and Gertrude Stein, 1927–1930
 edited by Jane Malcolm and Logan Esdale
All This Thinking: The Correspondence of Bernadette Mayer and Clark Coolidge edited by
 Stephanie Anderson and Kristen Tapson
"A Serpentine Gesture": John Ashbery's Poetry and Phenomenology by Elisabeth W. Joyce
Evaluations of US Poetry since 1950, Volume 1: Language, Form, and Music edited by
 Robert von Hallberg and Robert Faggen
Evaluations of US Poetry since 1950, Volume 2: Mind, Nation, and Power edited by Robert
 von Hallberg and Robert Faggen
Expanding Authorship: Transformations in American Poetry since 1950 by Peter Middleton
Circling the Canon, Volume I: The Selected Book Reviews of Marjorie Perloff, 1969–1994 by
 Marjorie Perloff
Circling the Canon, Volume II: The Selected Book Reviews of Marjorie Perloff, 1995–2017
 by Marjorie Perloff
Modernist Poetry and the Limitations of Materialist Theory: The Importance of Constructivist Values by Charles Altieri

For additional titles in the Recencies Series, please visit unmpress.com.

GEOPOETRY

Geology, Materiality, Ecopoetics

DALE ENGGASS

University of New Mexico Press | Albuquerque

© 2023 by University of New Mexico Press
All rights reserved. Published 2023
Printed in the United States of America

First paperback printing 2025

ISBN 978-0-8263-6558-3 (cloth)
ISBN 978-0-8263-6803-4 (paper)
ISBN 978-0-8263-6559-0 (electronic)

Library of Congress Cataloging-in-Publication data is on file with the Library of Congress.

Founded in 1889, the University of New Mexico sits on the traditional homelands of the Pueblo of Sandia. The original peoples of New Mexico—Pueblo, Navajo, and Apache—since time immemorial have deep connections to the land and have made significant contributions to the broader community statewide. We honor the land itself and those who remain stewards of this land throughout the generations and also acknowledge our committed relationship to Indigenous peoples. We gratefully recognize our history.

Cover photograph by USGS on Unsplash

Designed by Felicia Cedillos
Composed in ITC Berkeley Oldstyle Std

For my parents

Language is a perfect Geology.
—*Walt Whitman*

Poetry agrees with science and not with logic.
—*Ernest Fenollosa*

Contents

Acknowledgments ix

INTRODUCTION. The Language of Geology and the Geology of Language 1

CHAPTER 1. Printed Matter: *Robert Smithson's Depositions* 20

CHAPTER 2. "The World Soul / Slumbers in Matter": Gunslinger *and* The Magic Door 39

CHAPTER 3. Bedrock and Drift: *Earth, Language, and Bodies in J. H. Prynne and Maggie O'Sullivan* 68

CHAPTER 4. "Clastic Mates": *Sedimentary Language in Clark Coolidge and Steve McCaffery* 99

CHAPTER 5. Cropping The Desert: *Erasure, Erosion, and Reclamation in Jen Bervin and John C. Van Dyke* 121

CHAPTER 6. Crystal Gazing 144

Notes 163

Works Cited 173

Index 179

Acknowledgments

The research and writing of the present text go back several years. What began as a dissertation at the University of Utah has arrived at its present form after a long process of rethinking and revision. Throughout its conception and writing, Craig Dworkin kept me going at many difficult junctures with his unflagging enthusiasm for the project (even at times when it may not have deserved it) and his uncanny ability to solve any impasse with a single, perspicacious question. This book would not have been possible without his insight and generosity. The deep knowledge and stimulating company of Maeera Shreiber, Monty Paret, Lance Olsen, and Kathryn Bond Stockton have shaped this book profoundly, and I am grateful for their patience and advocacy at many critical moments. For over a decade now, Anne Royston has been the best of intellectual companions.

At the University of New Mexico Press I am grateful to Matt Hofer not only for taking on this project as a series editor but also for first introducing me to the difficulties and delights of experimental writing as an educator. I am lucky to have stumbled into his "Politics of Form" class at UNM many years ago. I would like to thank senior acquisitions editor Elise M. McHugh for being a delight to work with throughout the editorial process and Christopher Hellwig for his careful attention to the final manuscript. I am also thankful for the thorough and incisive feedback from my two outside readers.

I am indebted to the many friends and colleagues who provided commentary, conversation, and emotional support as this book was being written: Jessica Alexander, Aaron Beasley, Lillian Yvonne-Bertram, Mandy Bloomfield, Jace Brittain, Sarah Dyer, Molly Gaudry, Robert Glick, Todd Goddard, Michelle McFarlane, Brenda Iijima, Paula Mendoza, Miriam

Nichols, Ali Pearl, Jennifer Power, Brian Reed, Andrew Shaw, Anna Thompson, Adam Tipps-Weinstein, Angela Toscano, Mary Toscano, and Rachel Zavecz. Thank you.

An earlier version of chapter 5 appeared in *Interdisciplinary Studies in Literature and the Environment* (Fall 2020), published by Oxford University Press.

Finally, thank you to my parents for their unwavering love and support.

INTRODUCTION

The Language of Geology and the Geology of Language

> Language is a messy object not because it is disorganized, or at best partly organized, but because it is made up of a sedimentation of meanings and rules.
> —Jean-Jacques Lecercle

This book examines writing that treats language as if it were a geologic structure. It argues that by presenting language as geologic and geology as linguistic, certain texts seek to enact a strong, nonarbitrary bond between word and thing, and thereby to enact geologic processes such as deposition, sedimentation, erosion, and stratification. In the following chapters, I demonstrate that this geologic understanding of language is central to works by an interconnected set of poets and artists including Robert Smithson, Ed Dorn, J. H. Prynne, Chris Torrance, Maggie O'Sullivan, Clark Coolidge, and Jen Bervin. When read collectively, their works—which range from sculpture and art criticism to poetry and artist books—model a meta*morphic* and not a meta*phoric* engagement with geology. That is, these are not (or not simply) works that use geologic terms metaphorically to point to human truths or thematize ecological concerns. Rather, these texts attempt to embody geologic movements through their formal attributes. In doing so, they are offshoots of a broader modernist tradition that privileges linguistic materiality and autonomy. However, if the now familiar invocation of the materiality of language inevitably calls up a post-Saussurean world of the arbitrary sign and endless *différance*, a unique feature of what I am calling "geopoetic" texts is their insistence on the possibility of a natural language, a language necessarily rooted in the earth.

This book thus makes two fundamental claims: that language's material aspects are germane to ecocriticism because they reveal how language outstrips human intentionality and that the writers in this study use geology to establish an innate connection between words and things—even as this connection is undermined by language's arbitrary effects, which they hope to transcend. Against a certain trepidation regarding the "linguistic turn" in some recent ecocritical and new materialist theory, then, I will argue that the texts covered in this book articulate an ecopoetic position through their assertion of language's material embeddedness in the world.[1] Moreover, if a revaluation of matter and the decentering of human agency are goals of ecopoetics, and of ecocriticism more broadly, then texts that present language as a thing operating beyond human control not only complicate our picture of human agency but also broaden a new materialist rethinking of "material" to include language itself. And they do so not by anthropomorphically finding human language everywhere they look, but by locating a nonhuman autopoiesis already operating *within* language.

The present study consists of six chapters organized by distinct geologic processes. Chapter 1 focuses on deposition—the process of depositing sand, salt crystals, or other types of sediment into layers—in the writing and artwork of Robert Smithson. Looking at visual texts like *A Heap of Language*, and multimedia, multisited works like the Nonsites and *Spiral Jetty*, I argue that several of Smithson's central conceits, including his presentation of time as an irreversible entropic flow and words as "printed matter" no different than rocks or minerals, are attempts to enact the process of deposition and thereby to challenge the related concepts of origins and historical progression. The depositional logic in Smithson's *Spiral Jetty* introduces, furthermore, a hint of natural language, in that the spiral lattice of the salt crystals, which precipitate on the jetty's basalt rocks when it is submerged under water, replicates in miniature the helical shape of the sculpture.

In chapter 2, I look at two book-length poems, Ed Dorn's *Gunslinger* and Chris Torrance's *The Magic Door*. *Gunslinger*'s implosion of historical periods and literary styles is often read as a postmodern rejection of place in favor of a meditation on time, but I show that in attending to the geology of the American Desert Southwest, Dorn's poem is far more specific about both matter and place than previous readings have indicated. *Gunslinger* contains extended passages describing the region's hoodoos—distinctive rock formations in which sandstone has been weathered over eons by wind and water into eerie, humanlike shapes—and the coalfields near Madrid, New Mexico, countering the deliberately generic and jokey depiction of the Wild West that dominates the poem. *The Magic Door* is likewise concerned with coal mining and the metamorphosis of matter, though Torrance fuses these interests in a Jungian exploration of myth and archetypes. For Torrance, the ancient menhirs, or standing stones, of South Wales (like hoodoos for Dorn) are lithic signifiers of deep, cyclical time. I demonstrate how each poem presents place as a *matrix*, a crucial word for both poets that they use to designate environmental surrounds and to trope on the word *matter*.

Chapter 3 examines the contrasting concepts of bedrock and drift in the work of the British poets J. H. Prynne and Maggie O'Sullivan. Beginning with Prynne's correspondence with Charles Olson in the 1960s and their shared interest in the theory of continental drift that was then being codified in England, the chapter shows that the sense that words derive directly from topography is central to Prynne's (and Olson's) poetics. This view presumes that etymology is bound up with the geophysical forces of earth formation, particularly, in Prynne's case, with the glacial drift, or deposits, that were left behind by the last major glaciation event in the Pleistocene and that formed the base for what would become the British Isles. For Prynne and O'Sullivan, the etymological and geodynamic dimensions are additionally bound up with physiology, and both poets propound an analogy between human skin and the Earth's surface, with Prynne going even farther to suggest a direct connection between language and physiognomy. While O'Sullivan's *A Natural History in 3 Incomplete Parts* extends Prynne's and Olson's project to get back to the roots, or bedrock, of the earth and language, the intricate sonic and homophonic play in her poems also revels in the contingencies of language. Instead of walling O'Sullivan's work off from ecopoetic urgency, however, this linguistic play opens onto sociopolitical issues of Thatcher-era England, including labor strife in the coal industry and the violent response of the state.

Chapter 4 returns to North America to sift through the clastic arrangements and embedded sediments in the work of poets Clark Coolidge and Steve McCaffery. I explain that Coolidge's arrangements of words into geologic structures like clastic rocks or colloidal solutions and McCaffery's experiments in a stratigraphy of language reflect a model of reading borrowed from geology. This model completely eschews conventional reading methods geared toward extracting meaning in favor of attending to the chance patterns of linguistic particles. I contend that reading language through the lens of geology emphasizes the unstable, excessive, and nonhuman alterity of language—the contingencies of language that McCaffery calls the "protosemantic."

Chapter 5 places Jen Bervin's artist book *The Desert* under the sign of erosion. Bervin employs a unique sewing method to produce an erasure of John C. Van Dyke's 1901 book of the same name, and I argue that Bervin's materials (needle, blue thread, and handmade paper) function as wind, water, and sand respectively to enact the process of erosion, creating a palimpsest that both dissolves and preserves the original text much as erosional forces weather and rearrange rock. Through her text's manifestation of fluid dynamics similar to those proposed in the work of Luce Irigaray, Bervin develops a porous and noisy space wherein humans and nature (or industry and deserts) are inextricable. In this way, Bervin complicates Van Dyke's romantic depiction of nature as an inherently pure realm free of human interference.

Finally, chapter 6 concludes the study by following the trajectory of the subgenre of the "crystal text" in works by Smithson, Coolidge, Christian Bök, Craig Dworkin, and Melissa Mack. Coolidge's *The Crystal Text* and Bök's *Crystallography*, I argue, display Smithson's marked influence through their attempt to construct a mineral language that adopts the very structure of the crystals it references. The conceit of mirroring, which appears consistently throughout this subgenre, plays on the connotation of transparency in the term *crystalline* to mark the opacity of the texts' language and their inability to adequately represent crystals and crystallization. Mack's *The Next Crystal Text*, however, updates this trope to offer a more socially and politically charged account that foregrounds the labor, exploitation, and environmental stakes of mineral extraction and processing that are often occluded from more rigidly aesthetic considerations of crystals.

Geologic Modernism

In *Imagining Language*, their vast anthology of the literary exception, Jed Rasula and Steve McCaffery document a wide array of linguistic experiments that hope to arrive at what they call "pansemiosis"—language and signification as "an encompassing feature of the planet" (471). Geologic concepts and metaphors feature prominently in the editors' introductory notes as they track the conceit of language-as-nature through Coleridge's wish "to destroy the old antithesis of *Words and Things*," Emerson's insistence that "language is a fossil poetry," Novalis's work as a mine inspector, and Whitman's affirmation that "[l]anguage is a perfect Geology, with its strata, formations, and developments" (471–74). In the search for a kind of primeval language where "words are conceived as arising from below," Rasula and McCaffery see geology as a "convenient analogy," though the prevalence of the geologic analogy indicates an abiding fascination among poets with seeing words as rocks (473). At the same time, their commentary complicates this picture of a "fossil poetry," as it also invokes the modernist conviction—repeated from Mallarmé to Paul de Man—that holds "that language achieves an autonomy exceeding that of its users" (471). In other words, there is a tension beneath the surface of the geologic analogy: a "natural" language—a nonarbitrary, intrinsic relationship between words and the world—is simultaneously subject to language's unmotivated flux. The art historian T. J. Clark, in an essay that touches on de Man's prospect of nonhuman language, articulates this paradox precisely when he writes, "The moment at which a text or depiction reaches out most irresistibly to a thing seen or expressed is also the moment at which it mobilizes the accidents and duplicities of markmaking most flagrantly, most outlandishly—all in the service of pointing through them, and somehow with them, to another body that is their guarantor" (99). The more writing attempts to be the thing it represents, the more it exercises accidental, chance congruities. The upshot, as we will see again and again in the following chapters, is that language can only ever be *as if* geologic, not simply because words can never completely coincide with the thing they refer to, but also because such linguistic experiments inevitably produce the very contingency they aspire to escape.

Writing in the context of modern American poetry, Carla Billitteri calls the desire for an imminent meaning in language in poets such as Charles Olson part of the "the American Cratylus" and sees in the efforts to arrive at such meaning the long shadow of Plato's dialogue on "the correctness of names" (15).[2] There is indeed a Cratylic aspect to the texts I focus on in this study, with their insistence that words and earth are inextricable. As efforts to escape what Olson labels the "UNIVERSE of discourse," (qtd. in Billitteri 124) which, Olson further claims, has severed humans from bodily, immediate, concrete experience, such Cratylic texts comprise one strand of a broader modernist project aimed at "the reclamation of a primordial sense of oneness with nature" (Mellors 2–3). One catalyst for such plans in Anglo-American modernism is Ernest Fenollosa's *The Chinese Written Character as a Medium for Poetry*. As compiled and edited by Ezra Pound, Fenollosa's research depicts Chinese ideograms as "shorthand pictures of actions or processes" or "transferences of force" grounded in natural relations and rhythms (qtd. in Latter 53). In its seminal influence on Pound's poetics, Fenollosa's study figures significantly in the development of modernist poetry in both America and Britain, in particular Olson's understanding of poetry in "Projective Verse" as a transference of forces.[3] Geologic metaphors are crucial to Fenollosa's theory of language. For instance, Fenollosa asserts that "the whole delicate substance of speech is built upon substrate of metaphor," suggesting, *pace* a Saussurean, structuralist account concerned with describing the general features of a *langue* and not the usage specific to a *parole*, that these facets of language are inextricable (qtd. in Latter 53). Indeed, Fenollosa contests that there is not, in fact, an arbitrary relationship between the substance of speech and its metaphorical substrate: "Abstract terms, pressed by etymology, reveal their ancient roots still embedded in direct actions. But the primitive metaphors do not spring from arbitrary subjective processes. They are possible only because they follow objective lines of relation in nature herself" (qtd. in Latter 53). This is a view of language as a set of dynamic relations that find their source in the earth itself. In Fenollosa's model, "The wealth of European speech grew, following slowly the intricate maze of nature's suggestions and affinities. Metaphor was piled upon metaphor in quasi-geological strata" (qtd. in Latter 54). Sounding almost like Smithson in this passage, Fenollosa turns metaphor itself into a geologic formation and avers that his articulation of processes of nature with those of language "is more than an analogy, it is identity of structure" (qtd. in Latter 54).

The identity of words and earth, of language and geodynamics, becomes, as we will see in chapter 3, a central tenet for Olson and Prynne and, through this Poundian and Olsonian lineage, informs to varying degrees the work of poets such as Dorn, McCaffery, and Coolidge. In other words, the works in the present study make it possible to track the development of a poetics in which language is embedded in the earth and the earth embedded in language. The geologic metaphor, which is at the same time more than a metaphor, "shifts the focus from discrete objects to the dynamic 'relations' that determine their standing to one another" (Latter 54). The "identity of structure" between these dynamic relations and language—a natural, non-arbitrary language—might seem to imply a mimetic model of language, and indeed, Pound's interpretation of Fenollosa's unfinished theories has been widely criticized for its misunderstanding of how Chinese ideograms actually work, not the least by Prynne, who, writing to Olson in 1963, lambasts "the complete wrong-headedness of the thing [. . .] (i.e., the 'pictographic' thesis)" that ignores "the absence of any subject-predicate analogy in Chinese 'sentence' structure" (Olson and Prynne 59–60).[4] Mediating these positions, Alex Latter argues that the Fenollosan model, as it was taken up by Olson and Prynne, "is perhaps not so much a mimetic theory of language as one that insists that, in their most fundamental relation to one another, language and the world are synonymous" (55).

As this model was developed in Olson's essays, poems, and, above all, his correspondence with younger poets such as Prynne and Dorn, geology, as Latter puts it, would become integral to "a recovery of shared meanings of words through etymology," a desire for linguistic renewal "focused not on budding innovation, but on the revitalization of the roots of language" (37). This reinvigoration of language emphasized "an ideal of correspondence of forms—that is, a mythic, restorative order that inhered in certain forms of language use" (38). The restoration ultimately aimed at was, in its most utopian expression, nothing less than the supposed origins of human society, in this case through the theory of a gift economy explicated by Marcel Mauss. Significantly, Mauss himself uses a common geologic metaphor when he writes that in this economy of symbolic exchange and obligation "we touch the bedrock" of human societies (qtd. in Latter 44). As an index of the lowest layer or foundation, whether of solid rock, etymological roots, or the basis of human culture, bedrock—or the drive to reach this bedrock—organizes and motivates the mingling of geology and linguistics in the Fenollosan and Olsonian tradition.

Instances in modernist poetry of excavations into the earth in search of bedrock are surprisingly common. For example, in "A" 22, Louis Zukofksy begins to "dig" into the strata of interrelated human and geologic histories, which overlap in a "lettered pebble" or "table of / law" (510). This literally wordy rock recalls the "[r]ipped up pebble stones of our tessellation" all the way back in "A" 4, a pun on the stone tablets of *Mosaic* Law housed in the Ark of the Covenant (13). The vast gap between the allusions to the pebble itself enacts the multitemporal layers that Zukofsky builds into the poem, as this gap is spatial, in terms of the nearly five hundred pages separating the moments in the complete "A," as well as temporal, in terms of both the time of the reader and that of the poet, who composed "A" 4 and "A" 22 over forty years apart.[5] Zukofsky marks these coexisting temporal scales at the start of the poem's long, columnar descent into the earth in the line "Late later and much later" (511). Here, however, we are actually taken back in time for a kind of condensed creation story of the earth that unfolds across geologic, rather than biblical, time. The poem's geologic litany details how "surge sea erupts boiling molten / lava island from ice" and indexes its own stratigraphic arrangement whereby

> earliest mountain the lowest the
> seas moil, thin earth crust
> resists less, thickened thrown highest;
> stone, coral time evoke chitin's—
> word time a voice bridled (511)

The "stone" resting on "word" repeats the "lettered pebble" that occasions this cross section of geologic strata and implies the literal identity of word and rock. The dynamism in the verbs "thrown" and "moil," moreover, provides a sense of what Rasula has noted as the Smithsonian "presentiments of language as heap" in "A," which allow for the "very tight, even elliptical, syntactic condensation" that enacts, in Rasula's terms, "*language indiscriminable from earth*" (142, 85; italics in original).

A similar sample of the search for bedrock appears in book 3 of William Carlos Williams's *Paterson*. Under the heading "SUBSTRATUM," Williams displays, in descending columns labeled "Depth" and "Description of Materials," a "tabular account of the specimens" recovered from a series of borings made in the "Artesian well at The Passaic Rolling Mill, Paterson." Williams's table is resolutely "unpoetic" in its laconic recording of feet below the surface and the type of rock encountered at each depth: "110 feet . . . Red sandstone, coarse / 182 feet . . . Red sandstone, and a little shale / 400 feet . . . Red sandstone, shaly" and so on (139). The list, which continues through thirty such entries to a depth of 2,100 feet, enacts, in a manner much more visually literal than Zukofsky's, the motif of digging into the earth. This "tabular account" of strata is a visual echo, albeit in a more rigid structure, of the arrangement two pages previous. There, Williams describes the water of the Passaic River (which drives the mill mentioned above) as "at this stage no lullaby but a piston, / cohabitous, scouring the stones" and "undermining the railroad embankment." As if in an enactment of this fluvial erosion, certain of the proceeding lines are set at slight angles such that the page seems to depict the "substratum" indexed by the borehole samples. At the center of this earlier passage sits "a red-butted reversible minute-glass / loaded with / salt-like white crystals / flowing"—a curious detail that anticipates the note at the bottom of the bore samples observing "[t]he fact that the rock salt of England, and of some of the other salt mines of Europe, is found in rocks of the same age as this [i.e., at 2,100 feet], raises the question whether it may not also be found here" (137, 139).

Williams's geologic survey of the Passaic, with its repetitive register of raw materials and association of salt with time, is a clear precursor to Robert Smithson's work, particularly his description in the essay "Spiral Jetty" of the "Mud, salt crystals, rocks, water" that stretch out in every direction from his sculpture on the Great Salt Lake (149).[6] Smithson is a hinge figure in this study, as he is both an inheritor, through his connection and response to Williams's geologic interests, of the Anglo-American modernist tradition I'm tracing here and a key influence and fellow traveler of later-generation poets, such as Clark Coolidge, through his affiliation with the journal *0 to 9*, edited by Vito Acconci and Bernadette Mayer. Specifically, one of the main assertions of Smithson's work that aligns it with works I am calling geopoetic is, as Rasula writes in relation to Zukofsky and Olson, the "dynamic recognition of thought *as matter*" (88; italics in original). This recognition is not just one of seeing written language as "printed matter," but more fundamentally one of recalling that the human brain itself is a function of material interactions.[7]

Invoking the materiality of thought—and language—by way of geology raises two central and related tensions. First, there is the interplay of surface and depth. Geology and stratigraphy are often thought of as studying the depths of the earth: strata are said to "descend" both spatially and temporally. Geologic time suggests "deep" time. While this depth model is no doubt true of certain aspects of geology, such as petroleum exploration and the taking of core samples, it is important to remember that in reading strata (at a road cut, for instance) geologists are also reading surfaces—horizontal cross sections of the earth. A similar point holds regarding the effect created by a geologically informed poetry. As Rasula remarks, in relation to Olson's stratigraphy of Dogtown in *The Maximus Poems*, "It becomes possible to read layers of earth as multitemporal surfacing" (86). That is, in place of a depth model of strata—with its attendant resonances of human psychology—we might see geologic strata, and the texts I consider in this book, as a set of layered surfaces the material features and relations of which can be described. As I will discuss in chapter 1, this is precisely how Smithson views strata: as the ongoing accumulation of time on a surface and not as a descent into the depths (of earth, meaning, or psychology). The buildup, and opacity, of surfaces is what Smithson refers to when he writes in "A Museum of Language in the Vicinity of Art" that "language 'covers' rather than 'discovers' its sites and situations" (78). A geologic language holds the promise of both a univocal bedrock and the proliferation of polysemy.

In chapter 2, this friction comes to the fore in Ed Dorn's *Gunslinger* through the dichotomy of inside and outside, which Dorn's poem hopes to undermine by melding word and world, while Chris Torrance's *The Magic Door* embraces a Jungian, depth-psychology model of geology. My readings in this study likewise take their cue from the descriptive aspect of geology as well as from the material form of the signifier foregrounded by the texts themselves. In other words, the opaque, linguistically dense surface of these works requires modes of reading that parallel a descriptive, geologic approach. The methodology of this book, then, consists of close readings that track material aspects of language such as sound, the composition of the page, the material supports of the book-as-object, and the tangled webs of (occasionally spurious) etymological genealogies. While I am not suggesting that surface must always be preferred to depth, or that there are only surfaces, my mode of reading here reflects my sense that if a language is composed of layers of sedimented meanings, this sedimentation remains visible on the words' surface, not buried within words from where it must be excavated. The sedimented history of etymological relations can be traced by attending to the words as they appear on the page.

The second tension concerns the competing notions of bedrock and drift. The geopoetic attempt to recover a natural language—one bound to and deriving from nonhuman forces and rhythms—presumes that language forms a solid fundament, a bedrock or origin, coextensive with a particular topography. If "[t]he repeated metaphor of geological layering seems . . . borne from a desire to establish something solid," or, as Prynne puts it, seeks to acquire "access to the pressure of solid bedrock," then the primary method writers like Prynne and Olson use to locate this bedrock is etymological: they trace words back to proto–Indo-European roots (qtd. in Latter 58–59). I will have more to say about this method and its presumptions in chapter 3, but here I will simply note that this conception of a bedrock language derived from the nonhuman world is inseparable from linguistic drift, and in this it parallels a similar contradiction in geology. The articulation of a nonarbitrary language rooted in the earth relies upon the very contingencies of signification (such as, for instance, the chance material convergence of words in homophones or orthographic similarities) that this etymological approach is supposed to abolish. Likewise, the seeming solidity of geologic bedrock belies the fact that the earth's crust rides, or drifts, atop the plastic fluctuations of the mantle. Indeed, these parallel tensions are united in Olson's and Prynne's well-documented attention to the theory of continental drift as it emerged into the scientific mainstream in the 1950s and 1960s, and their hope that it could help reconstruct a formerly coherent, unified world. A further corollary of the tension between bedrock and drift is the lingering anxiety that words can never coincide with the objects they signify. In other words, attempts to regenerate a natural language imply that the geologic metaphor is more than a metaphor, that words *are* rocks and vice versa. As in Fenollosa's theories, the texts covered in this book want, at least at times, to propose geology and language as not analogous but identical.

Nonhuman Language

Ironically, the failure of words to be identical to things, far from invalidating the ecocritical purchase of the works in this study, reveals a nonhuman dimension of language that subverts uncritical claims of human agency. Words are thinglike not because they hold immanent meanings but because they produce autonomous effects. As Rob Halpern argues regarding George Oppen, a "geological imagination" wavers between despair regarding the inevitable triumph of the "idiot stone" over the human universe and the poetic possibilities for clarity in "the mineral fact" (42). For Oppen, the "stone" is a marker of the nonhuman realm that exceeds human temporality; the stone was here before humans and will be here after the end of human history. Oppen, however, wants the poem, in its encounter with a nonhuman outside, "to be the equivalent of the autonomous stone," the radically other that, in an echo of Heidegger, constantly withdraws from humans into an incomprehensible opacity (58). As Halpern further explains, the upshot of Oppen's realism—his attempts to render "the mineral fact" of the outside—is that "words bear the burden of impossibly coinciding with phenomena one can never immediately apprehend" (52). As a result of words' failure to be the objects they replace, poetry is left with the pursuit of a radical clarity, where clarity refers less to an easy transmissibility, according to Oppen, than to a "great mineral silence" aspiring to, while of necessity never reaching, "a word with no sound" (qtd. in Halpern 51–53).[8] Or, as Oppen himself puts it in widely noted lines from *Of Being Numerous*, "Words cannot be wholly transparent. And that is the / 'heartlessness' of words" (*New Collected Poems* 194).[9]

The perception of language as a nonhuman force that speaks humans as much as humans speak it, is not, then, simply a holdover from the "theory decades" in literary criticism, an overly abstract and, paradoxically, nonmaterialist time from which we have thankfully moved on.[10] Rather, it is a fundamental and wide-reaching feature of modernist poetics, the other side of the dream of a natural language.

Indeed, the importance of language's nonhuman, material aspects for ecocriticism can be discerned in as resolutely poststructuralist a tract as Jean-Jacques Lecercle and Denise Riley's *The Force of Language*. Echoing decades of poststructural linguistics, Lecercle and Riley describe language as a *délire* in which words signify beyond the intentions or desires of readers, writers, or speakers. Moreover, they present language as thoroughly material. Against what they deem the essentialist (i.e., genetic) and ahistorical concept of language developed by Noam Chomsky, Lecercle and Riley posit an unorthodox Marxist view wherein language is always entangled with history and ideology as well as being utterly corporeal. Language is produced by bodies and, as Riley's examination of "bad words" and hate speech attests, language pierces bodies, making our "inner speech" always already outer (39). In their account, language is quite literally a material force bound up with the other material forces of the world. Most relevant for my argument here, Lecercle, in his section of the book, contests any theory that fetishizes language, that is, that reifies the open-ended, collective process of language into a fixed thing or fact. To counteract the spread of language fetishism, Lecercle prescribes the "continental pragmatics" of Gilles Deleuze and Félix Guattari, for whom "[t]he central concept of linguistics, the source of utterances, the entity constituted by language as it speaks is not the individual speaker but the *collective assemblage of enunciation*" (Lecercle and Riley 140). The key strength of this theory, for Lecercle, "is that, far from separating language from the rest of the world into a reified system, it involves *ontological mixture*" of "bodies (of speakers and addressees), institutions . . . [and] utterances" (140–41). This "ontological mixture" not only corresponds to the image of language as intertwined with the dynamic processes of the earth detailed in *Geopoetry* but also resists the melancholic stance that humans are hopelessly "spoken by" language. Rather, Lecercle and Riley contend that humans are both interpolated by language and, in turn, interpolate language. Humans may be subject to language, but this situation is what allows for language's noninstrumental, noncommunicative (that is, creative) possibilities. My point is that this nonhuman dimension of language does not have to be a terrifying dystopian agency and could, instead, be embraced as an inherent feature of our collective contingency.[11] Both the mixing of nonhuman with human bodies and the contingency this mixing indicates are fundamental propositions of ecocriticism. Attending to language's nonhuman features can therefore be a productive ecocritical project in that it reveals how language is itself a material force, and, as such, "is never an instrument" and "is not necessarily, not even centrally, meant to allow the exchange of information" (Lecercle and Riley 85).

Geopoetry thus expands this long-running account of linguistic materiality by extending it to the sphere of ecocriticism. If ecocriticism and related projects such as new materialism have helped reassert the rights of the nonhuman world, they have not paid particular attention to writing and art that foregrounds language as itself an object. This lack of interest in language may stem from the fact that, from Lawrence Buell to Jane Bennett, ecocriticism has situated itself as a return to matter and the nonhuman world after poststructuralism's supposed fixation on abstractions like signification and inscription. Thus, if the materiality of language feels obvious, its implications in an ecocritical context, where literature and art are still mainly written about in terms of content and a piece's potential political efficacy, have hardly begun to be appreciated. I'm convinced, however, that ecocritical and radical formalist approaches are not mutually exclusive. Indeed, work in the ecopoetic subset of ecocriticism, such as that undertaken by Jonathan Skinner, founding editor of the journal *ecopoetics*, or Brenda Iijima, to name only two, has attended more closely to formal concerns and possibilities.[12] Even in this context, however, language as itself a material force has not come in for extended treatment. Despite this, texts that foreground the noncommunicative, nonrepresentational side of language might amplify ecocriticism's ethical imperative to decenter a humanist perspective. Writing about the use of texts in earth art by artists such as Smithson, Amanda Boetzkes argues,

"A crucial aspect of the textual artwork is . . . to reveal the impossibility of subsuming the earth into representational form" (57). In "consider[ing] . . . how nature troubles representational form," such texts concur with "what in eco-philosophy is known as recessive ethics: a stance of retraction from and receptivity to the earth that forgoes the propensity to actively subsume it within the parameters of our preexisting logic" (4). The texts I analyze in *Geopoetry* undertake a similar project, eschewing representation for the material excess of both language and earth. Just as the artworks, performances, and texts Boetzkes discusses "rather than presenting the spectator with information (scientific facts about ecosystems or environmental degradation)" instead ask her "to stand, watch, and wait for elementals to reveal themselves" (45–46), the works in this study do not present conventional arguments *about* ecology (or geology) as much as they demand that the reader attend meticulously to language as matter. I hope, therefore, that *Geopoetry* can show how the materiality of language, however long a critical precedent it might have, remains relevant for understanding the range of methods by which writing grapples with ecological questions and environmental crisis.

"The Geologic Turn"

In his 2011 article titled "New Cultural Geology," Mark McGurl sensed a "geologic turn" in the humanities (381). Citing the accelerating effects of global warming and our extractive fossil fuel economy, McGurl argues that the era of postmodernism, which he defines as the domination of poststructuralist thought fixated on questions of language—and by extension uninterested in realist ontological claims—has been superseded by a newly relevant awareness of deep geologic time he calls the "exomodern." This new epoch confronts humans with "a state of affairs that long predated human consciousness" and announces that "what we call the 'ground' is no ground at all, but the result of a process whose own ground is another, antecedent process extending backward in time" (384). For McGurl, the exomodern unearths a frightening realization: the advent of the Anthropocene reveals humans as "the terror . . . but only insofar as [humans] are discovered to be 'non-human' in precisely the way a stone is—in being careless of the fate of the other" (388).[13] Put slightly differently, the nonhuman is revealed to be already *within* humans, exposing the contingency and instability of humans' supposed dominance of the planet. Despite his concern with the impact of this "turn" on the humanities, McGurl does not explicitly discuss what our newfound nonhumanity means for the study of language. Part of my argument in the present study is that an unconventional, experimental literature has been engaged with nonhuman language for quite a while, and it can thus help show us what such a "turn" looks like for language and for humans.

The elucidation of the material aspects of language thus contains important parallels to theoretical work in posthumanism. Rosi Braidotti, for instance, defines posthumanism as not so much the end of the human as the end of humanism, a paradigm in which "the human is a normative convention . . . instrumental to practices of exclusion and discrimination." The humanist subject, for Braidotti, expands "a specific mode of being human into a generalized standard, which acquires transcendent value as *the* human," assumed to be male, European, and heterosexual (26). Following the Foucault of *The Order of Things*, Braidotti exposes the human as "a historical construct" and argues that given this universalized figure's legacy of colonization and climate disruption, "'Man' requires a form of estrangement and a radical repositioning on the part of the subject" (88). Braidotti's appeal for "estrangement" recalls the Russian formalist literary critic Viktor Shklovsky and his famous assertion that art defamiliarizes the everyday and is thus able "to make the stone *stony*" (12). We might say, instead, that geopoetic writing makes the *word* stony—and the stone *wordy*.

Indeed, the presentation of language as geologic challenges not only humanist thought but also much ecocriticism through its deviation from an organic to an inorganic emphasis. That is, much of the most prominent ecocritical thought decenters human agency by insisting on a vitality of matter and investing the nonhuman with a lively presence. Geopoetry, by contrast, bypasses organicist models of matter—and their implicit privileging of life, whether human or nonhuman—to foreground rocks, stones, deserts, and rubble. My articulation of geopoetry diverges, then, from other recent theories of "geopoetics," such as that developed by Kenneth White, which champions deep ecology through a "higher unity" of poetry with geography (174), or that of Joan Elizabeth Brandt in her study of mimesis in postmodern French poetry, which primarily concerns questions of human geography and mapping. Instead, the "geopoetry" of my title designates writing in which the enactment of geology reveals language's material, nonhuman operation.

The inorganic force of nonhuman language is an illustration of what Kathryn Yusoff calls the "micropolitical" incitement of "geologic subjects," an awareness that the nonhuman is "not a step beyond, but within the very composition of the human" ("Geologic Subjects" 383). For Yusoff, this "possibility to think different relations with the earth" in excess of human subjects (389) is arrived at through, in the words of Claire Colebrook, "attend[ing] to those differences that we neither intend, nor perceive, nor command" (qtd. in "Geologic Subjects" 399). Building on both Georges Bataille's theory of general economy and Maurice Blanchot's definition of "communism" as a welcoming of the impossible, Yusoff further contends that if we are "to break [the] reproductive logic of utility, language as a *relation* must be fractured and those breaks intensified." This reimagined language will "speak 'beyond the horizon of the familiar, to that which is unpredictable, undecidable, and irreducibly multiple in its consequences and effects'" ("Politics of the Anthropocene" 268). *Geopoetry* hopes to illuminate how certain literary works of the past fifty years have managed to "intensif[y]" this erosion of familiar language.

If Yusoff echoes the geologic approach to the materiality and nonhuman facets of language characteristic of the works I focus on in this study, she also shows that geology itself is far from being a neutral discipline separated from its social and historical contexts. Tracing the emergence of the science in Europe in the late eighteenth and early nineteenth centuries, Yusoff elucidates the ties between geology, extractive economies, and the slave trade.[14] Yusoff's larger point, then, is that the discourse of geology is inextricable from this history of violence, dispossession, and the burgeoning of extractive economies—and, thus, the social, political, and economic foundations of the Anthropocene. While I will go into greater detail about geologic "golden spikes" and the contested beginning of the Anthropocene in chapter 1, here I only want to point out the ironic twist in which the science so bound up with extractive practices such as mining and petroleum drilling—arguably two of the main drivers of climate change and habitat loss—is centrally involved in determining the start date of the Anthropocene. As Yusoff puts it, the "planetary analytic" of geology "has failed to do the work to properly identify its *own* histories of colonial earth-writing, to name the masters of broken earths, and to redress the legacy of racialized subjects that geology leaves in its wake" (*Billion Black Anthropocenes* 2).[15]

For now, however, I want to tie these concerns to the related matter of these texts' political and ecological import. That is, the texts I am concerned with in this book do not, in the main, seem to point to or address ecological issues in any thematic or rhetorically conventional way. They do not contain an obvious ecological message or agenda. Smithson, in particular, expressed skepticism about the goals of the expanding ecological movement in the early 1970s, and his interventions such as *Spiral Jetty* have been regarded—by both Smithson and his critics—as directly antithetical to ecological objectives.[16] However, as I detail in chapter 1, Smithson did not decide to build *Spiral Jetty* on the north shore of the Great Salt Lake simply so he could incise the surface of an otherwise undisturbed shoreline. Instead, that specific site intrigued him because it was already disrupted by the rusting machines, scattered industrial debris, and tar seeps from an abandoned oil-drilling camp and thus suggested a jumble of different times and speeds that his sculpture could engage and transform with. Far from inimical to ecological issues, then, Smithson's insistence on a "dialectical landscape" that is always already shaped by the co-interaction of human and nonhuman forces, feels even more relevant now in the third decade of the twenty-first century, as humans face accelerating ecological and environmental disturbances that cannot simply be reversed through conservation or undone by "green" consumer habits (157–71).[17]

In a similar fashion, the works in this study may initially appear to have little to do with pressing ecological or cultural affairs. But in their attention to the material qualities of words—their disruption of language as a transparent medium for communication—and their enactment of geologic processes in language, they divulge an assortment of specific political and ecological concerns, including the destructive legacy of railroads and mining (chapters 1 and 2), miners' strikes and police violence (chapter 3), water reclamation and industrial agriculture (chapter 5), and the lucrative market for rare earth minerals (chapter 6). In other words, there need not be an opposition between texts that foreground the materiality of words and their sociopolitical resonance; these works enact an ecologically minded politics in enacting geologic processes.

While the texts I cover have not typically been read in ecocritical terms, this book demonstrates that they extend the ecocritical project of closing the gap between language and the nonhuman world. Lawrence Buell, in his foundational work *The Environmental Imagination*, argues that for most of the twentieth century, literary discourse sought to render the text an artifact cut off from world and adrift in the "spacious domain of textuality" (86). Writing after successive waves of new criticism, structuralism, poststructuralism, and historicism, and before the resurrection of new materialism, Buell wants to affirm that literature (especially nonfiction) can represent nature, even if that representation is necessarily imperfect or incomplete.

Against the view that assumes representation can only mean mimesis, Buell recommends "what the poet-critic Francis Ponge calls *adéquation*: verbalizations that are not replicas but equivalents of the world of objects, such that writing in some measure bridges the abyss that inevitably yawns between language and the object-world" (97–98). I contend that the geologic texts in the present study speak to Buell's concern with the strict separation of text and environment. Yet, as I discussed above, they are also not especially interested in "representing" nature. Rather, these geopoetic texts reorient representation from a matter of correspondence to one of the text's internal relations. Smithson's depositions or Coolidge's clastic constructions do not depict, but instead attempt to create textual *equivalents of*, geologic phenomena. These texts envision language along the lines of the philosopher Alfred North Whitehead, who, as Astrid Lorange explains, "suggests that language ought to be considered as a part of the world, as something that is already coexistent in the things it is perceived to represent" (80). In bridging Buell's abyss, this view of language rejects the human/nonhuman—and even organic/inorganic—binary and reminds us of our material (un)grounding in the world.

CHAPTER 1

Printed Matter
Robert Smithson's Depositions

> Every landscape appears first of all as a vast chaos, which leaves one free to choose the meaning one wants to give it.
> —*Claude Lévi-Strauss*

An exploration of fractured, ruptured language and landscapes permeates the work of the artist Robert Smithson, whose writing and sculpture center concepts from geology—such as deposition, sedimentation, crystallization, and golden spikes—to display the thinginess of words. Or, arguing from the opposite angle, Amanda Boetzkes explains that in site-specific sculptures like *Spiral Jetty*, Smithson uses materials and elements from the site such that "the impenetrability of light and the fragmentation of earth enact the instability of signification" (77). Smithson's material approach to language and his insistence on process over discrete, bounded objects explain a large part of his influence on avant-garde poetics from the 1960s onwards, and his conflation of words with rocks will reverberate throughout this book. For Smithson, if geologic materials enact the volatility of signs, geology also reveals the earth's own instability and fragmentation, the awareness of which has immense consequences for the artist's understanding of time, material, and language. For each of these three categories, Smithson foregrounds a model of deposition, the buildup of fragmented sediments that forms strata.[1] In his work, deposition presents the accumulation of time not in the sense of an orderly progression of events but as an accretion of entropic heaps. Similarly, Smithson treats language more like a slag pile from which to gather shards than a rational tool for communication: words are always in the process of losing their meanings, their senses disintegrating and recombining under the pressure of Smithson's mineral and material practice.

Books on geology, mineralogy, and crystals featured prominently in the index of Smithson's library compiled by Valentin Tatransky, and from these texts Smithson developed a view of matter as fundamentally fractured.[2] In his essay "A Sedimentation of the Mind," possibly the most comprehensive summation of Smithson's artistic theory and praxis, he asserts that "no materials are solid, they all contain caverns and fissures. Solids are particles built up around flux, they are objective illusions supporting grit, a collection of surfaces ready to be cracked" (107). The advances of quantum physics, or, moving in the opposite direction, the theories of the pre-Socratic philosopher Heraclitus, whom Smithson was fond of quoting, are plausible sources of Smithson's thoughts about materiality. However, geology is at the core of his insistence that artists familiarize themselves with the nonsolid solids of the earth. If an artist resists the impulse to process and otherwise refine these materials, Smithson suggests, then "the artist begins to know the corroded moments, the carboniferous states of thought, the shrinkage of mental mud, in the geologic chaos" (107). This chaos, the telluric mess that the artist merges with, would become increasingly central to Smithson's art and writing in the late 1960s and into the 1970s.

Heaps and Nonsites

The conflation of mind and matter implied in the phrase "mental mud," and brought about through attending to the earth's geology, bears directly on Smithson's practice of institutional critique. As is well known, Smithson, along with contemporaries such as Nancy Holt, Michael Heizer, Walter de Maria, and Donald Judd, began in the mid-1960s to think beyond the confines of studio and gallery spaces and to devise projects intended for specific sites outside of the museum. As far as Smithson was concerned, the space of the museum was itself antithetical to a geologically inflected practice.

Smithson holds that the museum is a product of the nineteenth century and conceived in terms of Renaissance history; therefore, "Time had yet to extend into the distant future (post-history) or into the distant past (pre-history)—nobody thought much about 'flying saucers' or an Age of Dinosaurs" (85). But while the (art) museum keeps "modern art . . . trapped in temporality" (84), this is not necessarily true of Smithson's beloved American Museum of Natural History:

> [T]he "meanings" in the Museum of Natural History avoided any reference to the Renaissance, yet it does show "art" from the Aztec and American Indian periods—are those periods any more or less "natural" than the Renaissance? I think not—because there is nothing "natural" about the Museum of Natural History. "Nature" is simply another 18th- and 19th-century fiction. (85)

If art museums are limiting not simply in their institutional imperatives and spatial parameters, but also in their erasure of both pre-and posthistory, the Museum of Natural History demonstrates, perhaps counter to its own interests, the artificiality of human categories, especially the category of "nature." The Museum of Natural History thus comes closer than modern art museums to approximating Smithson's injunction that art "must instead explore the pre- and post-historic mind; it must go into the places where remote futures meet remote pasts" (113). Smithson implies that his fascination with the geologic past is equally a fascination with the distant future and signals his desire for a museum devoted to times before and after the human.

Indeed, for Smithson, the earth itself plays this role: "The strata of the Earth is a jumbled museum" (110). Unlike the rational organization of the typical museum, which tends to lead visitors through a linear progression and group objects according to period or style, Smithson's stratigraphic museum upends pretensions to order and linearity. In strata, the overlapping layers of time and sediment, Smithson saw the disintegration and not the coherence, the wreck and not the creation, of the earth. Smithson's vision here is remarkably similar to Jussi Parikka's description of geologic history: "For Darwin . . . the fossil record is like a book with only fragments left; it is only a fragmented part of a totality that cannot be discovered" (117). Like the ruin in the account of allegory developed by the art critic Craig Owens (to which I will turn shortly), the fossil record points, for Parikka, to an irrecoverable whole. The entropic construction of strata, Parikka adds, "demonstrates the essential: the archaic and the current are entangled through such fossil monuments" (117). While we may imagine geology to be a science that discovers and orders the earth's history, Parikka and Smithson counter that in so doing, geology also unearths the significant and ongoing role chance and contingency play in the arrangement of the world. In other words, Smithson—like the writers in this study and theorists such as Yusoff—is intrigued by the ways in which a geologic perspective can disrupt the illusions of stability, history, and human suppression of the nonhuman.

Throughout the latter half of his abbreviated career (he died in a plane crash in 1973 at the age of thirty-five), Smithson worked to document this sense of disruption in sculpture, installations, texts, maps, site-specific earthworks, and films. Key to each of these disparate approaches is the continual movement and mediation provoked through strategies of displacement. This is demonstrated most succinctly in his famous Nonsites. Beginning in the mid-1960s, Smithson created a series of sculptures meant to "contain" or "give evidence of" the artist's experience of working outside the studio amid the "physical abyss of raw matter." To construct a Nonsite, Smithson would, for instance, collect rocks from the "uncontained" site of a slate quarry and then place these rocks in a sort of trapezoidal enclosure. This container—the Nonsite—was then displayed in a gallery setting, accompanied by a mixture of photographs, maps, and other textual material that seems to point back to the site but in fact registers yet another displacement from any unmediated, original ground for the piece. In this way, Smithson "tries to give evidence of this experience [of the site] through a limited (mapped) revision of the original unbounded state" (104). The containers, which crucially for Smithson function as three-dimensional maps, "gather *in* the fragments" that the artist collects from the site. Nonsites, then, enact deposition in two senses: as a sculpture, they are rocks that have been deposited in a container; as a conceptual apparatus, meanwhile, they present a literalization of the word "deposition." In their melding of inside and outside, Nonsites *de-position* the observer, suspending her between gallery space and extraction site, site as textual representation and text as material site. In this way, the project instigates an unresolved dialectic between the artwork (ostensibly the container of rocks and dirt) and its textual supplements (the photographs and maps). In a note appended to his essay "The Spiral Jetty," Smithson traces the parameters of this "Dialectic of Site and Nonsite," juxtaposing the Site's open, scattered, and indeterminate status with the Nonsite's closed, contained, and abstract qualities. For Smithson, the appeal of the dialectic is that "[b]oth sides are present and absent at the same time" and chart "a course of hazards, a double path made up of signs, photographs, and maps that belong to both sides of the dialectic at once" (152–53). As Smithson's explanation makes clear, both the container and the maps are, in fact, maps of the site—that is, they are both texts.

This deployment of maps and other means of mediation indicates the centrality of language and text in Smithson's practice. Many commentators—most prominently Craig Owens, Lytle Shaw, and Richard Sieburth—have detailed the way Smithson (and other minimalists of his generation such as Sol LeWitt) erased the boundary between artwork and textual apparatus.[3] Owens, in his seminal essay "Earthwords," argues conclusively for what he calls "the reciprocity of [Smithson's] verbal and visual" practices, and for how this eruption of language into image, and image into language, renders Smithson's work allegorical in the sense Walter Benjamin employs to describe language that is fragmented and atomized (124).

While the importance of language in Smithson's output is clear, far less has been said regarding his distinctly linguistic approach to geology and geologic approach to language. If rocks create abstract, cartographic signs in the Nonsites, then words produce a cracked, fissured sediment in Smithson's written texts. Extending his analogy of the earth's strata as a "jumbled museum," Smithson claims, "Embedded in the sediment is a text that contains limits and boundaries which evade the rational order, and social structures which confine art. In order to read the rocks we must become conscious of geologic time. . . . When one scans the ruined sites of pre-history one sees a heap of wrecked maps that upsets our present art historical limits" (110). Here again are the basic tenets of Smithson's geologic vision: the telluric is both text and map; specifically, a disturbed, disrupted map that obscures rather than delimits boundaries as it fuses the prehistoric and the speculative future. Reading the rocks results in "a rubble of logic" rather than the rational, carefully historicized discourse favored by formalist critics of the time such as Michael Fried. For Smithson, "A sense of the Earth as a map undergoing disruption leads the artist to the realization that nothing is certain or formal. Language itself becomes mountains of symbolic debris" (110). The analogy of language to lithic detritus—which seems to simultaneously transcend the realm of analogy in Smithson's insistence that language "becomes" rock— leads directly to Smithson's well-known assertion: "My sense of language is that it is matter and not ideas—i.e., 'printed matter'" (61). Appearing as a kind of postscript to a Dwan Gallery press release for a 1967 show tellingly titled *Language To Be Looked At and/or Things To Be Read*, this statement is perhaps the clearest announcement of the familiar (if nebulously defined) phrase "the materiality of language." For Smithson, at least, "the materiality of language" means that language and semiotic systems more broadly are simply another potential material with which to make art. Words are equivalent to paint, steel, sand, or rock.

Yet what is most striking about these passages is the matter-of-fact manner in which they combine the seemingly disparate fields of language and geology. In fact, while Owens does not focus on this aspect in his "Earthwords" essay, an image borrowed from geology lies at the heart of Benjamin's own description of allegory. In "transform[ing] things and works into stirring writing," allegory, says Benjamin, "opens up a gulf in the solid massif of verbal meaning and forces the gaze into the depths of language" (qtd. in Owens 124). For Benjamin, there is a double process of destruction and creation—or, we might say, of erosion and sedimentation—at work in allegory that disperses rather than consolidates meaning. The mountain ("massif") of meaning is eroded not to eradicate meaning altogether but to then concentrate and deposit meaning in a series of fragments that, crucially, is never complete (Owens 124).

Smithson echoes Benjamin's imagery of erosion and cavernous language in a passage from "A Sedimentation of the Mind" that I take to be the keystone of his view of printed matter:

> The names of minerals and the minerals themselves do not differ from each other, because at the bottom of both the material and the print is the beginning of an abysmal number of fissures. Words and rocks

> contain a language that follows a syntax of splits and ruptures. Look at any *word* long enough and you will see it open up into a series of faults, into a terrain of particles each containing its own void. This discomfiting language of fragmentation offers no easy gestalt solution; the certainties of didactic discourse are hurled into the erosion of the poetic principle. (107)

Smithson describes language the same way he describes solids: as riven by fractures and refusing the stability implied by logic, the logos. Moreover, Smithson makes the analogy between print and matter (or words and minerals) literal, insisting that a name and the object it names do not differ; signifier and signified cannot be distinguished. At first glance, this account of language, which Owens calls allegorical, might appear as a naïve linguistic essentialism, as if Smithson were arguing that there is an inherent and necessary relation between a word and its referent. But Smithson is quick to point out that there is "no easy gestalt solution," no original or final substance on which either language or matter rests. It's fissures all the way down. This almost Derridean disavowal of the solidity, or self-presence, of language (not to mention matter) encapsulates Smithson's radical poetics, in which "the poetic principle" is more about the erosion than the creation of sense. The paradoxical process by which objects can be eroded into being, or ruins can be constructed, influenced Smithson's theories of time, history, and entropy. At the conclusion of the passage quoted at length above, Smithson avers that poetry "is somehow a product of exhaustion rather than creation. Poetry is always a dying language but never a dead language" (107). In his writing and his artwork, which are not separate endeavors but two aspects of the same practice, Smithson sought to enact unending erosional movement of poetry over the illusory certainties of didactic discourse.

This attraction to a language that is disruptive and destabilizing, rather than language as a communicative tool, aligns Smithson with the other writers in this study. The connection is not necessarily one of direct influence—though Clark Coolidge's work, discussed in chapter 4, engages with, and often literally incorporates, Smithson's writing and mineralogical investigations. Rather, Smithson's geologically informed praxis makes one prominent node within a network of relations of artists and writers who experiment with language as primarily matter and not ideas. As Smithson puts it in an essay with another telling title, "A Museum of Language in the Vicinity of Art," the kind of language that most interests him "'covers' rather than 'discovers' its sites and situations . . . 'closes' rather than 'discloses' doors to utilitarian interpretations and explanations" (78). In a 1973 interview, Smithson states that "language is physical rather than mental" and contends that all language is "a sort of accumulation of languages; one strata—like stratas of language—and one just mines this strata. It's a matter of just rooting through the heaps of language that are around and then constructing language rather than trying to get at reality or something like that" (Roth 89). Anticipating Braidotti and Yusoff's calls to undermine utility, Smithson seeks language that abjures its usefulness. Language that is aware of its materiality, language that presents an impediment to reading, that makes one read as if one has sand in one's eyes or rocks in one's mouth—such is the printed matter that Smithson and, I argue, Dorn, Prynne, O'Sullivan, Coolidge, McCaffery, Bervin, and others produce through their enactment of geologies.

Perhaps the clearest example of Smithson's material approach to working with language is his 1966 piece *A Heap of Language*. This pyramid of self-reflexive words about words, handwritten in pencil, and spreading out across a 6 ½ by 22–inch sheet of graph paper, suggests a cross between a concrete poem and an architectural sketch. As Richard Sieburth explains, in terms that echo Owens's description of earthwords, the piece "can be viewed either as an artwork or as a word work, as an 'image' or a 'text.'" It is, of course, both. Reading it as a "thing"—that is, as an art object—Sieburth positions *Heap* "among the other productions of Minimalist or Conceptual art of the 1960s and 70s . . . alongside the work of Carl Andre, Dan Flavin, Donald Judd, Sol LeWitt, etc."; read as a work of verbal art, the piece earns a place within a radical modernist lineage of "visual poetics," which for Sieburth includes Stéphane Mallarmé, Guillaume Apollinaire, the Russian futurists, and "Ezra Pound's 'ideogrammic method'" as well as contemporary descendants such as Jackson Mac Low and Tom Phillips—a poetic genealogy that also happens to be relevant for Dorn, Coolidge, McCaffery, and Bervin (219). Indeed, Sieburth reads *Heap* as a poem, much as Craig Dworkin implicitly does when he removes the language from its pyramidal structure and reproduces it in a typical text block with forward slashes to indicate the line breaks, as if quoting from a lineated poem (Dworkin and Goldsmith 13–14).

Where Dworkin places Smithson alongside the conceptual artist Vito Acconci's experiments in writing through Roget's Thesaurus, Sieburth sees *A Heap of Language* as an example of "sustained parataxis," a list-poem that, summoning "the most ancient form of writing known to us," reflects Smithson's abiding interest in monuments and ruins, and displays "writing . . . at its most unproductively excessive and, thus, most entropic." Sieburth suggests another sense of the entropic, or random, spread of this heap with his own thesaurus analogy, describing how the word *language* is poised atop the structure "almost like a thesaurus entry (or dump truck) spilling out a cornucopia of synonyms" (222). While Sieburth doesn't make it explicit, his parenthetical comparison to a dump truck positions the piece as a precursor to later site-specific works like *Asphalt Rundown* (1969), in which an actual dump truck deposited hot asphalt down the side of a cliff in a quarry near Rome, and *Concrete Pour* (1969), in which Smithson conscripted a cement mixer to do much the same thing at a gravel pit in suburban Chicago. In each work, Smithson's intervention enacted the process of entropy: the asphalt, for instance, ran down the hillside and cooled, both preserving its chance shape and melding with the cliff face, while a similar hardening and fusing occurred in the case of the concrete. For Smithson, the fusion of site with poured material results in a state of dedifferentiation, a dispersed, homogenous zone. Smithson was enamored of such entropic zones, and would insist in several essays and interviews that "[t]he actual *disruption* of the earth's crust is at times very compelling, and seems to confirm Heraclitus's *Fragment 124*, 'The most beautiful world is like a heap of rubble tossed down in confusion'" (102). As a *heap*—"an untidy collection of things piled up haphazardly" in the *Oxford English Dictionary*'s definition—Smithson's word pyramid would seem to be an example of symbolic debris tossed down in confusion from the thesaurus entry for *language*. However, not only is the text rigorously arranged on its grid, as Sieburth notes, but the order of words is also not nearly as haphazard as one would expect if this was a list of synonyms discharged into a random pile. While many of the words Smithson chooses overlap with those in standard thesaurus entries for *language*, it is odd that *language* remains the headword. More to the point, not all of the terms are synonyms: words such as *dictionary* and *lexicon*, or phrases such as *word coiner* and *Mrs. Malaprop* are containers for or oblique references to aspects of language use but are fairly far from substitutes for the words themselves.

Instead, the range of words included reveals *Heap*'s stratigraphic structure. Read from top to bottom, the piece progresses from terms having to do with vocal expression (*Phraseology; speech*), to registers of speech (*lingo; vernacular; King's English*), translation (*Esperanto; pantomime*), literary expression and institutionalization (*belles-lettres; republic of letters*), and terms of linguistic analysis (*labial; palatal; vocable*). In other words, each line (occasionally two lines or more) of the edifice indicates a particular stratum of the massif of verbal meaning, to recall Benjamin's phrase. Smithson's stratigraphic arrangement also anticipates Steve McCaffery's poem "Lastworda," discussed in chapter 4, which descends through the strata of English morphology by means of the *Oxford English Dictionary*.

In contrast to McCaffery's unbroken block of text, however, Smithson's visual design emphasizes its construction. Smithson is really building with words here, not simply piling them up (or pouring them out) but measuring them to fit within the graph paper's mathematical constraints. And if we take seriously Smithson's investment in viewing words as "printed matter," then we might also view the piece's overall shape as a predecessor to the trapezoidal Nonsite containers he would begin building a couple years later. In fact, the work's design matches much of the criteria for the Nonsite in the "Dialectic of Site and Nonsite," including "Closed Limits," "An Array of Matter," "Inner Coordinates" (thanks to the graph paper, one could pinpoint which quadrant a particular word appears in), construction through "Addition," and "Contained Information." Just as the rocks collected in the Nonsite refer back to the Site, the words in *A Heap* refer back to the broad expanse of language, demonstrating Smithson's description of the Site-Nonsite dialectic as comprising "a network of signs" (152–53). As in a dictionary (or a thesaurus), one sign leads to another, in this case, the word *language* itself accumulating additional words about words, thus "cover[ing] rather than discover[ing]" its foundations.

Remote Futures / Remote Pasts

While *A Heap of Language* is not quite as entropic as its title implies, its accumulative, stratigraphic construction is also not at odds with Smithson's obsession with entropy. Strata and entropy are bound, in Smithson's oeuvre, by the dimension of time. "The Second Law of Thermodynamics," Smithson writes in the article "Entropy and the New Monuments," "extrapolates the range of entropy by telling us energy is more easily lost than obtained, and that in the ultimate future the whole universe will burn out and be transformed into an all-encompassing sameness" (11). The gradual, inexorable diminishment of energy in the universe results, at least in Smithson's science fiction–saturated imagination, in a state of crystallized, frozen *dedifferentiation*, the term Smithson takes from the art theorist Anton Ehrenzweig to denote the feeling of being submerged in this "all-encompassing sameness."

Smithson's simplest illustration of the entropic process comes at the end of his deadpan "Tour of the Monuments of Passaic, New Jersey" (1967), a mock–documentary essay in which he visits "monuments" such as "The Fountain Monument" (a waterfall of industrial waste pouring into the Passaic through six giant metal pipes) in a walk through suburban New Jersey that holds some striking, though probably unintentional, similarities to the concurrent situationist practice of the *dérive*. "The last monument" to which Smithson–as–tour guide directs our gaze "was a sand box or model desert." Adopting the authoritative tone of a stuffy physics professor, Smithson declares, "I should now like to prove the irreversibility of eternity by using a *jejune* experiment for proving entropy," and asks readers to imagine the sandbox "divided in half with black sand on one side and white sand on the other." We are then to picture a child running clockwise through the sand until the two sides are thoroughly mixed and the sand turns gray. If the child were to then run "anti-clockwise . . . the result will not be a restoration of the original division but a greater degree of greyness and an increase of entropy" (74). In other words, entropy—like time—cannot be undone; the original order of the sandbox cannot be restored.

Virtually all commentators on Smithson have written at length about entropy and its bearing on his work. My purpose here is to suggest that entropy and geology are closely connected through the processes of erosion, deposition, and sedimentation and that the resulting stratigraphic vision of temporality is key to my readings of the works in this study. For example, in the "model desert" of the sandbox, Smithson discerns "a map of infinite disintegration and forgetfulness" that charts "the sullen dissolution of entire continents, the drying up of oceans." As a kind of readymade Nonsite, the sandbox evokes the fragmentation, rather than coherence, of space. Moreover, this monument provokes "forgetfulness," not remembrance; in other words, deciphering—that is, reading—the monument, which Smithson argues is impossible as to do so would "take one through the false mirror of eternity," is an entropic process as much about the erosion as the fortifying of the mind. We inevitably forget more of what we read than we remember (74).

And what is lost cannot be recovered, leading to a certain apocalyptic strain in Smithson's thought. Smithson's sandbox invokes images of environmental destruction that were prevalent at the height of the Cold War (and that have reemerged with our growing awareness of the disastrous effects of global warming), suggesting the obliteration of "green forests and high mountains" and supplying instead "millions of grains of sand, a vast deposit of bones and stones pulverized into dust" (74). The sandbox's transformation into a "model desert" is not incidental to this apocalyptic vision, as it prefigures Smithson's own growing interest in the geographic desert that would culminate in perhaps Smithson's most famous work, *Spiral Jetty*. Matilde Nardelli claims that for artists such as Smithson and Michael Heizer, the American desert, in the context of both nuclear threat and ongoing nuclear testing at desert locations such as the Nevada Test Site, became a signifier for the end of the world. In Smithson's case, however, the world will not so much come to an end as endlessly disintegrate, and he describes the desert more in temporal than spatial or figural terms. That is, the desert, according to Smithson, gives the artist her time back: because, as Smithson writes, "[t]he mental process of the artist which takes place in time is disowned" by a commodity-based system that only values the singular, unchanging art object, and the artist is "cheated" of the dimension of time as an aspect of the artwork (111). Smithson, therefore, asserts that "[s]eparate 'things,' 'forms,' 'objects,' 'shapes,' etc., with beginnings and endings are mere convenient fictions: there is only an uncertain disintegrating order that transcends the limits of rational separations" (112). One of Smithson's primary goals as an artist and a writer, then, is to reduce such separations to rubble, disorienting the viewer or reader. I will return to Smithson's rejection of "beginnings and endings," but for now my purpose is to argue that the desert, as an eroding, perpetually disintegrating landscape is the epitome of an entropic site for Smithson. It is a location where time and its results are materially present in the form of erosion and deposition and thus a terrain wherein an artist could make use of time to enact this breakdown of limits.

Indeed, the deep time of geologic processes is particularly visible in desert regions. This nonhuman time, unimaginably vast, allows the desert, like the Museum of Natural History in Smithson's artistic imagination, to make possible an investigation of "the places where remote futures meet remote pasts." Nardelli articulates this idea slightly differently when she observes that the American desert's "signification . . . as a landscape of the end differ[s] in crucial respects from its image as a primeval space, prevalent up until the mid-twentieth century and popularized perhaps above all by the Western film genre." In its prenuclear guise, the desert was, at least in North America, primarily associated with the frontier. In contrast to the postapocalyptic desert of nuclear war, the frontier marked "a spatial limit, the place beyond which civilization and the rule of law ended; it was not only unstable, shrinking as the frontier line moved, but it also stood as a space of beginnings." Smithson would likely contest Nardelli's emphasis on limits and beginnings here, because for him the deep geologic time one encounters in the desert shatters these human-imposed categories. As Smithson writes, citing the Victorian art critic writing in the wake of geology's emergence as a distinct science, "It was John Ruskin who spoke of the 'dreadful Hammers' of the geologists, as they destroyed the classical order. The landscape reels back into the millions and millions of years of 'geologic time'" (105).

Spirals and Golden Spikes

One facet of human-imposed time is the notion that history develops progressively. In the verb *reels* above we might, then, hear a pun rejecting this straightforward image of time through a reference to film, a medium that Smithson saw as provisionally able to reverse the seemingly progressive flow of time and a central component of the multimedia project that is *Spiral Jetty*. Back in the example of the black and white sandbox turned grey, Smithson speculates that "if we filmed such an experiment we could prove the reversibility of eternity by showing the film backwards" but then quickly adds the caveat that "sooner or later the film itself would crumble or get lost and enter the state of irreversibility" (74). Despite the impossibility of truly reversing time, Andrew Uroskie contends that, with the film *Spiral Jetty*, Smithson signals a shift from the Nonsites and written works to a medium that would allow him to grapple more directly with temporality. Uroskie argues persuasively that Smithson's film *Spiral Jetty*, which Smithson produced shortly after he completed the sculpture on the north end of the Great Salt Lake in 1970, was a direct response to Chris Marker's 1962 avant-garde science fiction film *La Jetée*. In Marker's film, time is neither reversed nor accelerated, but rather seems to stand still, moments accumulating across a montage of still frames documenting the ostensible travels of "a protagonist [who remains] strapped to a table for the entire length of the film" (Uroskie 62). Marker's experiment in rendering the dislocation of space and time in film—what Smithson elsewhere calls "a cinematic atopia"—provided Smithson with "a blueprint for his own *Jetée en Spirale*" (Smithson 138; Uroskie 63). Indeed, both films include a scene at a museum of natural history that encloses geology behind glass and thus, in Uroskie's resonant reading, encapsulates "man's futile attempt to classify, order, and understand a history of the world outside his own making" (63).

Yet, without contradicting any of Uroskie's conclusions, I would suggest that Smithson's interest in film forms an extension of and not a departure from his geologic preoccupations. As Owens observes, *Spiral Jetty*, like the earlier Nonsites, is a text; that is to say, the artwork is really a composite of the physical sculpture, the film, and the essay, each of which is titled *Spiral Jetty* (128). More importantly, while Uroskie understands the *Spiral Jetty* film as a turn toward time and away from materiality, his argument demonstrates how the film envisages a specifically stratigraphic model of temporality. Developing Deleuze's theory of the "time-image" in *Cinema 2*, Uroskie writes that in Smithson's film "[r]ather than the kind of organic description that would present an object, location, or process within the spatial and material terms we would expect of the documentary genre, Smithson's form of description in the *Spiral Jetty* perpetually seeks to complicate the referentiality it establishes." In other words, the machinations of the Nonsite are operative not only in *Spiral Jetty*'s dispersal across multiple media, but also within the film itself, refusing the viewer a stable sense of the site. For Uroskie, Deleuze's posthumanist theory of cinematic time "helps us to consider how this very indeterminacy, rather than lacking all form, can give rise to a mode of description analogous to the layered or stratigraphic quality of temporality itself" (64). The upshot of temporal layering is that it allows the viewer "to inhabit multiple 'presents' existing outside of any overarching chronology," thus shattering her sense of linear, progressive time altogether (67).

Deleuze's stratigraphic time accretes through a "double movement of creation and erasure" that recalls the process of erosion and deposition. Smithson depicts this double movement in his film in a scene showing an eroded cliff face covered with the torn pages of a geology textbook. On the soundtrack, a clock ticks and Smithson compares the geologic history of the earth to "a story recorded in a book, each page of which is torn into small pieces" (qtd. in Uroskie 65). In his account of this layered episode, Uroskie remarks, "While sheets of a book fall to the earth in a kind of sedimentation, Smithson's voice-over suggests this sedimentation is diffuse, scattered and, to an extent, irrecoverable" (65). These pages falling to the cracked surface of the desert embody the entropic process, and the entropic process is, for Smithson, equated with the geologic processes of erosion and deposition that combine to construct stratified sediments. In this sedimentary mélange, words, rocks, maps, dirt, and paper do not differ from each other, to recall Smithson's phrase about minerals and their names, and spread instead into a spectrum of strewn fragments—a jumbled museum assembled by chance.

A similar logic of accumulation surrounds the jetty itself. The art historian Jennifer Roberts has identified this aspect of the sculpture in relation to the key role salt plays in the piece's ongoing evolution. In 1970, when Smithson constructed the spiral out of 6,650 tons of basalt and earth, the Great Salt Lake was at historically low levels due to prolonged drought. In the following, wetter years, the lake level rose, submerging the jetty and coating it in salt crystals so that when it resurfaced over twenty years later, its black basalt was "clad in glistening white armor." As Roberts explains, these fluctuations in lake level, and their attendant effects, far from inflicting unfortunate damage on the jetty, instead form part of its ongoing production. Smithson, Roberts writes, included salt crystals in his list of the sculpture's materials, anticipating that "[t]he sheltering arms of the spiral would increase the concentration of brine in the surrounding water, allowing for a higher rate of crystal deposition." In Roberts's expressive phrase, the jetty "was built, in short, in order to be salted" ("Taste" 97). These salt crystals embody two crucial facets of Smithson's overall program: scale and time. The spiral growth of the salt crystal reproduces at a microscopic scale the structure of the jetty, much as the sandbox can, if magnified, replicate a desert. As Smithson observes in his essay "The Spiral Jetty," "each cubic salt crystal echoes the Spiral Jetty in terms of the crystal's molecular lattice. Growth in a crystal advances around a dislocation point, in the manner of a screw" (147). Roberts elaborates on this point, explaining that the Jetty's scalar symmetry "alludes to a common flaw in crystal structures known as the screw dislocation" in which "a slip or misalignment in the normal sequence of molecular deposition perpetuates itself throughout the crystal by causing a pattern of growth that spirals around the initial dislocation" ("Taste" 97). For Roberts, the screw dislocation is important because it models "time as an opaque encrustation around a fault or fracture." In its fractal reiteration of the spiral, the salt imposes what Smithson terms "the crystalline structure of time," which, in Roberts's description, "disregards linear, progressive, or triumphalist models by imagining time as an opaque encrustation around a fault or fracture" (98). The important point here is that in this model, time is literally *deposited*. Furthermore, this sedimentary accumulation of time, enacted through the deposition of salt, indicates the process of entropy: the "salting" of the *Spiral Jetty*, while likely anticipated by Smithson, nonetheless occurs through a chance combination of events not under the artist's control and dramatizes the jetty's always changing and forever incomplete status.

Roberts astutely observes that the unfinished, accumulative nature of *Spiral Jetty* places it in tension with the nearby Golden Spike National Monument. Named for the ceremonial spike marking the completion of the Transcontinental Railroad in May 1869 (almost exactly 101 years before Smithson traveled to Rozel Point to build his jetty), the monument's visitor center mounts an hourly reenactment of the joining of the rails replete with replica steam engines. In contrast to the monument's model of time, which seeks "a return to a privileged point in historical space," *Spiral Jetty* instantiates a vision of time as "sheer opaque accumulation," rejecting a nostalgic, retrospective theory of history for one that emphasizes irreversibility ("Taste"

99). Put another way, the jetty is not a monument but a ruin. Owens reminds us that Smithson's romantic affinity for ruins derives from their resistance to "the totalizing impulses of art" (124). Like fragments, ruins are allegorical, exhibiting, in Benjamin's words, "[t]he calculable result of the process of accumulation" (qtd. in Owens 124). In a strange way, then, ruins both result from a process of accumulation and embody Benjamin's assertion that "history does not assume the form of the process of an eternal life so much as that of irresistible decay" (qtd. in Owens 129). If, as Benjamin attests, "[i]n the process of decay . . . the events of history shrivel up and become absorbed in the setting," then Smithson's jetty performs the goal of merging remote futures and remote pasts. The jetty is in dialogue with not only Golden Spike National Monument but also the geo-economic history of Rozel Point, which, as Smithson makes clear at the outset of "The Spiral Jetty," he chooses not because it is a "pristine" location—for him there could be no such thing—but because it already contains "countless bits of wreckage . . . trapped fragments of junk and waste [that transport one] into a world of modern prehistory" (145–46). The remnants of a former oil-drilling camp that hoped to exploit deposits of tar seeping from the sand (which can still be witnessed today) allow Smithson to see in the site overlapping strata of past, present, and future. Rather than restage an origin story like its neighbor, the jetty seeks to obliterate beginnings and endings altogether.

Smithson's stratigraphic conception of time becomes especially relevant when we consider that in geology, the term *golden spike* refers to a marker designating the boundary of a geologic epoch. While Roberts makes no mention of this, given Smithson's considerable reading in geology he must have been aware of this resonance. In recent years, the golden spike most in question is, of course, that of the Anthropocene and where to locate its starting point. Smithson might seem far removed from this ongoing discussion, but his work's complication of linear time speaks directly to the kinds of concerns raised by theorists like Yusoff. In a chapter of her book *A Billion Black Anthropocenes or None* titled "Golden Spikes and Dubious Origins," Yusoff explains that "the search for the Golden Spike is a disciplinary endeavor to geologically map the material relation of space and time according to stratigraphic principles and scientific precedents." However, she challenges the presumption that geology is a neutral science with the reminder that it developed, after all, in tandem with the same extractive economies that have helped precipitate global warming. Wherever geologists agree to place the spike thus makes an implicit argument about the origins of climate change, who or what is to be blamed for its effects, and what practical and political recourses are available. Yusoff cautions, then, that "these spikes are not real places as such; they are trace effects in material worlds that infer the event/advent of this most political geology" (24). In other words, the Anthropocenic golden spike indicates a point of origin that has been constructed by humans in more senses than one.

As with any marker of an origin or boundary, a golden spike creates "borders that define inclusion and exclusion" (24). At stake, as it were, in the determination of where to place the golden spike marking the end of the Holocene and beginning of the Anthropocene, is what, and who, is included or left out of the narrative that geologists and governments construct by choosing one date over another. As Yusoff details, for instance, by locating the advent of the Anthropocene in 1945 with the deposition of plutonium after the Trinity Site detonation (currently the marker of choice for the Global Standard Stratigraphic Age), climate scientists elide the *longue durée* of social and ecological transformation brought about by the mutual rise of the global slave trade and the opening of colonial mining in the Americas beginning in the 1450s (44).

At a more localized scale, a similar erasure of history accompanies the construction of the Transcontinental Railroad. At the peak of construction from 1868 to 1869, some eleven thousand Chinese laborers helped build the Central Pacific and Union Pacific lines amid brutal working conditions and exposure to disease, explosions, landslides, and other accidents. Though no precise count is available, certainly many hundreds died. Yet these workers were almost completely absent from the ceremonial driving of the golden spike in May of 1869 (at a site temporarily named Camp Victory, no less) and were, until the last decade or so, left out of most accounts of this chapter in American manifest destiny.[4] To be sure, Smithson does not mention the atrocities committed in the railroad's construction either. However, his view of time as a material, entropic deposition that, like language, obscures rather than reveals a site, makes Smithson's work just as relevant now in the age of the Anthropocene and global warming as it was at the dawn of the ecological movements of the 1970s. This is because a work like *Spiral Jetty* challenges not only the conceit of historical time as necessarily progressive, as both Roberts and Uroskie argue, but also the geologic stratification of time as such, which, as Yusoff shows, stresses the importance of origins and a human-centric perspective (*Billion Black Anthropocenes* 24). Roberts elaborates that for Smithson, "time has no connection to an animate origin or center; it begins with a 'dislocation' and merely accumulates from without" ("Taste" 98). In other words, Smithson's engagement with the process of deposition, which reveals time and materials to be the result of continual accretion, disputes the ability of either geologic or locomotive golden spikes to locate some original, unsullied state. To borrow a pun from Uroskie, Smithson tosses (*jeter*) the very concepts of origins and endpoints, along with their attendant connotations of wholeness and completion. Or, as Smithson himself puts it, "at the end, if there is an end, are perhaps only meaningless reverberations" (78). In place of the fixed moments of human progress marked by golden spikes, Smithson's work exhibits the nonhuman possibilities of endless agglomeration.

CHAPTER 2

"The World Soul / Slumbers in Matter"

Gunslinger *and* The Magic Door

> all poetry
> begins in mysticism
> & ends in linguistics
> —Chris Torrance

In the late 1960s and early 1970s, when Robert Smithson and fellow land artists were turning to the American desert as a site through which to stage questions of time and destruction permeating the postnuclear age, the poet Ed Dorn was starting to compose and publish *Gunslinger*, his book-length, mock–Western epic of the American Desert Southwest. If Smithson's pivot toward the desert was part of his broader effort to imagine a fusion of the distant past with the distant future and to present a nonanthropocentric, geologic view of history and language, Dorn's poem enacts this collapse of past, present, and future. Much as *Spiral Jetty* disrupts the linear model of history and time enforced by the Golden Spike monument, *Gunslinger*'s anachronistic narrative, which reimagines the early twentieth-century tycoon Howard Hughes as a nineteenth-century railroad baron, projects a panorama of stratigraphic time, though one that is more a jumble—a heap of objects thrown down in confusion, to paraphrase Smithson and Heraclitus—than an orderly set of strata.

At roughly the same time in the United Kingdom, several poets influenced by the archaeological and geologic method of Williams and Olson—and, as we shall see in the next chapter, in some cases in direct conversation with Olson and Dorn—began composing work that presented language as geologic matter. While J. H. Prynne and Maggie O'Sullivan will be the focus of chapter 3, in this chapter, I set *Gunslinger* side by side with Chris Torrance's *The Magic Door*, a work begun in 1970 and running to eight volumes. The former may be a jokey amalgam of TV Westerns and what seem to us now to be countercultural clichés, and the latter a far more earnest—though no less symptomatic of its time—exploration of alchemy, Jungian psychology, and Welsh mythology, but my motivation for mustering these texts stems from their mutual interest in the cyclical transformation of matter and their quite similar emphasis on topology—or *topos*, to use one of Olson's favored terms. Dorn's poem, while most often read as a postmodern implosion of styles which erases space in favor of time, exemplifies the geopoetic desire for a language derived from the earth and, in positing such a language, is far more specific about the topos of the American Desert Southwest than previous readings have allowed. With Torrance, we encounter the wish for psychological metamorphosis to mirror the metamorphic cycles of geology. Both poems investigate a topos through the trope of the pun; to posit a language motivated by geology, the poets must make recourse to language's motiveless materiality. Moreover, while *Gunslinger* has attained at least a certain familiarity in postwar American poetics and criticism, Torrance's magnum opus remains relatively obscure. My hope, then, is not only to show how these works practice a geologic approach to language (or a linguistic approach to geology) but also to establish a broader perspective on the drift of geopoetic ideas between North America and Europe.

The Literate Projector

Gunslinger is a book-length narrative poem whose narrative never gets off the ground.[1] While the poem's multitemporal structure and cacophony of overlapping discourses resists any simple synopsis, in its barest outline the poem follows an eponymous protagonist, most often referred to only as the

"Slinger," on a journey across the American Desert Southwest from Mesilla, New Mexico, near the Mexican border, to Las Vegas, Nevada, ostensibly in pursuit of the shadowy billionaire Howard Hughes. Along the way, the Slinger accumulates his own merry band of pranksters, including a talking horse named Claude Lévi-Strauss, an acid freak named Kool Everything, a wandering poet, a cabaret owner called Madam Lil, and a character whose name is simply "I." Together, this company drifts across the desert in a steed-powered "stage" that is both coach and coliseum, making a quick stop in Universe City (a thinly veiled Albuquerque, New Mexico) before meandering toward the Four Corners where any plot, such as it is, comes completely unglued. The Slinger's apparent mission to catch Hughes fades, and the dramatis personae (already rather nebulous) disperse into numerous aliases and simulacra. The traveling troupe of archetypes from the Old West and 1960s drug culture never even makes it to Vegas.

If *Gunslinger*'s narrative seemingly fails to take off, if its promised showdown of the swaggering Slinger and the mysterious, shape-shifting Hughes never arrives, this is because such linear storytelling is continually overwhelmed by linguistic excess. The poem's endless puns, neologisms, and obscure jokes render it at once obstinately opaque and relentlessly digressive. Indeed, the Slinger's alleged destination, Las Vegas, might itself be a pun: *vague* is a suggestive term, as it connects etymologically with *vagabond* and *wave*, from the French *vague* (wave) and the Latin *vagus* (wandering, uncertain, which, if pronounced with a long a, makes an exact rhyme with *Vegas*). *Vega*, in Spanish, refers to an expansive plain or valley, especially one that is fertile and grassy. In other words, the poem moves but doesn't get anywhere because Vegas is—not to put too fine a point on it—a mirage, the site of illusion and simulation par excellence, and, as toponym, the false promise of an oasis in the middle of a desert. I argue here that *Gunslinger*'s drifting, nomadic delight in the contingencies of language—those chance sonic and orthographic similarities that make such play possible—reflects its interest in geodynamics. *Gunslinger* presents language and the earth as similarly unstable processes.

The poem's conflation of language with geologic phenomena surfaces most blatantly in *Book II*, when the Slinger and his motley posse arrive in Universe City. There, in the central plaza, they encounter an advertisement for a device called the Literate Projector, "a revolutionary medium / . . . sure to turn everything around" (75). Intrigued, the Slinger instructs Kool Everything, who seems to have some inside knowledge, to describe its operation:

> Well, There's a *Literate Projector*,
> which, when a 35mm strip is put thru it
> turns it into a Script
> *Instantaneously!*
> and projects that—the finished script
> onto the white virgin screen
> and theyre gonna run it in Universe City tonight (76)

Kool claims that this unlikely contraption has the power to "Invent a whole new literachure / which was Already There," allowing one to "rerun I mean all of it / ¡atencíon!—Shoot a volcano, project it / and See the Idea behind it / sit down at the geologic conference / and hear the reasons Why / skip the rumble, move into the inference" (76–77). The Projector transforms images into language, and this speculative process immediately implicates geology. Indeed, it seems to propose that beneath geodynamic phenomena there lies a kind of platonic idea in the form of language.

The Literate Projector has occasioned little more than brief, bemused asides from the poem's major commentors.[2] When it has provoked sustained discussion it is usually read as an allusion to the lies and propaganda promulgated by American government and mainstream media regarding the Vietnam War. As Kool Everything cautions the Slinger, "They can distort the Projector / so that the script Departs / from the film," making the device a perfect propaganda machine (78). The Slinger supposes it "works best in University towns / and other natural centers of doubletalk" and allows its operators to "put funny music next to Death or . . . say something quick about the war / in, well you know where the War is" (79). The projector, in this view, is just a dark joke, an Orwellian apparatus of discourse control.

Dorn himself asserts in an interview that the Projector is "the most arbitrary thing in Book II. In some ways it violates the forwardness of the book. . . . In fact, when I republish the whole poem I think I might extract that" (qtd. in Davidson 132n8). Yet he never did remove the Literate Projector, and his word choice here, while probably coincidental, is nevertheless telling. For the Literate Projector is indeed "the most *arbitrary* thing" (my emphasis): beneath its propagandistic possibilities, it functions fundamentally as a means to reverse the Saussurean sign. That is, *pace* Marjorie Perloff and other commentators, the Projector does not, as it seems to do, bind a signifier to a single signified—or in Saussure's terms, a sound-image (*signifiant*) to a concept (*signifié*). If anything, it does the reverse, tethering a signified (a volcano, in the poem's example) to a transcendental signifier that exists as if it were behind, or prior to, material phenomena. For Saussure, of course, the sign—this union of concept and sound-image—is arbitrary. In his primary example, there is no necessary reason that the general concept *tree* takes the form of a particular sound-image. By contrast, the geopoetic aspect of Dorn's Literate Projector lies in its latent challenge to the arbitrary: it imagines a noncontingent language lying beneath material phenomena.

However, as I argue throughout this book, the poem's attempt to enact this natural, geologic language can only proceed by way of arbitrary correspondences such as those that motivate Dorn's most frequent trope, the pun—or what the Slinger at the very end of the poem refers to as "this marvelous accidentalism" (198). In other words, in trying to achieve the geologic language promised by the Literate Projector, the poem must make use of the very arbitrariness it seeks to transcend. An example of this dynamic occurs directly after the Projector is introduced: The Slinger insists on seeing "a *Littoral* instance" of the Projector's operation (80). Observing the Slinger's drawn-out pronunciation of *literal* (and which, of course, puns on *literate*), Kool Everything questions him about this sudden "drawl." It results, the Slinger tells Kool Everything,

> from the inertia of National Lunch
> and from the scatteredness
> of the apexed sun which attempts
> at that point to enter a paradox—
> namely, The West which is the East. (80)

For the Slinger, the *show*down at high noon—that cliché of the Western genre—becomes the *slow*down at high noon. And the organized space of the city, along with the organized time of its convention-bound inhabitants ("National Lunch" and its subsequent siesta), causes the Slinger's normally quick *draw* to resurface as a *drawl*. Registered on the page as "*Littoral*," an adjective referring to the shore of a lake or ocean, the Slinger's accent harkens back to his earlier recitation of the first line from Shakespeare's sonnet 60: "Like as the waves make toward the Pebbled shore." Sonnet 60 famously laments the unstoppable unraveling of time, depicting human life as an inescapable sequence of gradual decay—in other words, the same "well-worn road" of temporality and causality that the Slinger usually transcends yet feels weighing him down in Universe City (79).

The Slinger's drawl is an instance of Kool Everything's assertion that the Literate Projector's script "has to be read / to be seen" (79). The pun *littoral* is a prime example of this logic: it is a *literal* instance of an effect (the drawl) that "has to be read / to be seen"—or, more accurately, to be heard. What is more, this instance is arrived at through a pun on the word *literal*. That is, *littoral* literally indexes (at the level of the letter) the Slinger's pronunciation; it renders his accent visible in writing. The pun, then, is simultaneously literal and figurative: by indicating the Slinger's drawl, it demonstrates how language is grounded in material features such as sound and orthography. And yet, the excessive character of this materiality thwarts the attempt to reach a pure language-as-thing. As the poem's linguistic play and obsession with signs has drawn the most attention from critics, in the next section I briefly consider this aspect of the poem and what has been seen as its postmodern skepticism regarding the "real" before turning to the way *Gunslinger* situates its play of signs within a specific geographic and geologic region.

The Desert of the Real

The major critical treatments of the poem have, quite justifiably, emphasized its postmodern self-awareness, which manifests most clearly as the slipperiness of signification and its ironizing of the lyrical "I." Michael Davidson, for example, observes that for Dorn words "have only a differential function," thus reiterating Saussure's claim that "in Language there are only differences without positive terms" (Davidson 136). Further, Davidson contends that, in the poem, "words are not tied to discrete meanings" but drift, rather, from surface to surface, loosing themselves from reference seemingly at will (132). Similarly, Perloff asserts that the poem's proliferation of "paragrams, homonyms, portmanteau words, archaisms, nonsense words, parody tunes . . . are spliced together with countless variations so to produce a 'map of locations' in which meaning is endlessly deferred, endlessly called into question" (Dorn, *Gunslinger* xvi). This characterization resonates quite strongly with Smithson's description of his Nonsite sculptures as "a limited (mapped) revision of the original unbounded state" of a "real" site, access to which is "endlessly deferred," as well as Smithson's axiom discussed in the previous chapter that "[l]anguage 'covers' rather than 'discovers' its sites and situations" (78). A major—and much commented on—way this skeptical view of language and reference appears in the poem is the Slinger's (and Dorn's) delight in undermining the pronoun *I*.

Specifically, the poem transforms *I* from a first-person pronoun into a proper noun, in the process encapsulating the Slinger's rejection of referentiality. The Slinger introduces his theory of referentiality when he jokingly refers to I as "my singular friend" shortly after encountering this character (a coincidence of individual and inscription) at Madam Lil's cabaret in Mesilla, New Mexico (6). The Slinger insists on the joke further along in the poem when he pointedly asks I, "What's your name?": "i, I answered. // That's a simple name / is it an initial? / No it is a single" (32). The Slinger finds I's "singularity" rather odd, as it means he is fixed to a solitary time, place, and body; as the pun on *initial* suggests, *I* is both a grammatical marker for the singular form and the Roman numeral for one. Even more problematic, this proper noun is descriptive, which according to the Slinger's cosmic view is rather limiting. The Slinger advises, "Don't describe yourself," and in a passage that is often noted in *Gunslinger* criticism, the Slinger warns I that "it is dangerous to be named / and makes you mortal" (24, 32). This is the case because "[i]f you have a name / you can be sold / you can be told . . . // you become, in short / a reference" (32). Becoming "a reference" is fatal as it is a marker of stability: one becomes a citation and thus easily found and classified. The Slinger, it seems, avoids this fate and fatality because he is an outlaw, not only in the sense commonly understood in the Western genre the poem is playing with but also in the sense that he exists outside the supposedly universal laws of space and time, not to mention the conventions of grammar.

The Slinger's distrust of reference permeates the entire poem; the capitalist archvillain Howard Hughes, for example, morphs without warning into "Robart" and, seemingly interchangeably, "Rupert." The Slinger himself comes to be called in the final book of the poem "Zlinger," while I transforms into "eye" and escapes a singular state after being pressed into service as a living container (*I* being an otherwise empty placeholder) for Kool Everything's batch of acid. The poem's endless riffs on the slippage between common and proper nouns, as well as its disruption of referentiality, can, of course, be read as its embrace of a postmodern instability of meaning. But it is worth noting here that the Slinger's critique of reference also reinstates a desire for the exact correspondence between thing and name: the poem not only presents *I* as the proper emblem of singularity but also implies that referentiality is limiting precisely because it is too stable and persistent. The Slinger, not unlike the Literate Projector, can somehow see beneath the surface of things to what he calls (when commenting on the Projector's ability) the "one Logos" that subtends the "many Images" of reality (78).

Gunslinger thus balances on a fine line between wanting a nonarbitrary material language and deploying language's contingencies to endlessly defer (or create an excess of) meaning. It is this latter aspect that Perloff fastens on when she depicts *Gunslinger* as "a poetic Sourcebook on postmodern discourses—the discourses of atomic science and cybernetics, pop song and media-speak, Heideggerianism and high finance" (Dorn, *Gunslinger* xvii). We might mention that Perloff does not include geology in this roundup of subjects. To be sure, its absence is understandable, as geology is specifically alluded to only a handful of times in the poem. I am not claiming that geology is *Gunslinger*'s central concern. What I am arguing here is that a geologic discourse intervenes at crucial moments in the poem, such as the explanation of the Literate Projector, and in doing so indicates the poem's dream of a language at one with the physical earth—and, further, that to realize this dream the poem must, paradoxically, foreground the material, and thoroughly contingent, features of words.

Before focusing on another example where the poem proposes a nonarbitrary sign, I want to linger over two additional postmodern discourses that have a particular bearing on Dorn's depiction of the geography and geology of the American Desert Southwest: the simulacrum and the nomadic. To take the former first, the poem's embrace of the play of signs brings it into the orbit of contemporaneous theories of simulation and simulacrum, most prominent and influential in this realm being Jean Baudrillard's. Baudrillard's theoretical works of the late 1960s and early 1970s—the very same period during which Dorn was developing *Gunslinger*—portray a postindustrial world dominated by the sign-value of commodities and not merely their use- and exchange-value as in previous Marxist analysis. In Baudrillard's semiotic studies, the transition from a production-based to a consumer-based society proliferates products and generates new desires for goods whose primary purpose is to signal social prestige. Hence, everyday life becomes increasingly jammed with signs, spectacles, and other inducements to consume, creating a situation in which humans are subordinated to a system of objects and, as a part of their reification, almost totally absorbed into media and computer-generated duplications of reality. Indeed, such duplications, or simulations, become hyperreal, more real than so-called "reality," a succession of simulacra.

While evidence of direct influence is minimal, one can easily see a similar semiotic account of society at work in *Gunslinger*.[3] Most obviously, the poem's entire setup, and much of its dialogue and nomenclature, is deliberately derivative of genre Westerns. The presentation of the Slinger as a laconic outlaw comically (and cosmically) quick on the draw, the stock characters with names like Tonto Pronto and Portland Beel, the punning allusions to the *stage*coach the Slinger travels in: each of these point to *Gunslinger*'s indebtedness to, and satire of, pop-cultural representations of the American Wild West from movies and television—and to how such simulations supplant specific histories. The poem is rife with such archetypes of the American West, and as reproductions of a mythic America, the tropes of the Western genre are examples of Baudrillard's simulacrum, a replication based on a copy or model and not an existing original. Indeed, Baudrillard, in *America*, singles out the American Desert Southwest (along with Disneyland and California) as a kind of ground zero for his postmodern society of simulation. Death Valley and the Mojave Desert, so Baudrillard claims, convey a sense of pure speed and light that reflects "[t]he lyrical nature of pure circulation" of capital and commodities in the United States (27). The "power of simulation" that Baudrillard encounters in America is "obviously true of the desert," which he describes as "like the set of a western" (56). The desert was, of course, literally the set of numerous Westerns, as in the case of Monument Valley (close to the Four Corners), which served as the setting—or at least the mise-en-scène, projected behind actors on a Hollywood soundstage like the tableaux that shift behind the Slinger's stagecoach—for many classic Westerns and which Baudrillard thus experiences as a thoroughly reproduced landscape, a kind of icon or sign of the American West rather than a specific geographic locale. Baudrillard goes further, however, and insists on seeing the desert as an emblem of emptiness: "American culture is heir to the deserts, but the deserts here are not part of a Nature defined by contrast with the town. Rather they denote the emptiness, the radical nudity that is the background to every human institution." In deserts, Baudrillard finds an "an exalting vision of the desertification of signs and men," a sort of environmental reflection of the insubstantial, ephemeral character of what he calls "Astral America"— perhaps punning on Reagan's "Star Wars" missile defense system and new age spirituality (63). *Gunslinger* has its own astral dimension, called, in the subtitle to *Book III*, "[t]he inside real / and the outsidereal," *sidereal* denoting a relation to distant stars or constellations. Dorn's collapse of interior reality (and its presumed locus in a lyric *I*) with the outer, nonhuman world is one marker of the hyperreal, in which, to recall Baudrillard, there is an implosion of discursive and societal boundaries. This implosion (or dedifferentiation, to recall one of Smithson's favorite terms) creates a "desert of the real" as humans abandon the quotidian for the novel, seemingly more intense "astral" realm of "vectors and signals" (Baudrillard 27). For Baudrillard—and, to an extent, for Dorn—the American Desert Southwest, as filtered through popular media, is literally and figuratively the "desert of the real," the emptying out of meaning.

At times, the desert in *Gunslinger* is a similarly empty, dedifferentiated space, while at other times, the poem foregrounds a much more specific geology of the Colorado Plateau. Both takes on the desert dovetail in the poem's embrace of a nomadic ethos. I am using the term *nomadic* in the sense developed by Gilles Deleuze and Felix Guattari in *A Thousand Plateaus*, where they elaborate a theory of "nomadology" across a range of disciplines.

For Deleuze and Guattari, the nomadic stands for a nonhierarchical, nonpossessive stance toward space, in contrast to a "striated" stance that captures and divides territory with "walls, enclosures, and roads" (381). In striated space, the earth is reduced to being property; as Deleuze and Guattari put it, "Property is precisely the deterritorialized relation between the human being and the earth" (388). In other words, the concept of "the earth" as the ground human and nonhuman objects exist on is displaced (deterritorialized) and recoded (reterritorialized) as an object one can own. If striated space is designed "to *parcel out a closed space,*" as a means of organizing populations, then "smooth" or nomadic space "*distributes people (or animals) in an open space,* one that is indefinite and noncommunicating" (380).⁴ We might note the geologic resonance of "striated" and "stratum," as for Deleuze and Guattari geology is itself one stratum of discourse that attempts to organize the earth, an attempt that the unruly body of the earth is always in the process of escaping or deterritorializing. The nomadic, then, is a kind of effect or function of smooth space (and vice versa), a manner of traversing strata and resisting the pull of a bounded territory or discourse. Deleuze and Guattari also allege that deserts, along with oceans, are smooth spaces par excellence. One can see what they mean if one adopts an abstract view of deserts as seemingly unbounded, unpopulated expanses. But this perspective, like Baudrillard's, tends to reproduce the attitude that the desert is merely an empty wasteland, a space of pure potentiality divorced from a specific geography.

Dorn's *Gunslinger* adopts, while also subtly transforming, this "nomadic" perspective on the desert. As the Slinger's company leaves Mesilla and heads "[i]nto the dry brilliance of the desert morning" at the beginning of *Book II*, the Poet, whom the Slinger addresses as "nomad," sings a raga that celebrates the rising desert sun:

> Cool comes the greatness
> the scalar beauty intointoo
> oh our morning bright environment
> along the passage of our company
> into the hoodoos
> lying around the foot of our future (50)

From one angle, the Poet's lines render the desert as a simulated hyperspace of light and speed not unlike Baudrillard's astral desert. Accompanying himself on his "Absolute," the Poet's song presents "the stereoscopic world," a world that, as the adjective suggests, only appears to have solidity and depth (48). This world is "scalar," then, in the sense that it can only be described by a numerical value, lacking direction. The desert here is emptied of specificity and made into a kind of screen, a generic reproduction. At the same time, however, the adjective "scalar," through a pun, suggests the dry, flaky ground of the desert eroded by wind and moisture. This sense is reinforced through the raga's riff, in "cool," "intointoo," and "foot," of the double-*o* in "hoodoo," a fanciful term for a column or pinnacle of rock that has been weathered by wind and water erosion into an eerie, sometimes human-shaped form. These distinctive rock formations, in other words, reimpose a specific geology of the American Southwest on to what seems to be Dorn's deterritorialized desert.

The poem's reference to hoodoos—a prominent geologic feature of the Four Corners region and the Colorado Plateau—has gone largely unremarked on by critics.[5] The few scattered mentions that do exist relate *hoodoo* to the hybrid spiritual practice of magic or witchcraft, *hodos* as Greek for "journey or way," or *hodo*, supposedly stemming from Charles Olson's notion of method as "how-to-do."[6] To my knowledge, no source has considered the geologic definition of *hoodoo*, despite the poem's pains to make this lithic sense apparent. For instance, when requesting the Poet's raga, the Slinger asks him if he can also "sing the traditional Rock [song] / Oh Light; The Light!" and, in a typical bit of druggy wordplay, assures the Poet that "From your sweet voice / I am astoned" (48). The Poet concludes with the observation that ahead of the travelers "loom the hoodoos / beyond the canyon country," a clear allusion to the geology of the Four Corners region where the company eventually ends up.

These hoodoos, the temporary (geologically speaking) result of erosion over eons, in a sense unite the poem's linguistic and geologic interests. They function much like signifiers, a physical form pointing to a concept, or in this case they are an index of a process so slow as to be invisible to the human eye. As indices of erosion and deep geologic time, hoodoos imply the possibility of a natural language. Such a language calls up a nomadic approach to space, in that it desires to meld with the nonhuman landscape rather than striate space by abstracting it in an arbitrary language. The Slinger demonstrates his nomadic intention as soon as the Poet's raga is finished, when with the aid of some "mescal buttons" he "truly turned his eyes / into the landscape" (52). The journey "intointoo" the landscape becomes one of literally transforming *into* the desert and its landforms. It is this objective to be fully immersed in the landscape, rather than to dominate it, that distinguishes the nomadic Slinger from the poem's villain, Howard Hughes/Robart. The former is a benign metaphysical adventurer, the latter a ruthless robber baron with dealings in real estate, railroads, and coal mines.

The Real of the Desert

While it might often be true, as Perloff states in her introduction, that in *Gunslinger* "place . . . is itself a simulacrum" whereas "*time* . . . is central to Dorn's narrative," place does surface in a poem-within-the-poem that thematizes the ecological stakes of striation and enacts the geopoetic possibility of a language rooted in the earth (Dorn, *Gunslinger* vii). In a section titled "The Winterbook," which concludes *Book III*, the Slinger and his company pass through the town of Madrid, New Mexico, about fifty miles northeast of Albuquerque along the ancient Indigenous trading route that, in Spanish colonial times, came to be called the Turquoise Trail. Established after the discovery of lead and coal deposits in the nearby mountains, Madrid would have been basically a ghost town at the time of *Book III*'s composition.[7] As his stagecoach approaches the remnants of the town and its mines, the Slinger glimpses

> past the curtain
> a certain destruction
> the hills have been upended
> theyre no longer blended upon
> the plates of their own dynamic principles. (Dorn, *Gunslinger* 128)

Coal mining began in Madrid in the 1830s, transforming it briefly into a boomtown, and the lineation here reflects the resulting ordered destruction of the landscape through stepped lines that suggest the terraced cuts and slag piles of strip mining. As the Slinger observes, this terraced architecture does not result from the region's "own dynamic principles," but from human imposition in the form of an extractive industry. Of course, the coal deposits that drew miners to Madrid existed by means of this same geologic dynamism. "Plates," moreover, alludes to the lithosphere, the crust that moves and morphs minerals and other matter as part of the rock cycle (and echoes the discussion of the new science of plate tectonics in the correspondence of Dorn, Olson, and J. H. Prynne, the subject of the following chapter). However, the contrast created through the rhyme of "upended" with "blended," and their superposition in the stanza, intimates that the mines have disrupted the area's geologic order.

The Poet replies to these observations in an interpolated verse, "The Poem Called Riding Throughe Mádrid." The title's archaic, idiosyncratic spelling speaks to the collision of times occurring throughout *Gunslinger*. Indeed, it is difficult to determine what time period the poem is set in: are we "[r]iding [t]hroughe" the ghost town Madrid of the 1960s or the boomtown of the 1830s—or some superimposition of both eras? Geology is central to these questions of time and place because here the poem wants to divulge a scale of time deeper than that of humans. As in his earlier raga to the "Sunne," the Poet uses a repetitive, improvisatory style, exhorting his listeners to "visit The World" to "Talk with the Trees and / Speak into the Trees and / Get it on with the Trees / They know whats happening." Like so many moments in *Gunslinger*, the Poet's advice here is part caricature of 1960s "tree hugger" environmentalism and part serious appeal to processes that human activity threatens to erase. In the Poet's vision, trees offer a counterpoint to mining's extractive logic: "They go straight to heaven / And they have heaved in waves / Their deposits in the earth." They also provide an index to time through the layers of matter they leave on the ground and the set of rings found within their trunks: it is the trees "Who have given their flesh / To this thing /And this ring / And this ring" (129).

There is, however, another resonance in these "rings," one already hinted at in the sonic similarity of "heaven" and "heaved." The Slinger's horse, misinterpreting (that is, in a sense, mis*hearing*) the Poet's repetition of "ring," fashions himself "a Gong! / with his shoes" to prolong this echo (130).

Applying such literal logic, the Slinger makes a similar homophonic substitution: after the Poet recites, "The miner has brought up / The madder from their graves," the Slinger, in a (re)citation of his own, declares this poem to "have made my ears remember / 'the world soul / slumbers in matter'" (129, 130). In other words, "madder" rings a bell, as it were, in the Slinger's mind, leading him to think about matter. The *sound* of the word *madder* makes the Slinger's "ears remember" the word *matter* (and repeats the first syllable of *Mádrid* for good measure). This resonance prompts the Slinger to quote the Emersonian credo about "the world soul" and to posit, as Emerson also did, that "language is fossil poetry." In fact, the poem literalizes this dictum by mining language's material properties—in this case the play of sonic similarities between words. The ear, itself a kind of cavern, resembles the mine, yielding a subterranean logic of words lurking within other words.

The Poet's focus on trees in his ode to Madrid is especially apt: coal, after all, is carbonized plant matter. The organic is lithified; fossilized plants become fossil poetry. Thus, the miners have, in a double sense, "brought up / The madder from their graves." In heeding the poet's advice to "Speak into the Trees" (a phrase that recalls the earlier nomadic journey *into* the desert), the poem unearths a material substratum—the *lumber*, as it were, in which the world soul slumbers. This is literally so: in the kind of coincidence that could incline us, if we didn't know better, to reject the arbitrary status of signs, the word *matter* derives from *materia* ("substance" or "timber"). By way of a related etymology, *wood* in Spanish is *madera*, which once more recalls the toponym *Madrid*. As in the example of the Slinger's "littoral" drawl, the joke here is literal: it is a pun about materiality using the word *matter*. Even etymology itself returns us to trees and timber through the common analogy of "root" words. In moments such as this, the poem's wordplay opens onto the prospect of a properly geopoetic language: words reveal, rather than merely refer to, the material world. Linguistic tropes transform into topos, paronomasia morphs into place. And yet to do this, of course, the poem activates the arbitrary coincidences that inhere in language's materiality—its aural, inscriptive, and typographical qualities.

Materia ultimately derives from *mater* (mother), a meaning that may be hinted at earlier in *Book III* through the Poet's sardonic lines, "I promise my mother / I will not join the Sierra Club" (121). The familiar trope of Mother Earth points to one final variation on *mater*: namely, *matrix*. A Latin term for womb, *matrix* has come to denote both a grid structure and the "general material or environment in which something develops" (*OED*). As a "setting," *matrix* is the material surround of place. Passages such as the company's encounter with Madrid remind us that *Gunslinger*, for all its suggestion of simulation and play of signs, is also concerned with specific places and their geosocial histories. A similar matrix of geology and mining will play a critical role in Chris Torrance's decades-long mapping of the coalfields and standing stones of South Wales in *The Magic Door*, which I will turn to shortly. For now, I simply want to make the point that Dorn's poem is far more specific about place—the geology and geography that forms the topos of the Four Corners region—than it is typically given credit for. Madrid is far from the only specific locale Dorn references—others include the Rio Grande; the Sandia Mountains; Santa Fe; the Four Corners; Cortez, Colorado; and, last but not least, Placitas.[8] *Gunslinger* could even be said to adopt the same itinerary as an earlier, shorter poem, "West of Moab," published in the collection *Geography* (1965). As does *Gunslinger*, "West of Moab" charts a journey northwest from New Mexico to the Four Corners and beyond—a trip that corresponds closely to Dorn's move from Santa Fe, New Mexico, to Pocatello, Idaho, in 1961. The poem moves back and forth in time, but it opens where *Gunslinger* culminates, near the Four Corners in Cortez, Colorado, as "The caravan wound. Past the pinto bean capitol / of the world and mesa verde" (*Geography* 22). In *Gunslinger*, the "pinto bean capitol" Cortez (named for the Spanish colonizer) becomes "Beenville," occasioning numerous puns on the past participle of *to be*. More importantly, "West of Moab" establishes the Four Corners region as a charged location in Dorn's poetry. *Gunslinger*'s concluding pages return to the region to pay eloquent (and multilingual) attention to its geology. The Poet looks out over "La Lejanía" (the distance) and, in an echo of the passage on the Literate Projector, describes the desert floor "resting at the monuments to volcanic action / to the last peñasco, desprendimiento / de tierra, ash & lava" (rocky outcrops, landslides). The "paisaje magnífico" (magnificent landscape) of the Four Corners and the Colorado Plateau bares "all thats left of the plumbing / dikes, flues, the tubes of frozen magma," signifiers of the area's eruptive past. This panorama of volcanic plugs, hoodoos, and debris flows reads like "a worn and bitter fugue by Chaos" (178). Or, as the Slinger remarks in response to the Poet's verses, "This is old dinosaur country / a record full of sudden changes" (186). Recalling Smithson's "jumbled museum" of the earth, as well as Emerson's fossil poetry, Dorn's Desert Southwest is a paleolithic transcript detailing eons of metamorphosis, a matrix in which geologic formations are cast in the image of language.

The Matrix of the Neath

The emergence in the United Kingdom during the 1960s and 1970s of a poetry committed to drawing connections between geology and language shows that a geopoetic program indebted to Olson and Williams is not an inherently Americanist project. The long running cycle of works by Chris Torrance make for a striking, if little known, transatlantic parallel. In his afterward to *The Magic Door*, the work he began in the early 1970s and set amid the coalfields of South Wales, Torrance recalls the heyday of the Welsh coal boom in the 1960s, when "both deep mine & opencast methods were being used to obtain the coal" and "conditions for the workforce had gradually improved" (411–12). However, by the 1970s and 1980s, Torrance recounts, "there was 'trouble in the coal'" and the Neath Valley, the region whose terrain and transformations Torrance tracks across the eight books of *The Magic Door*, "went into decline" (412). For Torrance, these human and economic transformations participate in a broader set of cycles that inform his poetry: the seasons, weather, myths, rocks, and, especially, the carbon cycle. Coal, in Torrance's poetic universe, marks not only the transformation of organic to inorganic matter and back again but also the transformations attempted in alchemy and the geologic signature of the Neath Valley. Torrance's fascination with each of these cycles leads him to develop what poet Phil Maillard, in his introduction to *The Magic Door*, calls a "psychogeology," a process of "the outer world of rock formation and movement over time interacting with the inner, imaginative world of the poet" (17). If Dorn deconstructs the lyric *I* by showing how it is riven with preexisting discourses, then Torrance's psychogeologic investigations, with their dual emphasis on deep roots and continual change, attempt to locate the origin of the lyric *I*—and language itself—within the geologic realm.

Torrance's afterword provides a useful guide to *The Magic Door*'s psycho-geologic makeup in the form of a schema displaying the poetic concerns that circulate throughout the project:

trope	Neath Valley & surrounds		
type	upland country, split by fault		
	rich in coal		
topos		discovery	
		<u>terrain</u>	
		geology	glaciations
		climate	weather
activities	walking	gardening	making
		searching	the Celts
		stones	prehistory
		<u>evolution (411)</u>	

The terminology and layout of this chart immediately recalls Olson's triad of topos/typos/tropos, through which he hoped to document a detailed understanding of human situatedness in a specific corner of the world. What is more, the organization of the schema is similar to the formatting of Olson's verse essay "Proprioception," wherein categories such as "Physiology" and "The 'Place' of the 'Unconscious'" descend down the left-hand margin and correspond to explanations or instantiations (more verbose in Olson than in Torrance) on the middle-right side of the page (*Collected Prose* 179–99).[9] In Torrance's schema, Olson's somatically based theories are aligned with geologic, meteorological, archaeological, and mythological observations in order to create an encompassing map of a particular human located in a particular place.

The resonances with Olson continue in a literal map appearing at the beginning of the first book in the cycle, *Arcospirical Meanderings in a Tongue of the Time*. Drawn by Torrance's then wife Val, the diagram takes the form of a circle—suggesting again the theme of cycles—bisected by the cardinal directions and displaying, in a kind of azimuthal projection, the geology and geography of the valley. Around the map's circumference are small rectangular legends depicting the various rock formations and topographical features of the Neath: "Alluvium; Millstone Grit; Old Red Sandstone; Waterfalls; Carboniferous Limestone; Pennant Grit; Lower Coal Series" (28–29). The depiction of these different sets of strata and rocks, seemingly both riven and sutured by thick bold lines demarcating the River Neath and its tributaries, lends the map a striking visual similarity to Alfred Wegener's map of Pangea that Olson uses for the cover of *The Maximus Poems IV, V, VI*. As well, Torrance's use of the map as a prefatory figure establishes an approach to place that corresponds to Olson's understanding of topos; as Miriam Nichols puts it, place for Olson is "layered and dynamic, a series of moving *scapes* or regions of attention that geological, historical and mythical as much as they are landscapes" (31). These parallels between Torrance and Olson—and by extension Dorn—have been noted several times in the (still relatively slight) critical literature on Torrance's work. For example, in an entry on Torrance in his series "Black Mountain in England," Ian Brinton cites a description of Torrance as Wales's foremost "open-field" poet and later quotes from a review of *The Book of Brychan* (the fourth book in *The Magic Door* cycle) that compares Torrance's long poem to Olson's amalgam of "historical, geographical, geological, mythical and political" contexts. In an articulation of his working method that resonates with Olson's emphasis on energy transfer in "Projective Verse" and advice to "dig one place" in *A Bibliography on America for Ed Dorn*, Torrance explains that he tends to "take a subject, immerse myself in it and read it through till I feel I'm grasping certain rock-hard concepts in the middle of all the evidence, and these are the concepts I can use to propel what I feel lyrically onto the paper" (qtd. in Brinton). In this reply, Torrance uses a lithic analogy to indicate his search for a foundation on which to secure the *I*'s shifting experiences. As we will see, however, one such "rock-hard" concept in *The Magic Door* is that of metamorphosis itself. As a result, the poem employs geology as part of its search for both deep, abiding rhythms and continual change. In this section, I am going to adopt the trope/type/topos triad Torrance outlines in his afterword to spotlight how he generates an interrelated set of meanings of the word *neath* in *The Magic Door*. Much as Dorn deploys the trope of the pun to posit a nonarbitrary language, then, Torrance tropes on the various resonances within the toponym *Neath*, implying that the name is perfectly suited to the surroundings it specifies. Ultimately, Torrance ties the various senses of *neath* into a Jungian typology of the alchemical process, producing a topos that incorporates both the standing stones of Celtic mythology and the anthracite coal of modern-day mining.

I begin with *trope*. That Torrance places "Neath Valley & surrounds" under the category "trope" at first seems a bit odd; it would make more sense for the location, or ground, of the poems to appear under "topos." However, to recall Miriam Nichols's discussion of Olson's triad, *topos* can be glossed not only as the rhetorical term for a figure of speech but also as "the spin one puts on what one is given" (54). Thus, Nichols maintains that *tropos* involves a widening of "the Poundian field into the matrix of the various scapes of the human universe" and "a dialectical relationship between the individual and this matrix" (55). In this sense, "trope" comes first for Torrance because it identifies the "matrix" within which he finds himself in relation—hence, in the schema (itself a kind of matrix) quoted above, the item "& surrounds" is not simply a synonym for *environs* or *area* but marks, rather, this expanded sense of the field of forces in which the poet exists. While used sparingly in the poems, *matrix* is a crucial term that points to the rhetorical dimension of *trope*. To recall the earlier discussion of *matter* and *materia* in Dorn, *matrix* meant "womb" in Latin and is derived from *mater*, "mother." One of the clearest interlocutors for Torrance's work, aside from Olson, is Carl Jung, whose theories of masculine/feminine duality and the psychological allegory of alchemy permeate *The Magic Door*, especially as they posit the feminine as dark, chaotic, mysterious, womblike, and material. As Jung writes in *Psychology and Alchemy*, darkness "means chthonic, i.e., concrete and earthy" (177). The chthonic manifestation of the feminine that Torrance pulls from Jung allows him to trope on the concept of "Neath." Indeed, the Neath Valley is, poetically speaking, appropriately named, creating an onomastic play thrice over. First, the toponym *Neath* names the river (for which the valley is also named) and the Neath Disturbance, a set of faults and folds that gives south Wales its distinctive geology; second, it plays on the preposition '*neath*—as in *beneath* or *underneath*—suggesting both the geology of the region and the *nether* regions of darkness and chaos in Jungian psychology; third, Torrance repeatedly summons *Neith*, an Egyptian goddess associated with, among other things, motherhood. Neith becomes an increasingly prominent figure in the second half of *The Magic Door*, where Torrance invokes her as a sort of contrast to the "earthy," "dark" Jungian feminine. Thus, in his rather loose mixture of Celtic and Egyptian mythology, Torrance portrays Neith as "a sky goddess / with wheatstraw hair / who crosses the heavens / in a gilded boat" (223). In troping, or turning, the proper noun *Neath* in these various ways, Torrance torques Jungian psychology into a more explicitly geologic register. *Trope*, in this broader definition, includes what one makes of the place where one is (and how that place is named) and the decision Torrance made to leave a fledgling literary and professional life in London for the Welsh countryside.[10]

Geology and geologic formations are foundational to the wider matrix of the Neath Valley. Take, for example, an untitled poem in *Citrinas*, the second book of *The Magic Door*, in which we find the poet scanning the "utter clarity" of the horizon on Valentine's Day and watching "six white birds / rowing strongly / from horizon to horizon / sun reflecting bright / from pale underwing" (186). Intruding into this serene, imagistic scene is an abrupt cut to geologic description: "a rough grit conglomerate / broken off by ice action / sparkling with / rounded quartz pebbles / set into the matrix." In the geologic context, "matrix" is simply descriptive, referring to "a mass of fine-grained rock in which gems, crystals, or fossils are embedded" (*OED*). Within the broader scope of the poem, into which this detour into geology is dropped and then dispensed with as abruptly as it is taken up, the phrase "set into the matrix" illustrates the way this conglomerate appears in the poem. Like its rounded quartz pebbles, the rock is embedded, without being smoothly incorporated, into the midst of the poem's "matrix" of the Welsh countryside and—as the poem continues—the poet's social life of pubs, friendships, and romantic entanglements. Torrance uses the same phrase earlier in this book in the poem "Maen Madoc," which is one of several recounting his visits to the titular standing stone. At the site of this stone, Torrance sees "a few red sandstone erratics / ponder the retreat of the ice" before encountering Maen Madoc itself, "a sentinel on / the high & lonely moor / set into the matrix / of the Roman way, Sarn Helen" (144). Here "matrix," while hinting at its geologic meaning in the context of the standing stone, more generally refers to the "surrounds" of the site, as well as the infrastructural organization implied by the old Roman road named Sarn Helen. The stone and the surrounding "sandstone erratics" deposited by glaciers are "set" in the poem as sites of intensity, rather like the sandstone hoodoos in *Gunslinger*. Indeed, the standing rock of Maen Madoc, in the same manner as the hoodoos and remnants of volcanic activity in Dorn's poem, encapsulates the recurring dynamic of bedrock and drift: it features an immobile "standing" stone surrounded by "erratics," boulders carried and deposited by the glacier and thus serving as material traces of glacial drift. In a coda to this section of *Citrinas*, Torrance characterizes this standing stone as "1500 years a vibrant node / accumulating wind & water power / sun power, earth power" (158). As in the first example, the standing stone set into its surrounding context also describes its manner of appearance in the poem. While I don't have the space for an exhaustive catalogue of moments where geologic descriptions appear "set into the matrix" of Torrance's poems, it is a common pattern that sees strata, rocks, and individual stones as powerful, arresting nodes around which the wider context of the poems accumulates.

Archetypes and Anthracite

One final sense of *matrix* is relevant to Torrance's schema. In the craft of letterpress printing, a "matrix" refers to the mold used to cast a piece of type. Thus, the phrase "set into the matrix" evokes the casting of metal type and suggests, in turn, Jung's famous explanation of archetypes, in which he traces the word *type* to a Greek root meaning to "strike" or "blow." *Type*, for Jung, indicates a literal "imprint" in the psyche—an impression Olson, in "Projective Verse," will extend to include the strikes of the keys of the typewriter as a means for "scoring" (in the senses of both orchestrating and literally creating a mark or imprint on) the page (Jung 14).[11] Torrance's repeated use of expression "set into the matrix" mixes these geologic and typographical meanings with Jung's psychological sense, in which the matrix as womb stands in for the feminine half of the masculine/feminine archetypes that the self must learn to navigate as it progresses and regresses through the process of individuation. Throughout *The Magic Door*, Torrance displays an ambivalent engagement with Jungian archetypes, as he both organizes his poetic cycle around them and, at times, calls them into question. Generally, however, archetypes provide a method for Torrance's attempt to "get back to the roots," as he puts it in a section of *Citrinas* titled "Mirages," an effort that would presumably help the poet achieve individuation, challenging his repressions and integrating his opposing psychic energies (182).

The effort to find a kind of psychic bedrock by way of archetypes leads Torrance, at least in some poems, to abstract women in the poems into either earthy, mysterious enigmas or idealized figures—that is, into figures of the chthonic 'neath or the goddess Neith. We see this binary in his characterization of two standing stones, the Roman Maen Madoc, discussed earlier, and its Celtic counterpart Maen Llia. The latter is first alluded to in *Citrinas* in "Circumnavigating the Mountain," which directly follows the poem "Maen Madoc." Much later, in *The Book of Brychan*, the fourth book of *The Magic Door*, Torrance returns to the two menhirs, insisting that "certainly Llia the feminine lozenge / wide-hipped, ponderous, earth-wise / is more of an enigma / than the redbrown, fiery, upright" Madoc, associated with a certain "Dervacus, son of Justus" (270). In this sort of archetypal thinking, Maen Llia's diamond (lozenge) shape, presumably suggestive of a vulva, locates it in Jung's realm of the dark, material, chthonic, womblike, always mysterious feminine, in opposition to the "fiery, upright" masculine realm of Madoc. Such archetypal essentializing creeps into the poet's portrayal of flesh-and-blood women as well, especially in *The Diary of Palug's Cat*, the third book.[12] Torrance, separated from his first wife, becomes rather ambiguously involved with Sue, an intelligent and vivacious, though emotionally unstable, woman, and their volatile, erotic, and ultimately doomed relationship is played out over a series of diarylike prose passages. While Torrance often portrays Sue as mercurial and disturbed—and as a stand-in for the threatening cat of the book's title—after one of their more tranquil interactions, Torrance takes the other tack and elevates "Dazzling Sue" to immortal status: "God, she's so beautiful . . . / A goddess, Neith. / Why not. Any goddess ought to have a string of lovers. / As well as a magician to work spells for her. That's me: / Merlin" (230). In an even more obvious example of the poet's recourse to idealization to cope with Sue's complex humanity, in a postscript Torrance flatly notes that Sue later "took her own life" before immortalizing her again:

"lifted high like Neith the Sun / Goddess to whom I compared her in my vulnerable / model-making" (247). While there is a certain poignancy to this tribute, it tends to reinforce the depiction of Sue as less a real, complicated human being than a hybrid archetype of the perfect goddess and the dangerous, mysterious, hysterical other.

Indeed, Torrance's fondness for such archetypes and dichotomies makes his work, at times, an example of what Rachel Blau DuPlessis calls "patriarchal poetry." In her readings of several modernist and postmodernist male poets, including Olson, DuPlessis identifies on the one hand an urge to subvert normative expectations of masculinity by claiming an expanded range of positions and affects, including those which have been traditionally coded feminine, and on the other a failure to extend a similarly capacious concept of gender roles to women (5–6).[13] There is, I think, something of this pattern in Torrance's use of Jung. As constructed in the poems, at least, Torrance's persona inhabits an array of affects and variously gendered positions, including confidence, swagger, awe, gentleness, anger, insecurity, and anxiety—not to mention a general nonconformity to dominant societal norms in the early 1970s of a career-focused, breadwinning man. Lurking behind all of this, of course, is the Jungian concept of individuation—the integration of one's masculine and feminine, or light and dark, energies. While individuation has the potential to disrupt traditional gender roles, or at least challenge gender expectations, it's not clear whether this same possibility for integration can occur for women, as Torrance limits Sue to the dichotomy of goddess figure or "damaged," mysterious, and unknowable wraith.

Readers can recognize, however, the contradictions and illusions inherent in Torrance's archetypal musings. The comparison of Sue to Neith is qualified as "vulnerable / model-making," while, having cast himself as Merlin, Torrance quickly undermines his own bravado: "Shit. That's fantasy. But my role as writer / is involved." The poet may not be Merlin to Sue's Neith but, in his role as writer, he still must undertake "The recording of these actual events / The transformations taking place. The elements of myth & / legend" (230). Moreover, in what is an interesting counterpoint to DuPlessis, Nichols, elaborating on Olson's topos/typos/tropos triad, observes that in *typos*, or what Olson referred to as the allegory of the poet's life, "the *figure* is inevitably fallible and historically specific," but "[w]hat is essential in the presentation of an event is not the actor, but the actor as he or she brings forward the ground" (Nichols 60). Torrance writes in the first poem that appears in *The Magic Door*, "The New Territory," that with his move from London to Wales he hopes to fashion "a life of no more deceptions, of no more lies!" (31). Despite this aspiration, as Torrance admits in a poem written over a year later and in the frank glare brought on by a "Mushroom Fever," "Carrying my delusion like a material to be obtained, / or mined, from the obstinate soil of myself / the conflagration of opposites / – the problem is me" (55).

Torrance's mining metaphor demonstrates how the telluric is itself a type for the psychological. That is, if the aim of *The Magic Door* is to record "[t]he transformations / taking place" on multiple levels and at various scales, inside and outside the poet, then the "Neath Disturbance" designates not only the geologic formation but also, perhaps somewhat wryly, the poet's turbulent psyche. One of the effects of Torrance's psychogeologic practice over the course of *The Magic Door* is that inner and outer worlds become completely intertwined—a process we saw, if to much different effect, in *Gunslinger*. The internal machinations of the earth, often invisible to the human eye, nonetheless erupt onto and reshape the earth's surface in a process parallel to, if at much slower speeds (from a human perspective) than, human psychological change.

The observation of different levels and speeds of transformation marks how for Jung the metamorphosis of base metals into gold and the quest for the lapis philosophorum (the philosopher's *stone*) in alchemy anticipates the explorations of psychology—alchemy is a type, in the theological sense, of psychology. Torrance titles several sections and poems in the first two *Magic Door* books after stages in the alchemical process—the nigredo, albedo, rubedo, and citrinas, corresponding to the stages of chaos (or blackness), whitening, and brightness of the sun respectively—stages that Jung then maps onto the individuation process (Jung 230). In fact, Jung writes that the first alchemical stage, the nigredo, is inseparable from prima materia, the base element carbon: "the chief chemical constituent of the physical organism is carbon" (218). Carbon, which is "black—coal, graphite" is, according to Jung, both literally and figuratively the core of the self. For Jung and for Torrance, this makes the processes of alchemy and individuation analogous to the carbon cycle and its rhythms of decay and regeneration.

To turn to the category of *topos*, then, we can see how Torrance seizes on the centrality of carbon to the Jungian system in siting his observations of personal and geologic transformations among the coalfields of South Wales. Examples of Torrance's interest in coal and the carbon cycle are everywhere in *The Magic Door*. The poem "Arcospirical Meanderings in a Tongue of the Time," for instance, opens with the terse statement, "The tyranny of fuel," and finds, in the titular pulsations of "Up & down, round & round" a figure for "The insatiable fire" (37). In "'Day-by-Day Poem,'" which is composed of lines from other poets, Torrance remarks, "& I'm on the Northern tip / of the Welsh coalfield" and goes on to wonder, quoting from Barbara Guest's "The Location of Things," "'Am I to understand change, whether / remarkable or hidden?'" (43). Torrance's desire to apprehend cycles of transformation—whether psychological, alchemical, or geologic—forms the through line of *The Magic Door*. And here we can see once again the double movement that links geology and language: from one angle, geology, like etymology, offers a way to "get back to roots," to grasp the foundations of things, while from another angle, geology describes change—the drift of materials and the deformations wrought by planetary forces. Bedrock, despite its metaphorical suggestion of stability and permanence, is always undergoing metamorphosis. Language, for Torrance as for Dorn and Olson, likewise promises a correspondence between words and things, and yet trying to enact such ties, as Torrance does with *neath*, brings forth language's contingent, polysemic character. Both dynamics are present in the poem "Letter to Barry MacSweeney," where, writing to his friend and fellow poet, Torrance details the geology and mythology of the Neath Valley. Torrance's discursive geologic description, which is bookended, in the "set in the matrix" manner I noted earlier, by his relation of a boozy bike ride with multiple pit stops at pubs (another sort of "cycle," perhaps?), seems to emphasize the vast timescales, even bordering on timelessness, of the topography. In the poem's description, "Islands of the Basal Grit crop up / through the Drift," the nonstandard capitalizations lending the formations an air of permanence. Compounding the sense of a mythic, ahistorical landscape, Torrance ties these features to the nearby promontory "Craig Y Dinas, under which in / a cavern are reputed to lie King Arthur & his men," thus equating geologic time with that of local mythology. The dynamism of Torrance's verbs, however, belies the continual transformations occurring over millions of years. The "Grit" that seems to resist the "Drift" is nonetheless riddled with "swallow holes," revealing the porousness of the "Carboniferous Limestone / below." And, while this limestone is "folded up in a nose" (echoing, if inadvertently, Prynne's topological anthropomorphisms discussed in the next chapter), it is also part of "a sharply folded & shattered anticline with / calcite-ridden thrust zones that rears out of the / confusion of the Neath Valley Disturbance" (169). The rock, far from a stable presence, is an index of violent deformational processes that shatter, cleave, and surge across its only apparently solid exterior.

Of course, the cyclical transformations Torrance highlights exhibit their own sort of stability. The predictability and consistency of cycles, whether of seasons or of carbon, connotes the persistent rhythms of the earth, and, in contrast to Smithson's entropic sense of time, Torrance foregrounds a circular conception of time as repetition. The entire poem is labeled a "cycle," and the cyclical figure manifests in Torrance's attention to the weather, especially the "position / of the true polar front, the area / of cyclogenesis" (88). As we have seen, the circle also functions as a kind of emblem for Torrance's poetic cycle in the form of the circular map delineating Neath Valley geology that opens *Arcospirical Meanderings*. An "arcospirical meandering" could also describe Jung's fusion of alchemical and psychological processes. Jung refers to "the spiral of inner development" by means of which the alchemist (and psychoanalyst) advance toward the center, "the life-giving vessel" described variously as "the uterus" or simply "the stone," and "surrounded by the spiral, the symbol of indirect approach by means of *circumambulation*" (177–79). Likewise, Ian Brinton maintains that this spiraling movement is a key component of Torrance's poetry and, quoting Samuel Charters, compares *The Magic Door* to "the endless circling, eddying movement" of Olson's *Maximus Poems*. From these circles it is only a small step to the ebb and flow of circulation. In "Subsidence was Pulsatory, However"—a title which, in its simultaneous citation and decontextualizing of a discursive register, recalls several of Prynne's titles in *The White Stones*, not least "The Glacial Question, Unsolved," a focus of the next chapter—Torrance melds morphological and circulatory activities. The poem comprises a series of the speaker's imagistic impressions, loosely linked through the similarity of their rhythmic rise and fall. These include the "trough subsiding weakly above" (recalling the counterclockwise rotation of a low-pressure system or cyclone), "the marshy terrain / eroding away downslope" that is "both manuring / & killing the tree," and the way "the very stones reach out" to the poet. Prompted by the flash of "[a] roadwork / cut into subsoil" of "sandy-clay alluvium / or glacial till" (152), the poem condenses the geologic history of the Neath Valley into a rushed, tumbling geochronology:

> breccias & acid plutonic intrusions,
> tuffs & ashes & lava flows
> now an outwash of debris in intense rainfall
> the storms tearing the rocks apart
> washing the debris over arid plains
> quartz fragments driven seaward
> to mingle with mudswarm (153)

These metamorphic processes repeat again and again, the land settling ("subsidence") only to "now uplift" before being "again invaded by muddy seas," the cycle restarting. The cycles of sedimentation and subsidence join with the carbon cycle as these pulsations eventually create the "coal peat bed composites" that would form, as Torrance writes elsewhere, "the cradle of the Industrial Revolution" (153, 411). But while these larger, deeper cycles occur over the course of millennia, the poem also attends to the faster (relatively speaking), more localized processes of erosion, chemical weathering, and deposition. Hence, in the "metamorphosis of deposits / formation of the fine anthracites / of the Vale of Neath," as the closing lines of "Subsidence Was Pulsatory" put it, the terrain appears fully in flux: flowing, folding, cracking, seething, and surging around the equally ungrounded poet (153).

The product of these pulsating rhythms, the "fine anthracites" (also known as "hard coal") provide the final piece of the topos of the Neath Valley and suggest, as well, a final type of cycle: economic. More precisely, they augur the boom-and-bust cycle of capitalism and the extractive industries that drive it. Ironically, it is this economic imperative to extract and burn resources such as coal that may well put an end to, or at least significantly disturb, the stability of the seasonal cycles altogether. The global warming caused by the burning of fossil fuels is raising ocean levels and temperatures, melting glaciers, and disrupting the jet stream and ocean currents, each of which changes will massively affect the duration and timing of seasons. Even these seemingly inalterable rhythms are subject to metamorphosis. More locally, the economic decline of the Welsh coalfields Torrance notes in the afterword was accompanied not surprisingly by the ecological scars left behind when coal mines closed. In the poem "Terrain," Torrance writes of "the bleak moorland & coal spoil East of the / Hirwaun Industrial Estate" and notices how, as the mines are shuttered, "the violent wounds are even now being / landscaped as 'tone' / becomes ubiquitous" (121). With the "stone" removed, all that's left is "tone," a managed modulation of the terrain.

This enforced return of the land to a simulacrum of its unmined state cannot erase these "wounds." In his summation of the transformations wrought by the mining industry, Torrance provides a further analogy that resonates with Prynne's attempt to create a unified theory of anthropic, linguistic, and geologic morphology, with which I begin my next chapter. "The industrial base vanished slowly but surely like the Cheshire Cat," Torrance writes, "but, instead of a grin, leaving behind a furrowed brow" (412). In the work of Prynne and Maggie O'Sullivan, geopoetics finds a more explicit theory of embodiment than is present in Smithson, Dorn, or Torrance, one that raises the interrelation of marks and landmarks, words and world, welts and *welt*.

CHAPTER 3

Bedrock and Drift

Earth, Language, and Bodies in J. H. Prynne and Maggie O'Sullivan

In a February 14, 1966, letter accompanying a package sent from Cambridge, England, to Gloucester, Massachusetts, J. H. Prynne apprised Charles Olson in urgent tones that "[b]oth Ed [Dorn] and I have gone halves towards getting this to you, presuming after this small delay that you could not do without a political document of such current relevance" (Olson and Prynne 161–62). The crucial document in question was *A Symposium on Continental Drift*, the published papers of a 1965 Royal Society conference that affirmed in large part the controversial and much disputed theory of continental drift and plate tectonics first developed by the German geophysicist Alfred Wegener. The importance that Prynne and Dorn accord this geologic treatise is doubly revealing. For one, it reminds us that geology, far from a settled science, was undergoing something of an upheaval in the 1950s and 1960s as new evidence of continental drift led to the gradual acceptance of plate tectonics—something to keep in mind when considering why writers and artists like Smithson, Dorn, and Coolidge made geology a central part of their compositions in the 1960s and beyond. Second, it demonstrates how geology impinges on the poetics of Olson and Prynne, as well as on the era's political struggles. This chapter will argue that Olson and Prynne—and a subsequent generation of writers influenced by this Black Mountain lineage and epitomized here by Maggie O'Sullivan—sought a bedrock layer in culture, linguistics, and geology that could bind language to land and the body in a nonarbitrary relation.

However, as the texts I focus on in this chapter reveal, the poetic and political charge of geology for these writers is that it at once promises a bedrock foundation for language and manifests the utter contingency of materiality.

Moraines, Ridges, and Brows: J. H. Prynne and Charles Olson

Prynne had written Olson a month earlier, in January 1966, to inform him about the "very exciting symposium run by the Royal Society of London on Continental Drift" and note that the papers given at the conference "refer to Wegener unceasingly" (150).[1] This last observation is in response to Olson's earlier inquiries about obtaining a color version of Alfred Wegener's map of the original supercontinent Pangea. In his reply to Prynne's letter, Olson exclaims, "I can't tell you how useful striking this symposium has been to me" and he asks again about finding "a colored Wegener just when the jig-saw splitting shows of the original single Earth. Which, as you know, has been my purpose for the cover of the volume [*Maximus Poems IV, V, VI*]" (152). Olson's mythopoetic fascination with the possibility of an "original single Earth" forms the basis of his interest in geology, an interest that Prynne shares and that defines this period of cross-pollination between so-called new American poetry and the British poetry revival. Indeed, as Joseph Pizza argues, for Prynne and fellow British poets Andrew Crozier and Peter Riley "the concurrent enthusiasm over continental drift (particularly its positing of a word in constant movement, along with the likelihood that North America, Britain, and Eurasia were previously united), became for these writers a scientific vindication of Olson's poetic and the subsequent revolution in British poetry they sought" (283). Likewise, Alex Latter, in a study of the influential poetry worksheet *The English Intelligencer*—edited and produced in large part by Prynne, Crozier, and Riley—views their interest in geology as part of a late modernist project to "reinstate 'the question of origins' as one of the utmost urgency" and thus "recover an earlier, mythic understanding of humanity's relationship with the world around it" (61). As we saw in the introduction, this idea of a once unitary earth is grounded in a theory of natural language indebted to Ernest Fenollosa, whose geolinguistic analogies were elemental to writers informed by a Poundian, Black Mountain poetics. As Latter explains, much as geology, for these writers, suggests an original, unbroken supercontinent, a geologic conception of language "posits the existence of a mythically coherent language" (57). Language and geology are often intertwined in Prynne's and Olson's correspondence. To take just one example, a few weeks after first alerting Olson to the *Symposium on Continental Drift*, and after several letters back and forth alluding to specific papers from the meeting, Prynne writes Olson, "Just a note, as of a new (and rubricated) scholasticism: the stratigraphy of current language" (157). As we will see throughout this chapter, such linguistic stratigraphy—like geology itself—points in two directions: the etymological methods displayed to differing degrees by Olson, Prynne, and O'Sullivan hypothesize a foundational, natural ground for language; and yet, such procedures only work because they rely on the contingent and continual transformations language undergoes, precisely because it is arbitrary and not natural. A search for the bedrock of language uncovers the drift of words.

In both his correspondence with Olson and the poems written during that correspondence, Prynne presents language and its etymological accumulations and erosions as being analogous to geologic processes. He also, however, imagines that language and geology are more than just analogues, speculating that language itself arises out of (or at least concomitantly with) geomorphology. Prynne derives the grounds for this speculation from his and Olson's enthusiasm for Indo-European etymology. Thus, in this tangle of geology and linguistics, etymology is doing double duty: it enacts, on a condensed time scale, geohistorical processes like sedimentation and stratification even as it hopes to form the fundament of a deep connection between words and earth.

Prynne's development of a nexus binding human, linguistic, and geomorphic origins is apparent in a poem such as "The Glacial Question, Unsolved," especially if it is read in the context of Prynne's contemporaneous correspondence with Olson. The question of "The Glacial Question" refers to the exact timing of the most recent period of glaciation in the Pleistocene and the effect of its retreat on the spread of prehistoric civilizations in England. Prynne is particularly interested in the disagreement among geologists at the time regarding when exactly the Pleistocene ended or whether it had in fact ended at all. The poem is a metastudy, a review of the existing literature, as it were, on the delineation of the Pleistocene epoch and the geographic extent of glaciation in northern Europe.

The unresolved issue of temporal and geologic boundaries is suggested in the opening lines of the poem:

> In the matter of the ice, the invasions
> were partial, so that the frost
> was a beautiful head
>   <u>the sky cloudy</u>
> and the day packed into the crystal
> as the thrust slowed and we come to
> a stand, along the coast of Norfolk. (Prynne 65)

Prynne's notoriously difficult syntax here enacts the temporal confusion surrounding the Pleistocene. The first three lines present the problem in the register of a natural history, employing the past tense and using nouns such as "invasions" and "head" in their technical, geologic senses (the "head" is the topmost part of a valley glacier from which the glacier flows out and "invasion" refers to the advance of a glacier or ice sheet into a previously nonglaciated area).[2] However, the stanza break and indented fourth line creates a split, much as if two puzzle pieces—or continental plates—had just begun to drift apart. This visual rupture becomes a temporal one in the sixth line with the sudden switch to the present tense in "we come to / a stand." What began as a generalizing overview with language taken from geologist W. B. R. King's 1955 article "The Pleistocene Epoch in England," one of the "references" Prynne provides at the end of the poem, shifts into a more intimate register and abruptly brings the reader up to the present moment. In other words, while the spacing inserts a visual divide between past and present, the syntax makes them overlap. Which is, indeed, part of Prynne's point: the geology (as Olson might put it) leans into the present, deep time coexisting with humans' narrower temporal horizon.

The overlapping temporalities Prynne creates are further confused by the ensuing line's description of the "stand . . . along the coast of Norfolk" as "a relative point" (65). The exact nature of the "relative point" indicated here is ambiguous: it could be a feature of the coastal terrain, a claim in one of the geologic articles Prynne draws from, or a relative point in time. Moreover, Prynne uses the pronoun "that" at the beginning of this line, although it is not clear what antecedent noun it refers to. As many commentators on Prynne have pointed out, such ambiguity is one of Prynne's most prominent poetic strategies. For instance, in their monograph on Prynne, N. H. Reeve and Richard Kerridge pinpoint one of the most peculiar features of his poetry when they note the frequency of demonstratives that lack clear antecedents and observe that this "lack of specificity is often combined with a rigorously assertive tone." As Reeve and Kerridge argue, such an odd blend of "rhetorical authority . . . without an explicit or paraphrasable didactic purpose" has the effect of shifting the burden of how to orient oneself to and within the poem (and thus the world) to the reader (40–41). Prynne continually poses the question of orientation, or what Reeve and Kerridge call an Olsonian/modernist move "realigning oneself towards experience," through his mix of discursive registers. In Prynne, scientific discourse "has no status associated with claimed objectivity" (17). Scientific language is itself a "relative point." Implied in this "relative point" and "stand" that the poem arrives at in its opening lines is a sense of orientation or facing. Thus the "head" of the glacier/frost doubles as a point of view, a suggestion that is reinforced throughout the poem in terms such as "lobe," "interior," "sentiment," and "feeling." Prynne shows how seemingly conventional lyrical moments centered on the self are "already implicated in and mediated by a range of natural, social, and economic processes external to them" (Reeve and Kerridge 37). In an extended close reading of "The Glacial Question," Thomas Roebuck and Matthew Sperling note the way preferential or prejudicial language already resides within supposedly objective scientific terminology. They highlight the word "invasion" in the poem's first line, which, describing the ice's advance from the north, could "imply Danish and Scandinavian invasions of Britain (from the ninth to the eleventh century) which also brought with them northern words which were sedimented into the language" (44).[3] Thus, if the reference to the frost's "beautiful head" in the third line "is the first moment at which the technical geological language of the poem gives way to judgments of aesthetic and humane value," the poem's geologic terminology ("invasions") already deploys "a value-laden language" (45). I'll have more to say about the trope of words as sediment later, but here the point is that Prynne's poetry has often been read as bringing forth the implicit "stands," or traces of orientations, in technical language.

At the same time, the intimation of orientations and heads indicates a specific process of drift occurring in "The Glacial Question." I'm going to argue that the poem makes a series of metonymic displacements that flow from "frost" to "head" to the glacial ice itself. Crucially, this movement reveals Prynne's conviction, at least at this relatively early stage in his career, that language arises from specific topographies—that words, and the human bodies that use words, are nothing less than a material extension of a particular terrain. The poem first establishes this conceit in the stanza break between lines 3 and 4, which calls attention to the juxtaposition of "head" and "sky." The link between the geologic "head" of the ice and the human head is made more explicit through an echo in the penultimate stanza, when the speaker, reflecting on the scouring, land-forming action of the glacier as it retreated north, remarks on the resulting "hollows with sandy clay / as the litter of surface" and the postglacial terrain's cradling effect: "We are rocked / in this hollow, in the ladle by which / the sky, less cloudy now, rests on our / foreheads" (66). The lineation enacts the feeling of foreshortening the passage describes, as the line break after "our" allows "the sky" to literally rest on top of "foreheads." Moreover, in conjunction with the "face" in the "surface" traces the glacier has left behind, the poem posits an overlap of head, sky, and topography.

In fact, the strange motif of the sky resting on the forehead opens onto the poem's main crux and the unsolved question alluded to in the poem's title: namely, an end date for the Pleistocene. This geologic question is inextricable from earth's meteorological history. Prynne, quoting from W. B. R. King's article "The Pleistocene Epoch in England," states immediately after these lines, "Our climate is maritime, and / 'it is questionable whether there has yet been / sufficient change in the marine faunas / to justify a claim that // the Pleistocene Epoch itself / has come to an end.'" For Prynne, these climatic and geologic considerations are far from idle or academic: they bear on the interrelated concerns of transformation and temporality, of how land and language changes over time. After the end of the quotation from King,

Prynne continues, "We live in that / question, it is a condition of fact: as we / move it adjusts the horizon" (66). The retreat of the glaciers quite literally laid the "ground," or as Prynne puts it earlier in the poem, "what we hope to call 'land'"—that is, the land mass that would come to be called "England"—hence Prynne's perhaps nationalistic use the first person plural "we" throughout the poem (65).[4] The advance and diminution of the glaciers over vast periods of time are, in turn, driven by climatic change that "adjusts the horizon" in the sense that it both determines the shifting boundaries between land, water, and ice and the variations in cloudiness and rainfall that form a distinctive feature of England's "maritime" climate. As Prynne explains in an earlier stanza, the glacial and fluvioglacial deposits—the drift—that forms the strata and topography surveyed in the poem display "the facts / in succession, they *are* succession, and / the limits are not times but ridges / and thermal delays" (66). Thus, the horizon is a "ridge" in the sense of both a visual limit to a spectator's surround and a meteorological boundary marking high pressure. The "thermal delays" referenced here are, furthermore, *ridges*—that is, contour lines marking the boundaries between temperatures. In the poem's third stanza, Prynne refers to the advance and retreat of "the 50° isotherm" creating "that sudden warmth which took / birch trees up into Scotland" (65). Such ridges influence the weather that creates the characteristics of the horizon.

By an oblique route, these topographical and meteorological ridges return us to heads. In the second stanza, Prynne paraphrases his geologic sources to demarcate the extent of the ice's "invasion" by way of a "moraine" that can be tracked "right to north London" (65). A moraine is a type of ridge, formed from an agglomeration of rocks and sediment that is then transported and deposited at a glacier's "edges or extremity" (*OED*). Describing this moraine in the fourth stanza, Prynne observes how "the curving spine of the cretaceous / ridge, masked as it is by the drift, is / wedged up to the thrust: the ice fronting / the earlier marine" (65). Here, Prynne again yokes the imagery of bodies and heads to geomorphology, as in the enjambment that pushes "ridge" up against "masked" (the comma between them placing extra stress on the latter), and the depiction of "the ice fronting" or *facing* the marine sediments. As it happens, this collocation is apt from an etymological perspective, as *moraine* comes to English through *morre*, a term in French dialect for "snout," which in turn derives from the French *morion*, a type of helmet worn by sixteenth- and seventeenth-century soldiers (*OED*). Thus, the rounded morainal deposits left behind by the ice suggest a snout, providing yet another referent for the "beautiful head" Prynne invokes at the poem's outset.

More than simply an etymological curiosity, however, the concatenation of ice, frost, ridges, and heads I am following here leads to some of Prynne's central concerns in this period of his career, especially regarding his (and Olson's) linguistic theories. Indeed, Olson, in a June 3, 1966, letter to Prynne, records his enthusiastic reaction to "The Glacial Question, Unsolved" in his typical exclamatory, scattershot fashion: "Wow, the syntax, and the line: like Baudelaire said is there [I have to go look, from my very first poem: Voila, a Tide in the affairs of man to discern!" (189; underline and bracket in original).[5] Olson's Shakespearean reference, with a detour through Baudelaire, could refer to the passage in the third stanza of "The Glacial Question" noting "the eustatic rise / in the sea-level" driven by the melting of the glaciers as temperatures warmed. But for Olson the main upshot of the poem is the way the question of geologic epochs has the potential to reintegrate humans into their surroundings. As Olson asks rhetorically, "And isn't it beautiful the question that Pleistocene isn't over? That the intervallic is the short wonder of man." Olson is excited about a poetry which would demonstrate how this (hu)man could "resemble his own movements, that he not continue to treat all he knows as high-fallutin? get his nose to what he does?" (190). Olson closes the letter with a particularly ecstatic and vatic statement of artistic purpose: "It must be, that all the lights will go on. They do, + the noses: I am swept into the stream Fantastic. And like take it away!" (189–90).

Olson's repeated reference to noses in this note may be no more than coincidental, the (typically gendered, for Olson) injunction for "man" to "get his nose to what he does" merely an echo of his frequent recommendation, as related to Ed Dorn in *A Bibliography on America*, "to dig one thing or place or man until you yourself know more abt that than is possible to any other man." In fact, the nose as a figure for the dogged (male) historian or archeologist may be something of a trope for Olson, as, a few paragraphs later in the "bibliography," he reminds Dorn that it "all goes back to the ONE JOB [ie., to exhaust the primary and secondary sources on a given topic]—that's where one's nose is whittled" (*Collected Prose* 306–7). However, in the correspondence with Prynne, such facial features take on an added importance, as they engender a remarkable statement of Prynne's poetics. After a series of mainly short messages in which Prynne sends Olson academic articles on linguistics, toponyms, and prehistoric archaeology, on July 7, 1966, (a month after Olson's reaction to "The Glacial Question") Prynne sends a cryptic, one-sentence query: "What is the Outer Prêdmost?" (194). By July 16—without a response from Olson to this letter—Prynne is answering his own question, as he writes to Olson that "Prêdmost" is an "epipaleolithic site in Moravia," citing V. Gordon Childe's 1929 study *The Danube in Prehistory* (196). Two days later, Prynne writes again, adding a "postscriptum" in which he provides a recent (1962) chart of the Prêdmost area's "geochronology . . . with the C14 dates alongside and the glacial oscillations set in provisional order" (197). For Prynne, the issue is to establish when, precisely, glacial retreat allowed for prehistoric European cultures to take root and thus to solve "the problem of sequence" raised in "The Glacial Question."

Prynne had come across Prêdmost in reading *The Maximus Poems*—although in the correspondence he can't remember where the reference appears in *Maximus* and Olson doesn't remember using it at all. Specifically, the allusion occurs in *The Maximus Poems*, volume 3, poem 13, where Olson proffers a belief in "God / as fully physical / thus the Outer Prêdmost / of the World in which we 'hang' / as though it were wood and our own bodies are / hanging on it" (381). While the Christlike imagery in this brief poem is obvious, it's less clear how exactly Olson is deploying the archaeological site. Perhaps Prêdmost, as a location indicating an early proto-European culture, is presented here as both genesis and abiding structure of the Western world, the kind of grounding, or rooting, in prehistory (and proto-Indo-European languages) that Olson was hoping to resurrect.

For our purposes, what is important is Prêdmost's role in the correspondence and the development of Olson's and Prynne's thinking about morphology and language. On July 20, 1966, Olson responds to Prynne's original one-line inquiry with the information that his source for Prêdmost was C. F. C. Hawkes's study *The Prehistoric Foundations of Europe*. For Olson, of key interest is the discovery of the "Brüna-face skeletons there and the shouldered point" blade (197). Olson enthuses over this face shape, and asserts, on aesthetic if not archaeological grounds, "What seems to me attractive entirely—even about Outer—Paleolithic, of this group (or jump!) of men, coming toward the Mesolithic, even with my love for the more Sioux-like faces of Aurignacians of Crô-Magnon, is that these were of this shoulder-blade + narrower face" (198).[6] While Olson is on shaky ground—or thin ice—here, as I read him he is mainly interested, like Prynne, in what these different facial shapes reveal about temporal sequence, and not in any type of hierarchical arrangement of proto-European cultures. Olson's focus is on pinpointing when certain linguistic, cultural, and geologic changes occurred in order to establish a solid historical ground for his mythopoetic claims. In a follow-up letter penned the next day, July 21, Olson expands on this point, telling Prynne, "And ice [as you have yourself so successfully shown—exhibited] is history" so that "what you have shown, there, that that Island bounces—floats up + down. And it is ridged" (199; brackets in original). In other words, for Olson, "The Glacial Question" demonstrates the central role ice and the ridged moraines of its drift played in the literal formation of the British Isles.

Prynne, for his part, takes Olson's enthusiasm in an even more literal direction, linking the "ridged" postglacial landscape directly to physical and linguistic morphology. In his letter of July 26, 1966, Prynne comments, "Those heavy brow ridges are exciting, as any ridged bone is an extension of landscape and its necessities: change as deformation and the crustal folding" (199). In referring to "those heavy brow ridges," Prynne has apparently shifted from Olson to his source, Hawkes's *Prehistoric Foundations*. There, in a passing mention of Předmost, Hawkes notes that "human remains have been found of a long-skulled physical type with well-ridged brows but a narrow face," adding that for him, as for Prynne, the excitement of this discovery lies in confirming "an unbroken succession" from earlier to later Pleistocene cultures (30–31). Prynne extends and radicalizes this line of argument, speculating that these skull shapes directly reflect geomorphology. According to Prynne, the "well-ridged brows" index the ridged terrain left behind by the glaciers. This postglacial terrain is, furthermore, a sign of climatic change—that is, of temperature ridges. Indeed, the very fact that there is postglacial terrain suggests how ice, like the earth's crust in continental drift, is both fixed and flowing. A paradoxical river of ice, a glacier is always melting and moving; ice is always transforming from a crystalized to a fluid state and back again. In his explanation of the importance of ice later in this letter, Prynne echoes the beginning of "The Glacial Question": "I don't know why this matter of ice has not been got to before, as the Gulf Stream offers that exilic or borrowed warmth which makes frost into the history of the English spirit" (200). Prynne pushes this thesis still further in a letter of August 9, prefaced as "[o]n ridge, further to the last note." He traces the word *ridge* to its Anglo-Saxon roots, "referring to a raised strip of cultivated land" and observing that "lland can also be used in this local sense, as a measure delimiting the unit of rise and fall in arable terrain" (204). From here, Prynne cites two articles by the economic historian M. W. Beresford, "who advances an 'equation' by means of which open-field maps may be reconstructed from currently existing landforms," because, as he explains, quoting Beresford, "the single strip of the medieval fields is represented exactly by the ridge and furrow of the modern English landscape . . . this twenty-two feet or so is the selion, the land, the ridge, of all open-field documents from the 12th century to the 19th" (204; underscores are presumably Prynne's own).

Given that Prynne is writing to Olson, it is hard not to hear, in the phrases "open-field" and "open-field documents"—not to mention in the language of feet and measurements—an intimation of Olson's "open-field" poetics and projective verse, and to read this letter as Prynne's attempt to quite literally ground an open-field practice in the ridged landscape cocreated by glacial scouring and human tillage.[7] Indeed, as Prynne affirms later in the letter, "the turning and returning curvature of tillage is part of the language, our metric of repetition, tribal response as an immediate response to landform: the condition of being" (204). It's useful to recall here that the word *verse* itself comes from the Latin *versus*, "a turn of the plow, a furrow, a line of writing" (*OED*). The *verse*, or turn, of the plow and its metric repetition lies at the center of Prynne's mythopoetic account, in which "the ridge is the assertion and presence of style, land held like a tent or the ridge-pole of a shamanistic lodge." Drawing on influential accounts of shamanism by Mircea Eliade and A. F. Anisimov, while anticipating Dorn's insistence on a sidereal orientation in *Gunslinger*, Prynne locates his mythopoetic project on this ridge: "this idealized ridge-work is the touch of that sidereal presence, tracked in the heavens or some notion of <u>level</u> as where we are (standing forth, as a mode of <u>ek-stasis</u>). The myth and extent of this terrain is entirely literal." The etymological affiliation of *literal* with *letter* is a further reminder that the "ek-static," shamanistic poetics being espoused here is thoroughly bound up with a conceit that views language as, if not identical to, then at least arising from, the earth. In Prynne's poetics, then, the ridge becomes "the <u>lie</u> of our <u>world</u>, how far we can raise the entire <u>condition</u>: tillage is the shamanic relation to land and the ridge is its metric achievement" (Olson and Prynne 205).

Prynne may also be thinking here of Olson's frequent references to the postglacial topography of the Dogtown section of Gloucester in *The Maximus Poems*. A particularly prominent mention comes in "Maximus, From Dogtown – 1," one of the opening poems of *The Maximus Poems IV, V, VI*, which would first be published in London by Cape Goliard in 1968. This poem has been commented on frequently, though not often in the context of Olson's engagement with Prynne. In the poem (or "proem" as Olson heads it), there are several mentions of the "WATERED ROCK" underlying the "pasture meadow orchard road" in which the sailor "Merry" is killed in his wrestling match with a bull (172). Throughout his oblique telling of this mythic story, Olson repeatedly digresses to remark on the "soft rock" of Dogtown: for instance, Olson declares, "And down / the ice holds / Dogtown, scattered / boulders," referring to the glacial erratics, or isolated boulders strewn along the Atlantic seaboard by retreating glaciers (173). Further along in the poem, Olson situates Dogtown "high up on her granite / horst," the ground "this / terminal moraine: / the rocks the glacier tossed" (175). As Miriam Nichols explains, paraphrasing George Butterick's *A Guide to the Maximus Poems*, the poem's topos is the "'watered rock' of Dogtown—literally a moraine of glacial deposits permeable to water" (51). For Nichols, the jumps in the poem between historical, mythic, and geologic time frames show how "events" for Olson are processes "composed of spatiotemporal strata of varying velocities. . . . The earth is 'quick' and molten in the center and striated at its crust" (49). The layering of these different temporal speeds forms, Nichols notes, Olson's sense of *measure*, his way of placing the human within the wider "Open Whole" of the nonhuman world (56). Given that the time frame of the letters dealing with ice and ridges (May,

June, July, and August, 1966) is, per Butterick's editorial notes, precisely the time at which Olson was reviewing the proofs of the typescript Prynne had recently prepared of *The Maximus Poems IV, V, VI*, it seems possible that Dogtown's granitic moraines linger behind Prynne's "The Glacial Question."[8] In particular, Olson's image of "the roads / of Dogtown trickling like / from underground rock / springs" (*Maximus Poems* 173) finds an echo in the third-to-last stanza of "The Glacial Question," where "the roads / run dripping across" the glacial deposits of Norfolk. In this antepenultimate stanza, Prynne writes that "the rhythm" of this undulating terrain of moraines and depressions "is the declension of history" within which, to quote the beginning of the next stanza, "we are rocked" (66). In the pun on "rocked" as both mineral matter and cradling rhythm, as well as in declension's double referral to descending geologic strata and the grammatical morphology of words, Prynne suggests the metrics of moraines that he will later work out more discursively in his correspondence with Olson. Whether or not this echo is intentional, in both cases the image of fluvial routes layered upon postglacial strata is an effective figure for how the poems meld glacial and human, geologic and geographic, rhythms.

This rhythmic postglacial terrain is created by the fluctuation of the isothermal temperature ridges that mark, meteorologically, the advance and retreat of the last ice age and thus the advent of the Pleistocene. In fact, in yet another instance of serendipitous etymology, *ice* has a Germanic origin that can be traced back to the Old Teutonic *iso*, recalling the unrelated etymology for *isotherm* in the Greek *isos* (equal). Remarking on this etymology of ice (though without linking it to "isotherm"), Roebuck and Sperling observe that "Prynne frequently implies an analogy between geologic processes and the way words accumulate historical significance from their etymological root and across their developing history" (43–44). This is an accurate description of Prynne's method (and that of the other writers featured throughout this book). And yet, in creating a further connection between *ice* and *ridge*, the chance similarity between the prefix *iso* and the root of *ice* again underscores the dual nature of etymology at play here. Like geology, etymology provides Prynne with both a claim to a kind of bedrock—the grounding of language in common roots—and access to the contingent drift of signifiers which allows for fortuitous folds and overlaps.

Following the ridges and contours of this drift ultimately leads Prynne to an etymological chain binding the earth to the body. Later in the letter expressing his "excite[ment]" over "those heavy brow ridges," Prynne quotes a passage from the tenth-century Anglo-Saxon poem "The Wanderer," highlighting a line that he translates as "frost and snow falling, mingled with hail."[9] In this letter, he focuses especially on the Old English word *hrim* (frost) and posits that it "connects directly with rim, in the first sense of a crust (of a wound, which is again history as pain, the infliction of time." "Rim" may also be the infliction of *rime*, in the sense of both "rime ice"—that is, frost—and an archaic spelling of *rhyme*, an allusion, of course, to poetry. "Rim" brings Prynne to the Anglo-Saxon "hruse, earth, ground, the crust on which we walk" and adds that "[t]he ridge here is welt" (Olson and Prynne 201). With "welt," Prynne manages to tie together *rim* (as in the leather rim attaching the sole of a shoe to its upper), a bump or swollen trace of a blow to the flesh, and a pun on the German *welt* (world). Pushing this logic of flesh and crust to its conclusion, Prynne opens his well-thumbed edition of Julius Pokorny's 1959 *Indogermanisches etomologisches Wörterbuch* (Indo-European etymological dictionary) to find that "Pokorny takes it all back to I. kreu-, kreud-: kru, thick, clotted blood, leading to kreus-, krus-, ice, crust (or scab)," an etymology that Prynne uses to imagine geomorphology as "the infliction of time" (201). Linking human skin and the earth's crust in a mutual condition of wounded and scabbed vulnerability to change, Prynne implies, in a manner reminiscent of Smithson's insistence on the increase of entropy over time, that time is experienced physically as pain and disorder.

Many of Prynne's commentators have remarked on this streak of somatic intensity in his work. Reeve and Kerridge give the most succinct statement of this matter when they write, "Here is one of the central paradoxes in Prynne's work: that a poetry so cerebral, so full of abstract and technical vocabulary, so rootless in its shifting from discourse to discourse, should attend so assiduously to the body" (128). Likewise, Peter Middleton, in an essay titled "On Ice" that contrasts Prynne's and Olson's work to the many historical and topographical woundings in the work of Susan Howe, encounters in "The Glacial Question" "a fictional, subjective register incompatible with realist science" (88). Specifically, Middleton singles out the third stanza in which Prynne asserts that "[t]he striations" of glacial drift "are part of the heart's / desire." In the fourth stanza, Prynne reprises this subjective and affective turn, claiming, as if it followed logically from the preceding lines' highly technical description of the cretaceous ridge, "so that the sentiment / of 'cliffs' is the weathered stump of a feeling / into the worst climate of all" (65). These lines exemplify Prynne's thorough entanglement of geologic and affective discourse: the faint trace of the ridge provides only "the sentiment / of 'cliffs'" or the "weathered stump of a feeling" (where "weathered" suggests both the effects of erosion and the weather that helped determine the extent of the ice, and "stump" implies a possible wounding or cutting). "Sentiment," meanwhile, is a near homophone of *sediment*, the deposits of glacial drift (and a pun Steve McCaffery will also make much use of). Of course, as we saw earlier, this somatic, anthropomorphizing language is already present in the supposedly technical geologic vocabulary, as *moraine* is derived from a word for "snout" and the "curving spine" of the ridge is "masked . . . by the drift." For Middleton, however, poems like "The Glacial Question" fall short of displacing "authoritative wisdom" through a Kristevan shattering of the symbolic and ultimately "endorse . . . scientific discourses as propositional systems" (90). Middleton asks, then, "Can a geological history of the ice age be a means of thinking about otherwise intractable issues concerning history, memory, and language?" (89). Given that Prynne arrives at his imbrication of earth and flesh precisely through the drift of an etymology triangulating ice, crust, and scab, the answer to Middleton's question would seem to be *yes*, though Prynne accomplishes this in a far stranger manner than Middleton here gives him credit for.

Prynne elaborates a geomythopoetic image of a wounded, broken earth that might be put back together again by following the parallel paths of geology and etymology. Such a project finds perhaps its clearest statement in the poem "The Wound, Day and Night," which in the 2005 edition of *Poems* appears as the verso to "The Glacial Question, Unsolved." Moreover, while the order of composition is not entirely clear, the opening lines of "The Wound" seem to either echo or anticipate this undecided question: "Age by default: in some way this must / be solved. The covenants that bind / into the rock, each to the other / are for this, for the argon dating" (64). Determining the geochronology of strata brings one into contact with the "covenants," or laws, by which different minerals agglomerate to become rocks. In typical

Prynne fashion, the apparently religious or transcendental language here could also be taken as a description of the argon dating process, in which these elements are unbound by volatizing, or vaporizing, a rock sample and then measuring the amount of argon and potassium released. "Solve" thus carries its additional sense of "dissolve," a dispersal of gas that is measured in terms of *iso*topes (leading us back once again to both *ice* and *topos*, "place"). This "solving" of the rock will result, Prynne hopes, in a version of Olson's commitment to a "responsive," situated relationship to the earth:

> . . . withdrawn
> from every haunted place
> in its graveness, the responsive
> shift into the millions of years
>
> I am born back there, the plaintive chanting
> under the Atlantic and the unison of forms. (Prynne 64)

As in Prynne's and Olson's adaptation of continental drift theory, the idea here is that by tracking geochronology "into the millions of years" one will arrive at "the unison of forms," the fused landmass from which our current fractured topography emerged. The poem expresses the wish that "It *may* all flow again if we suppress the / breaks, as I long to do," and, "If we dissolve the bars to it and let run / the hopes" we can glimpse that "'in the variety of aspects / the sum remains the same, one family'" (Prynne 64). While their sentiment might sound somewhat platitudinous, these lines are telling because they also appear in a letter Prynne sent to Olson on February 11, 1966. There, they are revealed to be a translation (by the Latin scholar and Prynne's Cambridge colleague D. R. Shackleton Bailey) of a passage from Marcus Manilius's five-volume poem *Astronomicon*. In the full passage quoted in Prynne's letter, the Roman poet invokes "the vast frame of the universe" ruled by "a divine force, a soul" who "[s]ilently . . . governs, dispensing the covenants that bind each part with each" (161). The "covenants" referred to in the poem's opening lines, lifted from Manilius's pean to a thoroughly integrated and "responsive" universe, corresponds to Olson's and Prynne's desire to reestablish a geolinguistic "unison of forms." Not incidentally,

Prynne sends this passage of Manilius's to Olson in the midst of the latter's inquiries about obtaining the Wegener map of Pangea, and only three days before Prynne sends Olson a copy of *A Symposium on Continental Drift* and a draft of "The Wound, Day and Night." The "wound" of the poem's title, then, would seem to refer to the inability, for those of us limited to what Olson would call "the human universe," to actually reach back across the expanse of geologic time and experience this mythic cohesion. Indeed, viewing geologic strata and tracing the etymologies of words are perhaps the closest one can get to "the unison of forms," and, as Prynne aspires in "The Wound, Day and Night," to "be / born at long last into the image of love" (64). Here again, geology promises stable foundations, yet these foundations can only be inferred from the results of drift.

The end of "The Glacial Question" offers a comparable glimpse of a possible "unison" or sense of coherence, though it too is undermined by the language of fragmentation and wounding. In the closing lines of Prynne's poem, the speaker relates how "[a]s the dew recedes from the grass / towards noon the line of recession / slips back" (66). The "beautiful head" of "frost" covering the ground in the opening lines is here disclosed as a temporary illusion of the last glacial "invasions." As the sun rises the frost melts, becoming dew, and the "glacial ice" recedes again as if in a massively accelerated time lapse of the Pleistocene's climatic changes. Having been provided this brief peek at millions of years of geologic time, Prynne concludes:

We know this, we are what it leaves:

the Pleistocene is our current sense, and
what in sentiment we are, we

are, the coast, a line or sequence, the
cut back down to the shore. (66)

The tripping, fragmented syntax, particularly in the final three lines, indicates a hesitancy or uncertainty surrounding what "we are" after the momentary vision of the glacier melts away. Indeed, the syntax seems to make "we" synonymous with "the coast" as well as "the / cut back down to shore."

Notably, "coast," meaning the edge of land or the land/sea interface, derives, via Middle English and Old French, from Latin *costa*, "rib, flank, side" (*OED*). This derivation lends an extra edge, so to speak, to "cut" in the next line, suggesting both a narrow passage down to the sea and an incision in a fleshy flank. Completing this set of associations, "shore" has a possible connection to the verb *shear*, which in its original sense meant "to cut through with a weapon" (*OED*). Prynne has thus chosen three words related to cutting to describe "our" wounded condition in the Pleistocene. Like the land warped and scoured by glacial advance and retreat, "we" too are left sliced, split, and scarred by drift.

This language of woundedness and frustration regarding the geomythopoetic project to "shift into the millions of years" begins to seep into Prynne's communications with Olson in the late summer of 1966. For instance, in a letter of August 19, Prynne, as part of "the recent sequence of notes" on ice and ridges, says, "I do want the whole thing unfrozen or something broken out of it at long last," adding, "At the moment I sense this immense pressure, the Jurassic invasion leaving not enough time for the ice to form to proper place nor the time itself to become memorable. We are even setting (and breaking) our wage freeze" (206). It is hard to know what exactly Prynne is upset about here. As he often does in his poems, Prynne in this letter leaves the exact meaning of "the whole thing" vague; it is not clear what needs to be "unfrozen" and "broken out of": Work on the poems that will appear in *The White Stones*? The Pleistocene? Or, perhaps, the contemporaneous political and economic turmoil in Britain? Also reminiscent of the poems is the way Prynne collides different discourses, so that the process of glacial ice formation is conflated with the wage and price "freeze" implemented by Harold Wilson's Labour government in July 1966 amid its ongoing fight with trade unions and fears about inflation. In any case, the upshot is grim: "there is no useful hope for us, we will never get across to the Secondary Neolithic or anything else . . . The small hopes are all running sores: festering expectancy." Again, it is hard to tell whether the precise failure Prynne articulates is one of economics, archaeology, poetic method, or something else, but the image of the wound reappears, followed immediately by the desire for a reconstitution of some kind: "Who they are, the sequence of tenses. The icefloe is a model gerund but loose pack-ice is just <u>mush</u>" (207). The allusion to gerunds recalls Prynne's interest in naming as the Fenollosan bedrock of language discussed in the first section of this chapter, which, in Alex Latter's useful summation, recognizes "[t]hat terrain is not a stable, fixed point, but rather dynamic and relational: its names and its naming are gerundial—that is, of named happenings, a naming that enacts coherence" (67). In the mush of the present, however, Prynne seems less sanguine that such a process can be enacted in language. As he writes in the letter's closing, "the decay is multivalent, a complete system of values taking over the links of being and thus also the connections of language" (Olson and Prynne 207). Prynne again presents time as a kind of entropic deterioration, a devolution of human connection to both land and language. The loss of a foundational connection between humans, language, and terrain echoes Olson's exasperation with "the universe of discourse," the tradition of Western metaphysics that has subsumed spatial experience and the "connections of language" under abstraction and instrumentalization. Prynne's proposal of the comorphology of earth and language—of words arising, like human facial features, from a particular terrain—seeks to reinvigorate the sense of a natural, necessary language, a language not fundamentally arbitrary. And yet, Prynne's attempts to arrive at such a language through etymology expose the continual, contingent drift and transformation that makes both language and landforms possible.

Greif, Glazes, Graves, and Gravel: Maggie O'Sullivan

The 1966 wage freeze that Prynne alludes to in his letter heralded the beginning of serious economic decline and political turmoil in Britain, particularly in the coal industry, which is a frequent feature in the background of Maggie O'Sullivan's examinations of landscape and geology. A vocabulary of wounding and bruising, piercing and stabbing, strata and skin, foregrounds the triangulation of body, land, and language in Maggie O'Sullivan's *A Natural History in 3 Incomplete Parts*. More so than either Prynne or Torrance, O'Sullivan enacts this triangulation by treating each page as a sonic and visual composition: typographic experiments, the incorporation of photographs and other images, and dense sonic play all contribute to O'Sullivan's project of writing the body-as-land within the context of social and political upheaval in Thatcher-era Britain. O'Sullivan's careful consideration of the visual and material aspects of the book's production, moreover, places her work in the sphere of the artist's book (an aspect of her work that tends to be overlooked in favor of an emphasis on oral performance) and the specific visual and production choices she makes are indispensable to my reading of *A Natural History*. Written between June 1984 and April 1985, the book was published by O'Sullivan's Magenta imprint, and was, in the words of the curatorial note to the facsimile of the original chapbook available on Eclipse's online archive, "[p]rinted photostatically by Bob Cobbing at New River Project in multiple runs to achieve chromatic text that alternates per sheet between brick-red and cobalt" (*Natural History*).[10] The text is arranged into three sections, titled "Incomplete," "More Incomplete," and "Most Incomplete." In the table of contents, these sections are listed within a sort of scaffolding, or matrix, that resembles the type of segmented timeline—demarcating geologic eras, periods, epochs, and ages—that one might find in a geology textbook. This scaffoldlike structure is replicated throughout the book, often as the formatting for titles of subsections that seem to conflate linguistics and earth sciences: for instance, "Singular Verbs & Plural Subjects," "Lead Vocals," or "1) Rough 2) Common 3) Branchy" (*Body of Work* 109). Additionally, there are several other visual plays on the charts and classificatory diagrams of scientific texts, often seemingly incomplete as per the book's title, or at least misaligned in some fashion with the content that they appear to label. Thus, as in many of O'Sullivan's projects, *A Natural History* mixes text and visuals, displaying not only a grounding in the concrete poetry of the 1960s and 1970s but also an Olsonian attention to the field of the page, "a space which," as Mandy Bloomfield puts it, "embodies residues of the 'whirling . . . sedimentary layers' of concretised time" (23). Charles Bernstein echoes this geologic consideration of the page—as well as his earlier geologic characterization of Clark Coolidge's work as "clastic"—when he writes in his forward to *Body of Work*, a collected edition of O'Sullivan's early books, that her "embodied poetics" consists of "a seismographic incarnation of language as organ-response to the minute, shifting interactive sum of place as tectonic," and describes her use of archaisms as "a cross-sectional boring through time, whirling the sedimentary layers into knots" (8–9). Like Olson, Prynne, and Torrance, the time(s) O'Sullivan bores into on her sedimentary pages is at once the deep geologic time of the earth, the historical time of social and political movements, and the idiosyncratic time of the individual human body.

In *A Natural History*, these coexisting times are indicated by a rich lexicon of geologic, botanical, and archaic terminology, as well as through O'Sullivan's frequent use of neologisms. But the work also contains, throughout these discursive and temporal layers, a thread (and threat) of violence that would seem to be at odds with these other discourses. To take one example of this aspect, in a subsection of the book titled "Reading Writing (a Documentary) B. b." (a title that appears in the type of unfinished diagrammatic scaffold, noted above), we find the irregularly capitalized, underscored line "ARMS HEDGE Weal of LUPIN, Gliner, cleanseth:" (123). "Hedge" and "lupin" (in its British spelling) come from a botanical realm, although "weal," intruding as "a red, swollen mark left on flesh by a blow or pressure" lends a sharpened sense of "arms" as armaments, a connotation that will take on added resonance later in my argument (*OED*). Then again, "weal" could be used in its formal (and directly opposite) sense of "well-being" describing a wealth of lupines, or, in yet another gloss, describe one's arms brushing against a hedge of lupines, leaving a weal. In any case, "Gliner" and "cleanseth" fit uncertainly here, the latter being an archaism and the former having no discernible definition, being a neologism or possibly referring to a proper name. O'Sullivan's dense, audiogenic compositions require and reward this kind of reading where one tries to sort, and sort out, the types of words that appear and the associations intimated by their spatial and visual arrangement.

The implication of violence and bodily harm in "arms" and "weal" obtains some added weight considering the previous page's allusions to a "seam ripper" and "claw longered hunt of jutted sickle," as well as the blunt statement of the last three lines:

> wild plum ever silken, fucking shot
> knife took
> u/neath. (122)

While "seam ripper" could anticipate "silken" and thus suggest a textilelike thread, the reddish-purple color implied by "plum," takes on a more sinister cast (as both *blood* and *bruise*) through the sudden eruption of armed attacks as well as the echo of the pointed ("jutted") "claw" of the "sickle" in the preceding line. References to violent acts, or more specifically, to blood, wounds, red, and the fragility of the body in its envelope of skin, abound in O'Sullivan's oeuvre. Marjorie Perloff, for instance, has written of the use of text and imagery suffused with red in later works such as *Red Shifts* and observes an abiding pun on the homophone *read* that exemplifies O'Sullivan's close attention to discrepancies between hearing and reading through errant spellings, regional dialects, and orthographic drift. Nicky Marsh, meanwhile, argues that the "latent violence" in O'Sullivan's work critiques cultural associations of subjection, objectification, and artifice with the feminine, even while demonstrating the complicity of language in such gendered, and often violent, determinations (93).

O'Sullivan's emphasis on red, in everything from her imagery to her choice of chromatic text, points to the overlap of the material of language, the body, and the earth. O'Sullivan has given her definition of the "materiality of language" as "its actual contractions & expansions . . . the acoustic, visual, oral & sculptural qualities within the physical" (qtd. in Sheppard 165). Moreover, in an interview with Redell Olsen, O'Sullivan answers a question concerning "female artists who are working directly with the landscape in relation to their own bodies" by averring that she " draw[s] upon the earth and the other-than-human–voicing my body/bodying my voicings" and citing the Chilean artist and writer Cecilia Vicuña's maxim, "To feel the earth as one's own skin" (Olsen 205). The prominence given to the materiality of language, earth, and skin corresponds to the oft mentioned "shamanic" dimension of O'Sullivan's work, in particular its interest in ritual and the incantatory qualities of opaque or secret languages. As well, Bloomfield posits that O'Sullivan approaches "language not just in terms of the arbitrary conceptual links insisted upon by Saussurian linguistics, but also in terms of sensory, corporeal processes" (15–16). These concerns position her work adjacent to the more historical and archaeological fascination with shamanism in Prynne and Torrance as well as their trope of the earth as wounded or cracked skin, although O'Sullivan is far more visually and lexically radical than either Torrance or Prynne.[11] All these registers are operative in *A*

Natural History, but what I want to demonstrate now is how they are tied to specific geologic—and political—events.

Curiously enough, we start, as in Prynne, with heads. Or, more precisely, with faces: the first section of O'Sullivan's *A Natural History* opens with an epigraph in the form of the classic Zen koan, "Show me your face before you were born," a deliberately impossible demand that the first poem nevertheless tries to fulfill, beginning, "The Moon's w/BLACK BLACK eye of wasp/ BLACK black / Vanilla Scent. Skin of Open Fields, the" (*Body of Work* 71, 72). The poem appears to establish a set of contrasts, for example between the white of the moon and the bruising of its "BLACK eye," and gestures towards an indexlike format with "Skin of Open Fields, the." The sense of contrast and cataloging is completed in the final lines of the first page: "Fire, as in / the Sun." Moon and sun, night and day, hot and cold, are each installed here as the poles of the poem, the boundaries that mark the skin of the open field. Red enters the mix a few pages later in a "Crudely reddish red yellow / sedge under bridge, gold in / river, cut w/crushed vein, / stabbed running reeling" (76). The image of the reddish-yellow sedge growing in its riparian habitat leads to an association between the extraction of ore (the "gold in" or golden river) and corporal violence through cut/crushed/stabbed and the double meaning of "vein" as both blood vessel and a fracture in a rock containing a mineral deposit. A near echo of "vessel" can be heard in "vassal," the first word on the facing page. As is typical in *A Natural History* (and in O'Sullivan's work more broadly), on this page words proceed in rapid asyntactic streams amid a dense thicket of paratactic collisions and opaque emphases:

> Codices & flay lavish cinder brooches mark brow of black's
> dominant prone total cloud, cast quick, FLAKE hemming
> curr: render batter sea his fatally pierce, cut raspy
> churl. Choice open globe, (suburb. prowl. some size.
> prowl-mitt. be. nuss. kid. ease). (77)

In such passages, rather than reading for narrative, one must read in terms of types of words. So, for instance, we find more words denoting violence here, such as "flay," "fatally pierce," and "cut," as well as references to heat and fire in "cinder" and "cast." And, in one of the clearer instances of

O'Sullivan's interest in regional British pronunciation and its homophonic transcription, we can hear at the end of the passage a parent's warning to "be nice kiddies." However, in radical "open field" style, such excerpts do not function in isolation but rather in dialogue with the rest of the page. One striking feature of this example is the prevalence of terms either denoting or connoting fire and a reddish color juxtaposed with words suggesting cold, icy, or blue conditions. Take, for example, the next two verse paragraphs, which I will quote in full to give a sense of the crowded tapestry of associations O'Sullivan creates:

> MirrorBall.
> Being LAID.
> Sans Soleil swan simplest whispering sumach, arm's cold
> lustre swole Tango Pulsing. drill. grill. Boogie glacis
> fooled finial saliva, reflex of immediate immense cry.
>
> <u>describe.</u>
> <u>Thunder. Bleeding. The Sky Confessing It.</u>
> <u>& being</u>
> <u>Jobless.</u>
>
> Billow churn, jazzy curve. Bee zen. of Glovewort.
> Utter Glaze. fridge roseflocking mutagenic. fridge Acanthus,
> lash prim thistle twist of pure nutmace, low flambé lead
> split: erosion. But child, Bead & reel, yellowed air soft
> mightily, i bleed & soak & pool olive, <u>prolonging</u>
> sund sund sundering (77)

There is the intimation of a grooving, hedonistic intimacy, as the "MirrorBall" (like one might find in a nightclub or discotheque) conjures the prospect of "Being LAID." The sexual suggestiveness is amplified by the "lust" in "lustre" that instigates the tumescent arousal of "swole," while "Tango," "Pulsing," and "Boogie" (not to mention "Ball") round out the dance motif. Also notable is the profusion of words in some way tied to red: "sumach," "bleeding," "Glaze," "roseflocking," "nutmace," "flambé." The red-hot erotic sheen (or luster) sparked by this boogieing, pulsating passage is, however, contrasted with a glacial coldness; the possibly lunar "MirrorBall" implies the lack of sun in "Sans Soleil" (also potentially a reference to Chris Marker's 1983 film of the same name), while "glacis" is an oblique reflection (or reflex) of the mirror's glass surface, as well as an anticipation of "Utter Glaze" in the second line of the next paragraph, *glaze* being etymologically related to *glass*. A "glacis," however, is "a . . . bank . . . that slopes down from a fort, exposing attackers to the defender's missiles" (*OED*). From Old French *glacier* (to slip) and *glace* (ice), "glacis" creates an association between mirrors and ice that is reiterated two pages later in the line "slippage, mirror" (80). Continuing the ice and fire theme, in conjunction with violent, martial terminology, directly below this icy mirror we find "flecked scalping (flame hue) inflict." In O'Sullivan's continual lettristic and sonic shifts, "flame" brings us back to the "cinders" of the earlier passage and to "lustre," which in ceramics indicates an "iridescent glaze." In the phrase "Utter Glaze" it is not clear whether "utter" functions as an adjective or verb, and thus whether it is characterizing a total, finished glaze, or urging the reader to pronounce the word *glaze*. If we were to speak this word, we might hear how it resonates with other long *a* sounds that appear frequently in *A Natural History* such as in "blaze," "blade," "laze," and "daze." What is more, in its adjectival form, *utter* originates from the Old English *uttra*, "out" or "outer," and thus could, through one of O'Sullivan's characteristic vocalic shifts, refer to an "*outer* glaze" (*OED*).

In fact, one such "outer glaze" appears in the next line through the word "flambé." Deriving, as one might guess, from a French word for *flame*, *flambé* literally means "singed," though in English usage it typically refers either to the culinary party trick of covering some food (usually a dessert) with liquor and setting it alight or, more relevant to our purposes here, "a red copper-based porcelain glaze with purple streaks" (*OED*). To add one final twist to this imposing tangle, several pages later, below a stanza which refers to "broken Fields broken," there appears the mysterious trio "lamé orchids, cotton, skin" (86). Lamé is a type of fabric or garment "interwoven with gold or silver threads," though, notably for my argument, the word was adapted from *lamina* (as in *laminate*) and denotes "a thin layer, plate, or scale of sedimentary rock, organic tissue, or other material" (*OED*). That is, we have arrived back at the overlap of rock and skin and can see how the associative progression from "glacis" to "glaze" to "flame" might motivate the shift to explicitly geologic language in "split: erosion" at the end of the long quotation above: "sund sund sundering" enacts erosion's splitting or cleaving of rock and the literal breakdown of words into s(o)unds that propels O'Sullivan's compositional process.

It might seem unlikely that this diffused series of sonic and phonemic mutations would point to pressing sociopolitical concerns, but O'Sullivan signals that such is indeed the case through her incorporation of visual material and colored type. O'Sullivan's use of visual material such as photographs and news clippings to create a collage of text and image is quite different than the mythopoetic and archaeological methods of the other writers in this chapter, and it allows her to point directly to contemporary political events even as her language remains enigmatic. For instance, in a subsection titled "Moral Conditions" at the end of part 2, O'Sullivan reprints five pages from part 1—including the page that is quoted at length above—this time with images superimposed (using the same cobalt blue or brick-red ink in which the original page was printed) over parts of the text. Three of the five images pertain to social and political unrest and the state's violent response, while the other two bookending images are of a shawled woman covering her face with her hand (perhaps in a pietà or crucifixion scene) and a woman writing on a desk.[12] Across from the first poem in the book ("The Moon's w/ BLACK BLACK eye," discussed above), O'Sullivan places a portion of a map with the words "Greenham" and "AIRFIELD" visible—likely an allusion to RAF Greenham Common, where the British government's decision to store nuclear cruise missiles at the base ignited a wave of protests against nuclear weapons, including, most prominently, the Greenham Common Women's Peace Camp, which would occupy numerous sites on the base beginning in 1981.[13] On top of and perpendicular to this map, O'Sullivan prints a newspaper report listing "People Killed By Rubber and Plastic Bullets," most of them young men under the age of twenty-one in Northern Ireland from 1972 to 1984. On another page, the Northern Irish "troubles" are again referenced through a collage of two headlines that read, respectively, "Man killed after RUC 'go beserk'" and "Man dies as police fire in IRA riot" (102). The IRA, of course, is the Irish Republican Army, while the RUC names the Royal Ulster Constabulary, the British-backed, militarized, and largely Protestant police force that had an infamous shoot-to-kill policy regarding suspected members of the IRA and were apparently among the first forces to employ allegedly less lethal rubber and plastic bullets.[14] Through the social and political context these images provide, earlier phrases like "fucking shot" come into focus as snippets from this background hum of state violence and repression.

This violence becomes even more explicit in the image that overlays the page discussed in detail above. Obscuring most of the middle-right part of the page is a photo of a young man lying on the ground, blood pooling around his head and splattered across his clothes and outstretched left arm. The photo is positioned such that directly below it, as if captioning the picture, are the lines "describe. / Thunder. Bleeding. The Sky Confessing It. / & being. / jobless." In the acknowledgments at the end of the original Magenta press version of *A Natural History*, O'Sullivan provides the identificatory details: "Manuel Alvarez Bravo. Striking Worker, Murdered, 1934, Mexico."[15] This visual citation of historical, global labor strife, in conjunction with the threat of "being / jobless," invokes another major upheaval that was occurring at the exact period in which O'Sullivan was composing this book: namely, the UK miners' strike of 1984–1985. Beginning in March 1984 and lasting nearly a year, the miners' strike was the culmination of years of strife between miners, trade unions, and both Tory and Labour governments. The immediate cause was the National Coal Board's announcement on March 6, 1984, that, as part of the Conservative prime minister Margaret Thatcher's neoliberal program of downsizing and cost cutting, twenty coal mines would be closed, causing the disappearance of some 20,000 jobs. This effectively voided an earlier agreement arrived at after the strike of 1974 between the unions and the government and led the National Union of Mineworkers (NUM) to call for a work stoppage in coalfields across the country. Over the next 358 days, the Thatcher government would deploy mobile police units to respond rapidly (and brutally) to demonstrations and efforts by miners to block the transport of coal to electrical stations, and there would be numerous attacks by police forces on the striking miners in an attempt to violently suppress the picket lines.[16]

Marsh has noted the relevance of the miners' strike to O'Sullivan's work of this period, in particular *A Natural History* and her 1985 chapbook *States of Emergency*, tracing the strike's importance to the well-known influence of the artist Joseph Beuys on O'Sullivan. As Marsh details, O'Sullivan served as the researcher for a 1987 BBC *Arena* documentary on Beuys, which features a scene in which the president of the NUM at the time, and the man who called for the miners' strike, Arthur Scargill, is filmed reacting to Beuys's installation *Plight* at the Anthony d'Offay Gallery in London in 1985. Scargill, clearly preoccupied with the recent failure of the miners' strike (it ended in March 1985), views Beuys's claustrophobic, felt-lined room as an allegory of underground mining, and Marsh applies this context to O'Sullivan's interest in "the processes of coal and carbon" and her "attempts to articulate the complex web of associations—from primordial energies to state violence to the destruction of rural communities—that the Miner's Strike came to embody" (89).

While Marsh's reading is fruitful (especially for *States of Emergency*), there may be an even more proximate point of contact between *A Natural History* and the concurrent political turmoil in Britain. In a poem titled "Mountain," we find a familiar entanglement of earth, skin, and wounding:

> muscle & flin & bone, gotta
> Blood gotta Hill gotta Lung purple
>   dark thru
>   Jar O Skimmish Burn
>
>   <u>Or greave</u>
>   <u>it is</u>
>
> GREAT GREAVES OF HEAD, (107)

While I have not been able to trace the suggestive phrase "Jar O Skimmish Burn" to any likely source (though "skimmish" comes close to *skin* and *skirmish*, and "burn" aligns with other words for red or fire, as well as the "burning" of coal for power), the underlined "<u>Or greave</u> / <u>it is</u>" seems to be a more direct allusion to the so-called "Battle of Orgreave."[17] A key confrontation in the course of the miners' strike, the "battle" took place on June 18, 1984, (the very same time that O'Sullivan started composing *A Natural History*) when workers at the Orgreave Coking Works began picketing to stop the delivery of coal to the plant in solidarity with the striking miners. In addition to the workers, a further five thousand picketers arrived at the plant at the behest of the NUM, while in its own show of force, the South Yorkshire Police deployed a force of six thousand—officers, riot squads, mounted forces, and K-9 handlers. As later reporting and inquests would reveal, the police essentially trapped the overwhelmingly peaceful and compliant picketers in a field near the plant and then led several charges against them, beating the protestors indiscriminately and making dozens of arrests in what has been repeatedly referred to as a "police riot."[18]

The suppression of the picketing miners at Orgreave resonates throughout *A Natural History* in the repetition of near homophones that echo and amplify the place-name and its attendant violence: *grieve*, *grief*, and *grave*. O'Sullivan's use of the chance sonic properties of the proper noun *Orgreave* to allude to this violent event is a compelling instance of what Derrida has called "le Malheur de son arbitraire" of "Le nom propre" (the misfortune of the arbitrary character of the proper name) (qtd. in Dworkin, *Radium* 64). If we disarticulate *Orgreave* as O'Sullivan does, we might notice that *or* recalls the *ore* of coal, the black "gold" (*or*, in French) over which the miners' strike was fought. "Greave," meanwhile, designates a type of small shin guard, a suggestive item given that one of the aspects of the battle most remarked upon was the rows of police officers decked out in full riot gear to confront the unarmed workers. However, *greave* is also a homophone of *grieve*, a sonic coincidence that O'Sullivan emphasizes throughout the book. In the poem "Benedictional," for instance, O'Sullivan writes, "oil <u>arresting</u>: Aloe. Bold drome rind, harsh cordite, / <u>GRIEF</u> stun substance. Ash weed dripping vein, gone / <u>GRIEF</u>, the moon gone Grieve Eye" (95). Doubly stressed by being capitalized and underscored, and appearing at the start of consecutive lines, "grief" becomes a kind of chant; appropriately so, as this "benedictional" poem begins with the word *Kyrie*, a short, repeated invocation, and an allusion to "Kyrie eleison" or "Lord have mercy." Furthermore, the play on "greave" provides a new context for the image of a woman with her head lowered and her hand covering her face—Degas's *Old Roman Beggarwoman*—that graces the front cover and obscures one of the pages in "Moral Conditions": this seemingly stricken figure, in its resonances with a Pietà, resembles nothing so much as a grieving woman.

It is a short step, both thematically and orthographically, from the injury and death implied by *greave* and *grieve* to the grave:

grave (noisette) across marble

>   (or choking)
>   <u>dead slow</u>
>   (jangle) from
>   broken <u>Fields</u> broken,
>   prong w/icy lamming bone, Daisy. (86)

A "noisette" could be a small cut of lean meat such as lamb (hence the reference to "marble," as in "marbled meat"); however, it also suggests sound—a little noise, as it were, a sense taken up by the similarly parenthetical "(jangle)." It is fitting that this noisette is "<u>dead slow</u>," as in musical notation the Italian *grave* (pronounced with a long *a* on the second syllable) signifies "slowly; with solemnity." The sepulchral somberness supplied by "marble," as well as "(or choking)," which, given the context, is suggestive of mining—choking on ore, perhaps anticipating "gotta Lung purple," above—lends these lines a chthonic shade. "Choking" is also one letter away from "coking," intimating the Orgreave Coking Plant that was the site of the strike. As a verb, *prong* means "to stab or pierce," as with a fork, and to "lam" is to attack or hit someone hard. In its position below "broken <u>Fields</u> broken," (the second "broken" leading to "bone"), "lamming" summons the beatings police gave workers at Orgreave and points to one of the salient features of this battle, the fact that police tricked the striking workers into gathering in an *open field* near the plant and then, having trapped them thus, carried out charge after charge (including on horseback) against their disorganized and often fleeing (on the lam) ranks. We are left, then—to overlap O'Sullivan's disseminated impressions—with the "broken" "Skin of Open Fields," the bloodied bodies of grieving workers and blackened earth of British collieries.

"Lamming" also points back to "lamé" and "flambé," and, in appearing next to "icy," follows the pattern of fire juxtaposed to ice. We might also recall how "flambé" is itself intertwined with "Utter Glaze," a connection that is relevant given that the page I've been discussing here echoes this phrase in its opening words: "Utter Gravel" (86). The repetition, with a reversal, of these words at the beginning of the next line, "Gravel utter slow," anticipates the solemnity of "grave" music and leverages the adjectival and verbal functions of "utter." To "utter" (that is, speak) "gravel," to talk as if one's mouth was full of stones, would indeed be to enact the splitting, stuttering erosion of sound we might remember from "sund sund sundering" (77). Moreover, in returning us to "glaze," the poem comments on its chromatic text: the glaze of the "cobalt" blue (cobalt being an element derived of nickel and copper ores) and "brick-red" ink stages not only the contrast between sun and moon, ice and fire, glaze and glace, that I have been tracking throughout this section, but also, at a few degrees of removal, the confrontation between workers and police, miners and—to use the British slang for a police officer—coppers.[19]

Its thick weave of visual material and homophonic play makes *A Natural History* a more radical and disjunctive text than even Prynne's specialized parlance. The paronomasia pointing to the background context of the Battle of Orgreave undermines the sense of steady progression or innate order implied by the term "natural history"—history as *naturalized*, made inevitable. The title makes a wry comment on this connotation of stability, as there is nothing natural or necessary about the violent political repression, from Ulster to South Yorkshire, that informs the background of O'Sullivan's text. Instead of a naturalized sense of either geologic or human history, O'Sullivan presents us with an ongoing incompletion, an open-endedness that stresses transformation and orthographic drift. Thus, even as O'Sullivan seeks to move beyond an arbitrary, Saussurean conception of language to one that revitalizes the deep-seated connections between language and the body, the arbitrary, contingent similarities between words are what enable the drift from the toponym *Orgreave* to *grieve*, *grief*, and *grave*.

The density of language and disruption of syntax in O'Sullivan's oeuvre renders it, in the context of this study, a bridge between the attempts of Prynne, Olson, and Dorn to uncover a natural language and the more textually extreme efforts of Clark Coolidge and Steve McCaffery to enact geologic processes. In my next chapter, I turn to these latter writers and examine how their experiments in radical formalism extend the geopoetic aspiration for nonarbitrary language. The belief in a geolinguistic bedrock—a foundation that would secure a necessary set of relations between language, land, and body—is not abandoned but rather assumed, presenting words as lithic fragments that agglomerate into cliffs of opaque prose.

CHAPTER 4

"Clastic Mates"

Sedimentary Language in Clark Coolidge and Steve McCaffery

> If you look at a rock long enough you become sub-rock.
> —*Stephen Rodefer*

In an essay on Clark Coolidge's early book *Space*, Charles Bernstein identifies what he calls "a gooeyness and gumminess, a thickness of texture" that characterizes Coolidge's oeuvre. Bernstein is mainly thinking about the dense "word clusters" in Coolidge's work of the late 1960s and early 1970s, evocative but opaque phrases such as "clump bends trill a jam" that often seem to point recursively to their own effect on the reader. For instance, in Bernstein's example, "[B]ends trill" hints at Coolidge's abiding interest in the compositional model of jazz, which privileges improvisation and the repetition of patterns, while the bookends "clump" and "jam" suggest "thickness of texture"—the word clumps and noun jams in Coolidge that gum up the works of conventional reading. For Bernstein, these poems of word fragments and noun clusters are also "clastic," from the geologic term for rocks made up of the broken pieces of older rocks ("Maintaining Space"). That is, they are composed of particles and fragments of other texts that have been pulverized and sedimented by Coolidge's idiosyncratic manner of reading.

In this chapter, I track these twin gooey and clastic aspects of Coolidge's writing as they manifest in *A Geology*—a title that echoes, most likely unwittingly, O'Sullivan's *A Natural History*—part of a larger, decades-long project labeled the Longprose. I say "twin" because these qualities, far from being separate, function in tandem: not only does the fragmentary composition of clastic rocks imply a kind of glueyness holding the structure together, but also this gluey texture forms the very structure of Coolidge's writing, especially that of his prose experiments. Building on Bernstein's description of this clastic character in Coolidge, I refer to this gooey, gluey structure with the term *colloid*, which denotes a substance in which insoluble molecules or particles from one substance are dispersed through a second substance (*OED*). Thus, in Coolidge, words and phrases from one context are often dissipated throughout another context while refusing to fully dissolve. Deriving from the Greek *kolla* (glue) a colloid has a gelatinous consistency; and, I argue, the gooey effect first noted by Bernstein is the result of Coolidge's specific reading practice. To adapt a phrase from the poet and critic Steve McCaffery, whose own clastic compositions I will address later in this chapter, Coolidge is a writer of his unconventional readings of others' writings (*Prior to Meaning* xvi).

Coolidge's fascination with geology and geologic terms such as *clastic* is central to this manner of reading. One might say that Coolidge's colloidal writing style indicates his geologic reading style in that he eschews a linear reading geared towards extracting meaning for one that attends to the chance patterns of linguistic particles. Reading language through the lens of geology becomes a way to emphasize the unstable, excessive, and nonhuman alterity of the former and aligns Coolidge with his contemporaries McCaffery and Smithson, who also explore the implications of viewing language-as-geology. This insistence on the geologic, nonhuman aspects of language, while an example of a pataphysical imaginary solution, is in fact highly relevant to current debates within ecocriticism and philosophy as it anticipates recent critical writing that employs geology in order to present a philosophy of the unthinkable.

"Clastic Mates"

Coolidge's interest in, and use of, concepts from geology are well established if not always adequately accounted for.[1] In the 1977 talk "Arrangement,"

Coolidge relates that Aram Saroyan once referred to his poems as "cliffs of rock." While Saroyan depicts Coolidge's work as a material entity that is simply there, as a boulder might be, Coolidge goes on to explain that geology, in his view, actually requires a complex mode of reading. According to Coolidge, Saroyan was right but in the wrong way. Instead of "look[ing] at the rock as just one thing," which was apparently how Saroyan was thinking, "geologists," Coolidge notes, "*read* the rocks . . . and sometimes there are very complicated arrangements of strata and faults and things." Thus, for Coolidge, to say that his poems are like cliffs is to say that they "have that particular solid separate arrangement aspect and I *read* them, and I want people to read them."

In the same talk, Coolidge details his lifelong interest in geology, recalling childhood trips to the natural history museum in Boston that sparked an early fascination with rocks and minerals. As Rachael M. Wilson has documented, Coolidge also became active in the caving community, exploring many caves in the southern and northeastern United States during the 1950s and 1960s. Wilson charts his fascination with caves from his early "sketch-map of Knox Cave" from 1956, which would appear in *The Northeastern Caver* in 1974, to *The Cave*, a work he collaborated on with Bernadette Mayer between 1972 and 1978. Wilson observes that caving, like jazz music, provides Coolidge with a model of reading and writing: "[T]he poet, a sort of language-caver, wends his way through passages, dropping through semantic and structural 'levels,' following sound and syntax." Caving—and geologic pursuits more generally—presents Coolidge with a model of textual engagement that is interested less in looking for meaning than in observing the non- or presemantic features of language.

For Coolidge, "Words have a universe of qualities other than those of descriptive relation: hardness, density, sound-shape, vector-force, and degrees of transparency and opacity" (qtd. in Orange). That is, the material qualities of words—and the specific arrangements of words that bring out those qualities—is more interesting for Coolidge than words' communicative function. Writing—and, by extension, reading—appears akin to looking at various types of rocks, placing them side by side, weighing them, and noticing the different mineral arrangements of which they are made. Coolidge admits that when he chose to major in geology at college, he assumed a geologist was "[a]nybody who looked at rocks and collected minerals and got something out of that"; however, "in the late fifties, geology was changing from being a descriptive science to being a real high-toned mathematical" field ("Arrangement"). Again, Coolidge's rejection of the more abstract, theoretical side of geology suggests that he is less interested in geology as an applied science than as a method of reading, a way of attending to small details and patterns below the level of syntax or meaning.

To be sure, Coolidge's move away from geology as a discipline also stems from the way its "high-toned mathematical" aspect contradicted his romantic conception of being a geologist. With wry humor, Coolidge admits, "I thought I would be standing in the Gobi Desert with a pick, finding dinosaur eggs or something, like Roy Chapman Andrews" ("Arrangement"). Coolidge may have only meant to invoke Andrews's expeditions to the Gobi Desert and discovery of dinosaur eggs in the 1920s, but his word choice is striking, as it harks back to (or perhaps anticipates) the poem "Gobi" in *Space*. Orange sees a broken sonnet in this poem's fragmented, gridlike spacing, and he places it in the context of contemporary collage-sonnet projects by Ted Berrigan and Kenneth Koch. For Orange, however, the poem's "collaged units," such as "columnar mufflered huffs" or "tile ape ketch," point to the way "sound is leading sense here." The sonic qualities of words are the primary factor in play, and therefore, Orange contends, "Coolidge's words are quite intractable: what they resist is easy assimilation to any semantic fields than their own." This account is largely accurate, and it echoes Bernstein's description of gooey word clusters; however, there *is* a phrase in "Gobi" that both points to another semantic field and describes the construction of the poem itself: "clastic mates" (*Space* 18). As we have seen, Bernstein highlights the "clastic" nature of Coolidge's early work and "Gobi" provides a sustained instance of clastic construction. *Clastic* derives from the Greek *klastos*, "broken in pieces"—icono*clast* comes from the same root (*OED*). Visually, "Gobi" resembles a kind of broken tablet, its words spread out across the page and separated by extended spaces. What is more, its individual words function like clasts, constituent fragments that are combined to create clastic phrases. While the title "Gobi" remains something of a mystery, it is possible, given the allusion to the Gobi Desert in "Arrangement," that Coolidge the poet is fulfilling his romantic image of the geologist in the desert "smashing [words] with hammers."

In accounting for Coolidge's geologic interests, critics have highlighted the influence of Smithson on Coolidge, even reading Coolidge's early works, such as those in *Space*, "as literary analogues to Smithson's 'non-sites' and 'earth works'" (Golston 81–82).[2] More specifically, Coolidge and Smithson share a fascination with crystals, and both attempt to enact the growth and development of crystal structure in their works. As Coolidge explains in *Smithsonian Depositions*, crystals play a critical role in developing photographic film using emulsion: "The process by which Polaroid is manufactured turns all the crystals the same way. . . . But if one identifies and examines the words one finds them beginning to separate and to act independently" (qtd. in Golston 95). Coolidge replicates this process across several works of the 1970s, "developing" his language, as one would develop a photograph, until the reader begins to see clearer and clearer individual images (Golston 97).

The emulsion used for film is a type of colloid, and *Smithsonian Depositions* itself possesses a colloidal makeup. As the title indicates, the work contains *deposits* of Smithson's writing dispersed throughout a solution of multiple texts. For instance, a couple of sentences after Coolidge's description of how Polaroid crystals organize themselves, he writes, "A language must be carefully guarded and closed in sommon [sic] usage for its clastic energies to be held in check. Words and rocks contain a language that follows a syntax of splits and ruptures" (26). The first sentence is apparently Coolidge's own, its (chance?) typo undermining the guards of "[c]ommon usage." But perhaps picking up the geologic cue of "clastic," Coolidge lifts the second (and several subsequent sentences) directly from Smithson's essay "A Sedimentation of the Mind." While *Smithsonian Depositions* is less improvisatory and fragmented than other of Coolidge's colloidal writing, the basic concept is the same: from his reading of various literary and technical texts, Coolidge creates a solution made up of dispersed (but not dissolved) particles of those texts.

A Geology of the Longprose

Most of the criticism that attends to the importance of geology to Coolidge's work skips over the one work that would seem to be most relevant to explaining this importance: *A Geology*. The work was first published as a chapbook from Potes & Poets Press in 1981, a year after *Smithsonian Depositions* appeared. While it is always difficult to keep track of Coolidge's prodigious output and complex publication history, *A Geology* was likely written sometime in the mid-1970s, which would place it slightly after *Polaroid* and *The Maintains*, and roughly concurrent with *Smithsonian Depositions* and *Solution Passage*—that is, precisely in the middle of the photographic sequence discussed above. Not surprisingly, *A Geology* shares with these texts a fascination with geologic processes and the ways in which writing might enact a Smithsonian equation between words and rocks. Most important for my purposes, the text displays a colloidal structure not only within its own boundaries but also as part of a larger serial prose project. Known colloquially as the Longprose following a series of readings Coolidge gave during a 1979 residency at the 80 Langton Street Gallery in San Francisco, the complete (though unfinished) text was published by Fence Books in 2012 as *Book Beginning What and Ending Away*. That is, while *A Geology* was initially published as a stand-alone chapbook, it also forms one piece of a larger series of prose experiments.[3]

A Geology is itself a clastic fusion of several disparate registers. Its language ranges from improvisatory sonic play, as in "Tantamount to neighborhood slackhood, lath and plaster crogenies," to extreme syntactic disruptions, as in "Are, the rocks, apparently, move," to lineated more discursive passages that sound as though they have been excised from a geology textbook, as in "Seldom occurring as an independent rock" (Coolidge, *Book* 202, 206, 215). As in other of Coolidge's disjunctive prose works, the phrases often seem to be just on the brink of coming into semantic focus, but the work never quite resolves into a consistent meaning. Indeed, tension between flashes of semantic legibility—for example, "Seldom occurring as an independent rock"—and a more general sense of opacity is a primary feature of Coolidge's colloidal compositions. Particles of language from various sources may suggest possible meanings to the reader, but these possibilities never assemble into a definitive semantic system.

One of the few poets or critics to make a direct (albeit brief) reference to *A Geology*, Alan Halsey notes, "The opening section of *A Geology* reads as a treated text. Paragraphs as strata. Certain repeated words as stray deposits in any." The effect of Coolidge's geologic treatment, Halsey suggests, is a sense of "drift," individual words or phonemes becoming like "a loose unstratified deposit of sand . . . transported and deposited," and he sums up "[g]eology as gist of [Coolidge's] aesthetic." As Halsey indicates, much of *A Geology* seems to employ a restricted vocabulary, borrowing terms not only from geology but also from the fields of music, caving, and mechanical engineering. The most common words in the text include "stone," "rock," "tone," "car," "scar," "fold," "hill," "cut," "cone," and "road." Any attempt at a typology of these words is somewhat arbitrary, however, as many of them could fit in all three categories or at least imply multiple possibilities. For example, "tone" is four fifths of "stone," suggesting a further pun on "rock" as both mineral and music. The writing often seems to engage in these kinds of minute lettristic shifts, as in the phrase "Gone to the tone, and won't be about," which turns on the repetition of the words "one" and "on" before morphing into "out" (204). Possible musical terms proliferate from "tone" to include the frequent repetition of "scale" or "scaling" and repeated allusions to "sharps" and "flats." At the same time, the polysemic nature of Coolidge's language—for example, he likes to employ words that are both nouns and verbs—undermines such classificatory schemes.

Coolidge puns on the notion of typology in the line "Typing up the rock to its one day gone." Typing *A Geology* is another way of doing the geologic work of *typing*—that is, arranging and categorizing rocks. Coolidge also repeatedly compares rocks to books, suggesting that both display a kind of wholeness, as in the statement "Rocks are as all said as books" (213). At the same time, however, unlike the typical codex "Rocks have not insides nor outsides. Rocks are all edge," and part of Coolidge's project in *A Geology* is to compose a book that, like rocks, is "all edge," a jagged agglomerate of syntactic shards. Hence the article *a* in the title: the book does not simply enumerate the geologic features of a given area but actually tries to resemble the rocks at the tops of hills.

One clue to Coolidge's allusions can be found in the dedication to the original chapbook edition of *A Geology*, "for Ray Fletcher / and Thacher Park." Ray Fletcher was an old caving buddy of Coolidge's, while Thacher Park is a popular state park in Upstate New York near Albany. This latter dedicatee provides a good portion of Coolidge's language, which he tweaks and improvises as he goes. For example, within Thacher Park one finds the Indian Ladder Trail, Cliff Edge Overlook, and Paint Mine Trail. Often, it appears that Coolidge has broken these names up and dispersed them throughout the text: "Above Indian fossils form a ladder, less molds with level outcrops" (*Book* 192). Or, "Edges are the world of the book, of the film of speeds by the book cliffs" (206). Within the playful structure Coolidge has set up, potential connections and cross-references multiply. Accordingly, "ladder" also points to "scale" (as in "to scale a ladder"), which in turn leads back to the musical scale. Thacher Park is named after John Boyd Thacher, a New York state senator and mayor of Albany in the 1880s and 1890s whose widow, Emma Treadwell Thacher, donated the land to the state in 1914. Before entering politics, Thacher helped run his father's business, the Thacher Car Wheel Works, which manufactured wheels for rail cars. This detail might help explain the many references to "cars" and "wheels" in the text as well as the odd shift to the language of railways and irons near the end of *A Geology*, as in lines like "The railway grows to the reef of his farm" and "Men running railways through skylights, wires stitched to their iron arms" (215, 216).

The text is also preoccupied with one of Thacher Park's most famous features, the Helderberg Escarpment. Named by early Dutch settlers, "Helderberg" translates as "clear mountain," likely an allusion to its bare, rocky top. Two of the most common words in *A Geology*, "scar" and "car," are word particles present in "escarpment." In fact, "scar" is often a kind of abbreviation for "escarpment"—a steep cliff or slope usually made of limestone. Indeed, the Helderberg is composed of limestone and contains many fossils and a network of over forty caves. The embedded section titled "The Light on Lime," then, suggests the sunlight on this limestone escarpment as well as the sense of "light" implied in "clear"—a bright, airy vision that Coolidge contrasts with the "shadows" of caves and mines (203). Coolidge indicates a further link between limestone and escarpment that perfectly demonstrates his playful method. If from "escarpment" he gets "car," then from "car" Coolidge arrives at "carburetor," a word that appears several times in the text. "Carburetor" gets Coolidge to *carbon* (a word that doesn't appear in the text), which leads back to fossils and limestone—calcium carbonate.

Coolidge sketches a veritable carbon cycle, from the fossils that become sedimentary rocks to the fuels humans extract from them in order to burn more carbon, a process that is nicely condensed in the phrase "The dinosaur came through the carburetor" (202). In other words, while there is no etymological connection between *car* and *carbon*, Coolidge proposes one through an almost pataphysical line of reasoning. The word *car* is, by chance, related to the word *carbon* by way of fossil fuels. The particular relations between words in *A Geology* bear out Halsey's observation that Coolidge's approach to language "pays minute attention to the 'random,' watches for its patterns" and could be described as "[c]olloidal in American drifting repetition."[4] In other words, Coolidge's geologic approach instigates a nonlinear, drifting mode of reading, and this mode of reading in turn produces texts that possess a colloidal structure.

The centrality of this unconventional reading practice to Coolidge's method becomes even more apparent if we take into account the larger context of the Longprose. The twenty sections of this massive work, of which *A Geology* is the ninth, are bound by a multistep compositional process. As Tom Orange explains in an essay at the end of the complete edition, Coolidge would begin with "a section (typically 20–30 pages) occasioned by his immersion in texts and/or subject areas of his interest" and then compose "a transition section to a new subject area, then another section on the new subject area, then a final section combining elements of the three preceding sections" (Coolidge, *Book* 584). Thus, the "final" version of twenty sections charts five cycles through this four-part process, with *A Geology* marking the start of the third cycle.

A glance at the table of contents reveals a map of Coolidge's preoccupations in the Longprose. The five sections that begin a cycle are titled, respectively: "The Caves," "The Music," "A Geology," "Weathers," and "Movies" (a sixth, final section is titled "Another Life"). The subject areas that comprise the third entry in each cycle are focused on writers and artists important to Coolidge's style and poetics: "Beckett," "Creeley," "Dalí," "Bernadette," and, in a pun, "ForEigner," referring to the poet Larry Eigner. The intervening "transition" sections are numbered but not titled.

As Orange comments, this structure "grew increasingly complex and unwieldy," probably because after each subject and artist is introduced, various key words associated with it are repeated throughout the rest of the work (584). The entirety of the Longprose demonstrates, then, a kind of cumulative structure that almost resembles strata. However, for all of its Oulipian scaffolding, Coolidge holds rather loosely to his constraints, displaying a method that is less rigorous than improvisational. In his essay, Orange gives an example of this process in action, showing how Coolidge would write-through various texts he was reading and then combine the results with words, phrases, and sentences from earlier sections. Taking section 11, "Dalí," as an example, Orange compares Coolidge's second paragraph to the beginning of *The Secret Life of Salvador Dalí*: Dalí's confession that as a small child he was forbidden to eat in the kitchen and would thus "stand around for hours, my mouth watering, till I saw my chance to sneak into that place . . . [and] snatch a piece of raw meat or a broiled mushroom on which I would nearly choke," becomes, in Coolidge, "I wanted the chance to sneak by foot into the hot meat I saw with my maids" (585). This manner of writing-through is not as strictly procedural as that of a John Cage or a Jackson Mac Low. Rather, it is associative and playful: Coolidge here seems to turn Dalí's anecdote about his "sin" of stealing food into an appropriately surrealist (and Freudian) escapade involving his "maids." At the same time, the passage enfolds a pun on "food" and "foot," thus equating Dalí's famous "paranoiac-critical" obsession with food as erotic fetish with the foot as a "base," low, and yet still highly fetishized, part of the human anatomy. The upshot of such play is neither appropriation nor citation, exactly, but rather a hybrid text that fuses and distorts language from multiple sources.

The "Dalí" section of *A Book Beginning What* is relevant to *A Geology* because it forms the third of the four sections initiated by *A Geology* and thus contains fragments of the previous two sections suspended within its riffs on Dalí's autobiography. Or, looked at the other way, certain words and phrases in *A Geology* anticipate those in "Dalí." Reading *A Geology* in this context helps to account for the curious insistence on paint and painting that becomes prominent near the end of the text. The words "paint" or "painting" occur six times in the final three pages of *A Geology*, while only appearing once in the rest of the text. If in most of the text Coolidge is "typing" rocks, in the final three pages it is as if the text is trying to approximate a still life. For example, the passage, "Rice edges the broom, a botch on mountain greenery. A reef of that greenery in white paint in clear sun." Hinting at a kind of landscape painting, these sentences also point to the sudden prevalence of colors and the word "light": "This sun a mere particle, clear as no heat. Charts of light bending at hand. And the next day stones" (215). Elements of the upcoming "Dalí" section are suspended in a colloidal fashion within the flow of *A Geology*.

Coolidge's choice of Dalí—as opposed to another surrealist artist such as Yves Tanguy—hardly seems incidental, however. In a manner similar to (if more willfully eccentric than) Coolidge or, for that matter, Smithson, Dalí often writes about visiting the Museum of Natural History in Madrid as a child, and these childhood visits become central to several recurring fantasies and daydreams within his corpus. As Dawn Ades and Michael R. Taylor note in an exhaustive catalogue of Dalí's intellectual interests, "His father was an amateur geologist and instructed Dalí in the fossils of [Catalonia]" (447). Indeed, Dalí makes geologic imagery central to his paranoiac-critical method, as in his well-known interpretation of Jean-François Millet's painting *L'Angélus*. The painting sparks Dalí's "fancies related to the Tertiary period" and "a nostalgia for the end of the Carboniferous age" with its "fantastic geological cataclysms" (Dalí, *Collected Writings* 289–90). Ades and Taylor quote from Dalí's archived notes for a text on *The Persistence of Memory*, in which he discusses "the exceptional nature of colloidal substances." They write that for Dalí "the traditional distinction between the processes of growth in living entities and accretion in inorganic matter had been undermined by recent research into so-called 'fluid crystals' and into colloidal particles." These latter particles are "entities that did not follow the normal law of passing from a liquid to a crystalline state but that moved, Dalí noted, from a liquid state to either a gelatinous form or a granular structure" (460). Dalí thus emerges as a kind of precursor to Coolidge's desire to enact in art the geophysical processes of supersaturation and crystallization.

Dalí's interest in colloidal structures extended to what he called "soft-structures"—eggs, for example, in paintings such as *Fried Eggs on a Plate without the Plate*. While eggs have most often been viewed as erotic or uterine symbols in Dalí's work, they also point to his geologic obsession with fossils and "the origins of the universe" (Dalí, *Collected Writings* 290). Eggs are also tied to painting through the technique of tempera, in which an emulsive substance like egg yolk is used as a binding agent for paint. Aside from some early paintings produced using this technique, Dalí does not seem to have had much interest in tempera—indeed, he cautions young painters, "Tempera, fresco, egg painting, etc.—how it creaks! Those painful brush-smears of a Giotto or a Fra Angelico!" (356). Elsewhere, however, Dalí does single out a close contemporary of these Italian masters who painted primarily in tempera: Paolo Uccello. Uccello also shows up in Coolidge's *A Geology*, seeming to occasion the sudden appearance of "paint" in the text: "Timing and coating and so making a stitching the battery of running men to paint. Uccello eyed the table and rose, treed as in timbered" (*Book* 214). As a painter, Uccello is famed for his development of advanced techniques in perspective: Coolidge writes, "The written hinge, a spectacle, of mechanical division," with a characteristic pun on *vision* (215).

In *A Geology*, Uccello's vision, his "spectacle," is aligned with the interplay of surface and depth: "Must elongate to deceive. . . . A spectacle of the first water and the table rose" (215). On the one hand, Coolidge is slowly incorporating and rearranging word clusters—note, for instance, the repetition of "table" and "rose," which are repeated in various configurations several other times in the final pages of the text. On the other hand, Coolidge employs repetition to allude to the Dalíesque confusion of hard and soft entities. For instance, "table" increasingly appears with "water" nearby. Likewise, the text proposes, "That it is a matter of buttering stones in the mill room, friable as an attribute" (215). With its pun on "matter," this image of "buttering stones," rather than, say, buttering *scones*, is an apt approximation of Dalí's penchant for confounding hard and soft structures. What is more, "friable" (that is, crumbly) implies the prevalence of erosion in Dalí's imagery (especially if one hears the "butte" in "attribute") while also potentially hinting at the title of his *Fried Eggs* painting. The word "egg" appears only once in *A Geology*, but it occurs at least ten times in the subsequent transitional section that links the sections of *A Geology* and "Dalí." "Egg" then appears numerous times throughout "Dalí," including in the first sentence: "I wanted to grow from a town that extended an egg" (249). The overall texture of Coolidge's colloidal writing, then, is similar to that of tempera: the word "egg" itself serves as a sort of binding agent linking *A Geology* to "Dalí."

Reading *A Geology* in light of its place within the larger structure of *A Book Beginning What* allows us to see how Coolidge employs a colloidal method not just in individual works but also on a much more extensive scale. Pulling words and phrases from many contexts—in this case, from the realms of geology, caving, music, and art history, among many others—Coolidge disperses these textual particles throughout a series of prose experiments. The reader encounters these particles not as elements that can be pieced back together to form a coherent whole (as in a monumental work like Pound's *Cantos*) but rather as one might encounter an intrusion of rock in one stratum only for it to disappear in the next. Certain words will arise and repeat within a local area of the text, then gradually (or abruptly) disappear back into what Coolidge calls, following Beckett, "the mess" ("Notebooks" 44). And yet, at the risk of sounding like Dalí's paranoic-critic, who sees a vast, all-encompassing system of meaning as an objective reality, I want to suggest that Coolidge's emphasis on the nonsemantic aspects of language encourages a reader to see patterns everywhere. As in Dalí's observation that a colloidal substance undermines a clear distinction between organic and inorganic matter, Coolidge's use of geophysical concepts points to a nonhuman excess at the heart of language. While Coolidge does not make this nonhuman aspect of language an explicit mode of inquiry within his poetic practice, I turn now to a poet, Steve McCaffery, who has systematically embraced its implications.

Word Strata

The work of the British-born Canadian poet Steve McCaffery comprises a sustained attempt to treat language geologically and extends this geologic view of language into a philosophical stance about the limits of the thinkable. For example, in "Lastworda," the poem that closes his 1991 collection *Theory of Sediment*, McCaffery places language into geologic strata. As he explains in a note that appears after the poem, "Lastworda" undertakes "a journey back through an English lexicon along the sweep of a single continuum. Commencing with selected words current in contemporary usage the continuum retreats a few lines to each decade, in this way as far back as Anglo-Saxon" (214). The piece comprises a single extended block of text that lacks a clear syntactic structure and is devoid of punctuation except for a period after the final word, which is, fittingly, "lastworda." The result is a dense conglomerate of language that resembles, at least superficially, the more impenetrable passages in *A Geology* or *Smithsonian Depositions*: "An intervention buffer friendly to diskette that transit via chunnel sovereignty of fission" (201). While the text includes fragments of semantic legibility (for example, "transit via chunnel"), its overall effect is that of an uninterrupted flow of words with no clear syntactic relation. Moreover, as this flow proceeds (or, perhaps better, retreats) along a temporal continuum from contemporary to Anglo-Saxon diction, words are subject to increasing orthographic deformations and thus become increasingly illegible for the contemporary reader: "i-cleoped swetture wemme grundwal con vnderfonge bihote feolevolde" (212). In reading "Lastworda," one reads the visible (and hears the sonic, when performed) strata of language, much as a geologist reads the layers of rock in a cliff face or a core sample.

As Christian Bök explains, McCaffery's pataphysical practice "suggests that like a word . . . a rock holds a position within a grid of forms—a tabula, created by the horizontal axis of spatial ordering (i.e., the line) and the vertical axis of temporal layering (i.e., the page)" (*'Pataphysics* 96). In this "conceit that language is itself a subgenre of geology," the totality of a language aligns with "the mass of the earth" while individual instances of the language (*parole* in Bök's Saussurean vocabulary) function as a "node in the earth," a sort of "fold" in the overall topography. McCaffery's diachronic defamiliarization of the English language distinguishes his use of geology from Coolidge's. Thus, in contrast to Coolidge's colloid compositions, "Lastworda" reveals how language change itself resembles a geologic process of stratification. Individual words are sediment that coalesces into phrases, which in turn consolidate into a langue.

"Lastworda" resists aggregation into a molar structure such as that found in Coolidge: words here do not resolve into larger syntactic structures (sentences) or semantic units (paragraphs) but rather serve to index change over time, their positions in the text relative to their first appearance in print. In this way, the poem further demonstrates Deleuze and Guattari's contention that "strata are judgments of God (but the earth . . . constantly eludes that judgment)" (qtd. in Bök, *'Pataphysics* 115-16n9). That is, stratification undertakes "a royal process of capture that arranges disparate parts into long-range, large-scale orders of solidity," which is "always subject to a nomad process of rupture which deranges disparate parts into short-range, small-scale orders of fluidity" (115–16). "Lastworda" is what Deleuze and Guattari might call a line of flight from semantic constraints: one reads "Lastworda" not to arrive at a meaning but to experience the compressed temporal morphology of the English language.

This temporal point is worth emphasizing, as it both encapsulates and departs from Deleuze and Guattari's presentation of language and geology. On the one hand, geology suggests an exemplary process of becoming for Deleuze and Guattari (and, I would argue, for McCaffery). Geology is exemplary because it dramatizes the concept of rates of change or, as they would say, speeds of becoming. For instance, to the human eye, a mountain range does not appear to change very much from year to year; however, the mountain is rising or eroding or otherwise shifting at very small scales. The mountain is still becoming, but across nonhuman periods of time. A geologic stratum, then, is compressed time, and such temporal compression is precisely what "Lastworda" enacts. The poem speeds up the rate of linguistic change, graphing in some ten pages millennia of vowel shifts and morphemic erosion or agglomeration.

On the other hand, for Deleuze and Guattari, language (whether written or spoken) is always part of a collective assemblage of enunciation and thus only one stratum of many in the material world—and not necessarily the most important one. Unlike their poststructuralist contemporaries, Deleuze and Guattari are not especially fixated on signification and inscription, seeing instead a multiplicity of strata through which the real and the virtual (that is, actual and potential capacities of objects) can be organized. McCaffery collapses this distinction, combining geology and linguistic morphology on the same plane. Yet this very collapse is what allows McCaffery to foreground a nonhuman tendency in language. In pataphysical fashion, "Lastworda" features a rigorous organizational constraint. However, due to the inevitable (and always unfinished) change of language over time, which occurs independent of any particular writer or speaker, this mock–scientific schema leads to a poem that is increasingly difficult to decipher for most modern readers. Paradoxically, the poem disrupts semanticity through its overly meticulous attention to the material deformation of words.

As both a poet and a critic, McCaffery is interested in disrupting instrumental language and revealing what he calls the "proto" or "pre-semantic" qualities of words. For instance, in his critical study *Prior to Meaning*, McCaffery identifies "a limited autonomy of the written mark at a level both beneath and around the semantic" (xv). This "autonomy" consists in the ability of language to exceed its conventional function as an instrument of communication. In other words, for McCaffery, "Language is frequently the struggle to contain the errant vivacity of 'a living letter'" (xix). But, for all that, the endless movement of this "living letter" is not so much recognizably human as it is an alterity, something disturbingly other. McCaffery's descriptions of the protosemantic indicate its nonhuman qualities. McCaffery defines "writing as a material scene of forces" and repeatedly returns to characteristics such as volatility, instability, and displacement (xv). Proposing a "particle poetics," McCaffery argues that the protosemantic creates "shifts along fault lines" that demonstrate how "complex stable systems carry within them unstable subsystems" (xviii). In McCaffery's rhetoric, language is akin to the geophysical system of the earth: seemingly stable on the surface but roiled by chthonic forces. The protosemantic is language's geologic underside.

McCaffery's stratigraphic approach to writing has a precedent—though it's likely not a direct influence—in Smithson's 1970 piece "Strata: A Geophotographic Fiction," originally published in *Aspen* number 8 edited by Dan Graham. Smithson designs his text as a series of narrow strips that correspond to geologic periods ordered from the most recent (Cretaceous) to the most ancient (Precambrian). These layers are interrupted by blown-up photos depicting fossils and other rocks associated with each period. The text, while displaying more syntactic regularity than those of either Coolidge or McCaffery, is nonetheless paratactic. Indeed, each stratum is a collage of sources and stray observations that describe aspects of the corresponding period. For instance, the "Triassic" layer begins, "Obscure Valleys. Data from drilled holes. *He may even now—if I may use the phrase—be wandering on some Plesiosaurus-Haunted ollitic coral reef, or beside the lonely saline lakes of the Triassic Age* (H.G. Wells)" (75). In addition to forming a kind of intertext with Smithson's own work—"lonely saline lakes" suggests his abiding interest in salt lakes, in particular his contemporaneous *Spiral Jetty* sculpture, essay, and film—each stratum is an index of geologic texts.

If McCaffery produces a paleontology of language, Smithson constructs a sort of paleoepistemology, a stratigraphic study of documents concerning natural history. "Strata" points to depictions of geologic history ranging from "[a] display of plaster Triceratops eggs in a glass case" and "[d]igestive systems shown in diagrams" to entries in the "Dictionary of Geological Terms." Instead of a flow of words arranged diachronically, Smithson offers "[a] landslide of maps" and other second-order representations. (Indeed, the piece could potentially be read as Smithson's idiosyncratic tour through his beloved American Museum of Natural History in New York City.) This preoccupation with maps and diagrams aligns with Smithson's dialectical approach to place, in which he continually defers arrival at a specific location through the intermediaries of models, maps, and photographs. In its emphasis on mediation, "Strata" recalls Smithson's articulation of the Nonsite. As I detailed in chapter 1, the Nonsite, typically installed in a gallery, attempts to contain an unbounded site existing outside the gallery space by functioning as, in Smithson's words, "a three-dimensional map" (111). This abstract map indexes the site from which the materials were collected. However, as Smithson further explains in a note to his essay "The Spiral Jetty," the dialectic of Site and Nonsite never reaches a resolution. Rather, it comprises "a double path made up of signs, photographs, and maps that belong to both sides of the dialectic at once.... The Nonsite is a container within another container—the room. [The Site] is yet another container.... Is the Site a reflection of the Nonsite (mirror), or is it the other way around?" (153). In other words, with the Nonsite, Smithson proposes that human knowledge (and its documentation in texts, be they maps, photographs, or essays) is itself a "subgenre of geology," prone to deformations and chthonic shifts.

Indeed, through an erosional process that Smithson would have appreciated, the version of "Strata" that appears in *The Collected Writings* has been altered by time and circumstance, much as *Spiral Jetty* has undergone years of salt deposition and weathering. As Jack Flam, the editor of Smithson's *Collected Writings*, explains, "Some words are illegible in this article because of the worn folds in the pages of the only copy of the original available to us" (75). In short, certain words and lines in the piece have been effaced, as if demonstrating Smithson's insistence on entropy. It is also a literal instance of Amanda Boetzkes's point that in its proliferation of "textual artworks," earth art foregrounds "a failed recovery through texts that betray the expenditure and loss of the elemental forces they attempt to represent" and "reveal[s] the impossibility of subsuming the earth into representational form" (57). Of course, one might wonder just how accidental this damage was. For instance, the still-legible section of one damaged line reads, "In these natural traps they died, and were eventually buried," while another barely visible sentence notes, "Anticline is a type of strata fold." *Folds* (as in a book) are all to the point here, and while Smithson may not have foreseen this outcome, the erosion caused by these folds epitomizes his vision of a world in continual disintegration. At the very least, the weathered surface of this text presents a useful reminder of Smithson's statement that "[a] book is a paper strata" (75).

For Smithson, McCaffery, and Coolidge, a geologic treatment of words reveals the nonsemantic aspects of language. McCaffery emphasizes the paragrammatic aspects of language such as acoustic and orthographic play, while Smithson foregrounds the materials of the earth. In "Sedimentation of the Mind," Smithson observes that "[t]he breakup or fragmentation of matter makes one aware of the sub-strata of the Earth before it is refined by industry" (106). Following the logic that would read language in terms of geology, Smithson's fascination with the unrefined matter of the earth suggests McCaffery's exploration of presemantic shards of language that have yet to be polished by the writing industry's demand for communication.

In each case, the use of strata alludes to a broader process of articulation in which language links the mineral earth directly to thought. As the title of his essay, "A Sedimentation of the Mind," makes apparent, Smithson is interested in "the suspension of boundaries between what Ehrenzweig calls the self and the non-self" (103). Listing the effects of this suspension in the terms of his "abstract geology," Smithson explains, "One's mind and the earth are in a constant state of erosion . . . brain waves undermine cliffs of thought, ideas decompose into stones of unknowing. . . . Slump, debris slides, avalanches all take place within the cracking limits of the brain. The entire body is pulled into the cerebral sediment, where particles and fragments make themselves known as solid consciousness" (100). "Unknowing" is a crucial state in Smithson's writing and art, and his insistence on material processes is part of his interest in getting the artist out of the studio and extending artworks beyond the confines of the gallery. Smithson concludes that as "the fissures between mind and matter multiply into an infinity of gaps, the studio begins to crumble and fall like The House of Usher, so that mind and matter get endlessly confounded" (107). This passage anticipates the striking language of Smithson's comparison that comes just one paragraph later, between "the names of minerals and the minerals themselves." Here, "material" and "print" become "endlessly confounded" in "an abysmal number of fissures." This is, as Smithson might have put it, an entropic situation, one of increasing disorder and the erasure of boundaries between categories. Smithson, in other words, treats mind, matter, and language as subject to an erosive process that not only turns each into fragments but also disintegrates the boundaries between them.

Bök offers a similar dissolution of categories in his account of McCaffery's project. In the form of a "'pataphysical metaphor," Bök claims: "When the process of stratifying minerals becomes reflexive, it makes a protein; when the process of stratifying proteins becomes reflexive, it makes a cellule; and when the process of stratifying cellules becomes reflexive, it makes a thought. No fossil is simply a figure for a phrase; instead, every fossil can become a phrase." Bök does not so much confound mind, matter, and language here as he combines them to form a single process. Moreover, Bök's pataphysical metaphor ceases to be a metaphor altogether—the arrangement of language into strata is not "simply a figure" but actually one stratum in a wider mineral-neurological organization. In a sense, then, Bök literalizes Smithson's triangulation of mind with matter and language. By way of McCaffery's paleological approach to words, Bök is able to claim, "Language is just the latest update of a machine that has found its own diverse methods to replicate itself (be it through geoseismic fossilization, biogenetic hybridization, or semiologic symbolization—three processes which establish a kind of conjugal relation, a *paleosexuality*, between rock, life, and word)" (92). While neither McCaffery nor Bök mentions Smithson in this context, the horizon of entropic dissolution—of language, of meaning, of matter—binds their projects.

Such is the case even at the level of style. Compare, for example, Bök's insistence that a geologic perspective "eliminate[s] any *grounds* for the truth of meaning" (93) or McCaffery's observation that, in light of geologic time, "we can only enter into a philosophy of the unthinkable, where meaning is finally detached from the human mind and where words no longer mean anything," (qtd. in Bök 93) with the following passage from "A Sedimentation of the Mind," discussed in chapter 1:

> A sense of the Earth as a map undergoing disruption leads the artist to the realization that nothing is certain or formal. Language itself becomes mountains of symbolic debris. . . . The strata of the Earth is a jumbled museum. Embedded in the sediment is a text that contains limits and boundaries which evade the rational order, and social structures which confine art. . . . A rubble of logic confronts the viewer as he looks into the levels of the sedimentations. (Smithson 110)

These presentations of language as "symbolic debris" or "rubble" are delivered in similarly overcharged, almost millenarian terms. Each account is shot through with a kind of pseudoscientific seriousness that is either borrowed from, or a spoof of, science fiction and proposes a grand theory that seems to both rigorously apply and misunderstand the science it employs. Indeed, misunderstanding is part of the point of this pataphysical mode of research: it enacts the very disruption of categories it claims to discover while at the same time hiding its conflations behind a mask of conceptual rigor. However, the "mendacity" (as McCaffery calls it) of this pataphysical line of reasoning is in the service of imagining new configurations of language.

Or, indeed, of imagining the limits of human language and thought itself. McCaffery's assertion that geologic time raises the specter of "a philosophy of the unthinkable" anticipates in a rather striking manner the recent advent of "speculative realism." For example, Quentin Meillassoux contends that geologic time reveals an unthinkable "anteriority," a time that is prior to, and thus not a correlate of, human thought (122). This anteriority, which Meillassoux calls the "arche-fossil," signals the absolute contingency of the world: the world (and the universe) does not exist *for* humans; it contains no ultimate reason for being as it is, or for being, period.

While the relevance of McCaffery, Smithson, or Coolidge to current debates within speculative realism has not, to my knowledge, been remarked before, this work could be considered an important precursor to, and enactment of, this new articulation of radical contingency. Because geology affirms the existence of a world prior to human thought (and thus of a world indifferent to the presence of human thought), it forms a fitting analogue to language's own indifference. Or, to put it another way, treating language as if it were a geologic structure—as Coolidge, McCaffery, and Smithson do—accentuates language's nonhuman aspects, the way language patterns proliferate in excess of human will or intention.

For these writers, the use of geology returns to a question of reading. Textual processes like sedimentation, stratification, and colloids disrupt conventional modes of reading. The logical contours of—in Smithson's case—art criticism explode into "a jumbled museum" of fragments from disparate discourses—a kind of slow defamiliarization of genres and categories. McCaffery extends the connection between sedimentation and reading even further in his prose poem "Theory of Sediment," where he posits that the act of reading itself comprises erosion and sedimentation: "Sediment is a derivative from other material. Passing the way of words. Deposits" (*Theory of Sediment* 107). In this way, "Sedimentation is a process of denuding: the erosion of a land or text mass and its transportation to numerous environments of depositions; this leading both to stable and unstable forms" (104). McCaffery suggests that reading a text erodes that text; and, furthermore, that readers transport their readings into other contexts, thus mixing and remixing a range of texts.

Here we have a slightly different version of Roland Barthes's famous "writerly text," a text in which "it is language that speaks, not the author" (143). Barthes's proclaimed "death of the author" is, of course, overly familiar now. But what is not often specifically noted is that it presents the writer-as-reader (which Barthes calls the "scriptor") as a remixer of language, a kind of textual DJ who "performs" language. McCaffery picks up where Barthes leaves off—that is, with the figure of the reader who encounters the text as a "multi-dimensional space in which a variety of writings, none of which are original, blend and clash" (146). *Theory of Sediment*, like Coolidge's *A Book Beginning What*, is certainly such a space, ranging as it does from paratactic non sequiturs to more discursive (if pataphysical) pronouncements about the homology of geology and language.

However, whereas Barthes privileges reading and the reader as "the space on which all the quotations that make up a writing are inscribed without any of them being lost," (148) McCaffery views reading as a fundamentally entropic enterprise. As he describes it, "Reading provokes as a social act the release of turbid optical currents on a textual slope effecting both a lateral and vertical modification of the source texts. The eye is a fluvial force operator" (*Theory of Sediment* 104–5). The adjective "turbid" discloses reading as a disturbance: the eye discharges opaque flow that, rather than preserving meaning, disperses it. In the next chapter, we will see how Jen Bervin further develops this fluvial, erosional manner of reading through the creation of a palimpsest in her artist book *The Desert*. Whereas Bervin turns to the material support of the codex in her work, McCaffery produces a lettristic disturbance at the very core of his text: "The ambiguity thus arising in the referent produces a relief development of the text and pertains, of course, to the latter's sedimentary depth. (At first he heard sentiment.)" (106). As with pataphysics more generally, the poem enshrines a misunderstanding, replacing a depth model based on sentiment with one based on sediment (a switch that becomes all the more pointed when one recalls that it is precisely a *sentimental* model of authorial depth that Barthes seeks to dislodge with a more topological model of textuality). "Sediment" is thus another instance of McCaffery's abiding obsession with that aspect of language that exceeds fixity. The lettristic shift from *sen*timent to *sed*iment marks "an inferred catachresis" (114). Reading, rather than facilitating human communication, involves a breakdown in usage and proffers a glimpse into language's nonhuman autonomy.

CHAPTER 5

Cropping *The Desert*

Erasure, Erosion, and Reclamation in Jen Bervin and John C. Van Dyke

> Porosity, and its fullest responsiveness,
> can occur only within difference.
> —Luce Irigaray

In the summer of 1898, John C. Van Dyke abruptly abandoned his comfortable life as a librarian and professor of art history at Rutgers College in New Jersey and set off on a nearly three-year journey across the deserts of North America. He had no fixed itinerary, no companions other than his terrier Cappy, and brought only about fifty pounds of supplies. For an indefinite sojourn into some of the hottest and driest portions of the planet, he carried one gallon of water. Forty-two years old and by all accounts asthmatic, Van Dyke hardly seemed the type to embark on such an ambitious, one might even say reckless, adventure. Indeed, a certain air of mystery and rumor still surrounds his voyage: had he fathered an illegitimate child and was he thus fleeing a scandal? Did Andrew Carnegie send him to Mexico on a secret diplomatic mission?[1] Whatever precipitated the voyage—and despite his apparent lack of preparation—Van Dyke would survive his wanderings across California, Arizona, and Mexico to write *The Desert: Further Studies in Natural Appearances*. Originally published by Scribner's in 1901, the book was, for a time, extremely popular and is described by Richard Shelton in his introduction to the 1980 edition as "a touchstone, a model of accuracy, deep feeling, and simplicity" that "not even the poets" have "surpassed" (xvi–xvii).

As if taking up Shelton's latent challenge, in 2008 the poet and visual artist Jen Bervin produced an erasure of Van Dyke's text in the form of an artist book, titled simply *The Desert*. Retaining the original book's title, typeface, page numbers, and marginal glosses, Bervin, with help from the artist Jan Drojarski, digitally reprinted the first seven chapters on bleached abaca paper from Twinrocker Handmade Papers. She then used some five thousand yards of pale blue thread to machine-sew line-by-line across each page, deliberately leaving certain words and phrases uncovered to produce a found poem—or, rather, a set of poems—out of Van Dyke's paean to desert landscapes.[2]

This chapter argues that Bervin's specific material intervention, as well as the palimpsestic effect it creates, enacts the geologic forces of wind and water erosion and illuminates the central tension in Van Dyke's work between nature and human industry. That is, while Bervin presents her book as a meditation on Van Dyke's theory of deserts as silent "breathing spaces" which counteract the suffocating expansion of American industry and capitalism, I contend that her adoption of this concept produces an ambivalent text that melds geologic and mechanical forces. Specifically, the materials Bervin utilizes—needle, thread, and paper—enact various processes of erosion: appropriate to its desert subject, the book's materials operate variously as wind, sand, and water, abrading and preserving the original text much as these forces might weather and rearrange rock. Each of these items in turn creates particular material and thematic effects. To put it briefly here, the thread's role as air and wind erodes Van Dyke's descriptions of erosion, collapsing textual and geographic space; the sandlike pages, in conjunction with Bervin's sewing, produce a palimpsest that reveals the surprising ubiquity of water in the desert; and finally, as this water, the thread indicates a subterranean fluid dynamics similar to that proposed by the philosopher Luce Irigaray. The interplay of these erosions renders Van Dyke's text a porous and noisy space. Bervin thus complicates Van Dyke's ontological separation of human and natural realms and undermines his insistence on a gendered idealization of nature as virgin and pure. In place of Van Dyke's tidy ontology, Bervin's project exhibits, through its very means of production, a space wherein humans and nature (or industry and deserts) are inextricable.

Because features such as the loose ends of the thread and the holes made by the needles remain visible, the book also functions as a record of its own compositional process. And if an erased text about deserts seems a rather obvious gesture—as, in the popular imagination, deserts are already thought of as empty, barren, and blank spaces—Bervin does not exactly *erase* Van Dyke's text. Rather, her decision to employ a zigzag stitch allows the original words to peek through, enabling a patient reader to view both versions of *The Desert* at once. In this way, the book is reminiscent of Bervin's earlier project *Nets*, which uses a bold font to set off the minimalist poems she has fashioned from Shakespeare's sonnets while maintaining his original text in a fainter but still readable typeface. Unlike avant-garde precursors such as John Cage or Jackson Mac Low, Bervin does not arrive at her found poems through aleatory procedures—although, as I hope to show, she does utilize the palimpsest's interplay of absence and presence to reveal a mode of reading alive to chance occurrences.[3]

While her choice of Van Dyke's book could offer a veiled riposte to Shelton's enthusiasm over *The Desert*'s supposedly unparalleled poetic achievement, Bervin more immediately takes a cue from Van Dyke himself. In his preface he claims that his record of the Colorado and Mojave Deserts is "at least truthful. Given the facts perhaps the poet with his fancies will come hereafter" (xi). In her colophon, meanwhile, Bervin explains, "John Van Dyke writes of the American deserts as necessary breathing spaces; my sewn poem is narrated by the air." Her use of light blue thread as a "narrator" was, she writes, originally inspired by artist James Turrell's use of light, and she "composed an early draft of the first chapter for [a] reading at . . . Roden Crater." Indeed, Turrell's Crater, a monumental land artwork located inside the cone of an extinct volcano in northern Arizona's Painted Desert, combines an interest in the geologic formation of the desert with an intense awareness of light. As the work's caretaker, the Skystone Foundation, declares: "Roden Crater is a controlled environment for the experiencing and contemplation of light" in which Turrell has turned the interior of the cone into a series of "special engineered spaces where the cycles of geologic and celestial time can be directly experienced." In other words, Turrell has carved out spaces that reframe various portions of the desert sky, much as Bervin reframes Van Dyke's observations of the desert. In Van Dyke's *Desert*, then, Bervin finds, as she writes in the colophon, an "uncanny relationship to Turrell's concerns" with light and space, a relationship she means to visualize through the thread's suggestion of a clear blue sky, which "narrates" the poem by simultaneously veiling and revealing Van Dyke's language.

Turrell makes sense as a catalyst for Bervin's *Desert*, particularly in such passages as "The great get on with the least possible and suggest everything by light." It is tempting to read this statement as Bervin's ars poetica, for it articulates her book's intertwined themes of minimalism, veiling, and vision. The still rather slight critical literature on Bervin does precisely this, presenting her treatment of *The Desert* as a quiet meditation on light and nature. For instance, in a review of *The Desert* and Mary Ruefle's *A Little White Shadow*, Mary Hickman maintains that "Van Dyke's text exists as one man's record of his senses, which Bervin's attentive erasure excavates to further reveal a meditation on light, vision, composition, and ultimately, the body's absence in the landscape of the wilderness." This characterization of Bervin's work as in touch with "elemental" forces also appears in Travis MacDonald's article "A Brief History of Erasure Poetics." For MacDonald, erasure poetry obtains its license first and foremost from nature: "It seems only natural then, that the world's first erasure poetry was authored by the elements themselves and comes to us via the remnants of weathered stone carvings and papyrus scrolls." Anchored to the weathering of stone and the origins of writing, erasure in MacDonald's account becomes intrinsic to poetry itself. However, while neither Hickman nor MacDonald makes this point explicit, the most salient feature of Bervin's procedure is that it *enacts* geologic forces. Bervin does not create a poem *describing* erosion; she actually *erodes* Van Dyke's detailed descriptions of erosion.

Van Dyke's second chapter, "The Make of the Desert," focuses on the role of aeolian processes in the desert and provides a good example of how Bervin's interventions work in practice. In the original text, across from the marginal glosses "Barren rock" and "Saw-toothed ridges," Van Dyke gives an impressionistic description of the formation of mountains: "Rising as they do from flat sands they give the impression of things deep-based—veritable islands of porphyry bent upward from a yellow sea." For Van Dyke, the resulting crags suggest "needles that are lifted skyward like Moslem minarets or cathedral spires" and "shine like brazen spear-points set against the sky" (42). On the facing page, meanwhile, adjacent to the gloss "Seen from the peaks," Van Dyke extols the mountains as "Genii—spirits of the desert—keeping guard over the kingdom of the sun. And what a far-reaching kingdom they watch!" (43). Bervin's rendition, by contrast, maintains only a fraction of Van Dyke's language: next to "Barren rock," she removes both Van Dyke's more technical, geologic language ("porphyry") and his architectural imagery of minarets and spires, leaving the micropoem, "Rising as they do / of things deep-based—." In a similar fashion, across from "Saw-toothed ridges" she distills the description of the younger, less eroded peaks to the suggestive lines, "They / have needles that are lifted / brazen spear-points" (42). Here, there is an implicit pun on the past tense of *see* in the "sawtoothed ridges" that in Bervin's version are indeed no longer seen. The next page (which in Bervin's layout is always the recto), sharpens the motif of sight as Bervin commands the reader to "watch! / into the blue of the / fold / its / veilings / attuned to the key of / air— / There / questioning" (43).

By isolating the imagery of "needles" and "the / blue of the / fold / its veilings," Bervin makes obvious her conflation of book and landscape. Van Dyke's description of a mirage, "fold upon fold over the mesas the hot air drops its veilings of opal and topaz," becomes a reference to the "fold" of the book, while "needles," shorn of its original context, shifts from designating mountain peaks to implying the object those peaks are supposed to resemble—and thereby establishes a metonymic reference to sewing. At the same time, Bervin analogizes these sewing needles to "brazen spear-points" so as to indicate the physicality of needles piercing paper—in this sense, sewing allows Bervin to literally "poke holes" in Van Dyke's prose. Her "needles" are "brazen" in the sense of a "bold, piercing stare." Yet her practice is piercing in another sense: "brazen" can also denote "harsh in sound" (*OED*). Thus the "eye" of Bervin's needle marries sight with sound while calling attention to the noise her thread introduces into the silence of the desert.

For if, in its role as the air that narrates the poem, the blue thread is meant to create "breathing spaces," these spaces are not exactly the quiet and meditative spaces MacDonald and Hickman lead us to expect. In the example above, sound plays a central role in Bervin's selection of words to leave uncovered: in "veilings / attuned to the key of air— / There / questioning," "There" immediately repeats the long *a* in "veil" and "air," demonstrating how Bervin's erosions are indeed "attuned to the key of / air"—that is, driven at least in part by sound and chance textual adjacencies. Put differently, Bervin treats the page as an open field of relations rather than a strictly linear construction, uncovering new formations while obscuring (but never entirely erasing) others. Van Dyke describes a similar activity when he compares the effects of wind erosion in the desert to a skeletal emergence of the bare earth in which "the drift rolled high in one place was cut out from some other place; and always there are *vertebrae* showing—elbows and shoulders protruding through the yellow byssus of sand" (28). Bervin cleverly covers the word "byssus"—appropriate, perhaps, as it is a fine textile fiber—in other words, a type of *thread*. Bervin's sewing again erodes a depiction of erosion.

Bervin's conflation of textual space with geographic space illustrates book artist and media theorist Johanna Drucker's claim that all "[w]riting is a site" and "[d]ocuments are specific territories." Sounding almost as if she were discussing Bervin's play with the relation of text and marginal gloss, Drucker argues for a "topographic" treatment of the page, which attends to the text's "geometry of position" ("Un-Visual and Conceptual"). *Topography* designates a study of relations—the arrangement of the natural and artificial physical features of an area (*OED*). In Drucker's lexicon, topography "is about connections, juxtaposition, sequence, break, order, rupture, and all the many ways spaces and zones relate." Hence, as the "Un-Visual" in the title of her article ironically suggests, for Drucker there is no such thing as poetry that is *not* somehow grounded in its visual and graphic codes.[4]

This combination of topographical and sonic play in Bervin's text directs our attention to the paper that serves as the book's material support. Indeed, the decision to use bleached abaca paper is far from incidental to the project. Visually, the light tan color suggests the effects of prolonged exposure to sunlight as well as desert sand, while the abaca fiber, more commonly known as Manila hemp, is famous for its twin properties of strength and porousness: in addition to being a popular choice for specialty papers, abaca has been used for ships' rigging and tea bags.[5] In terms of *The Desert*, abaca's combination of toughness and porosity not only makes it a wise practical choice but also instantiates the processes of erosion and sedimentation. The perforations made by sewing machine render the paper literally porous—that is, the quality of "having minute spaces or holes through which liquid or air may pass"—and the blue thread creates a sort of visual pun on both air and, as we will see, water (*OED*).

What is more, the paper's appearance as sand recalls the material process that informs the very term *palimpsest*. Writing in a different context, Craig Dworkin establishes an etymological link between sand and palimpsest that is directly applicable to Bervin's project. In a discussion of Maurice Blanchot by way of Robert Rauschenberg's *Erased de Kooning Drawing*—which, rather than achieving a blank canvas, exhibits both the faint outline of de Kooning's original drawing and the marks made by Rauschenberg's eraser; in other words, the erasure in fact produces a palimpsest—Dworkin points out that "[sand], with its abrasive, pumicing ability to sponge, is an instrument of erasure" (*No Medium* 43). This is demonstrated in the verb *to sand*, meaning "to smooth, to rub out," and from here, Dworkin arrives at the term *palimpsest*, which "always enacts a double play of concealment and revelation, erasing one text to inscribe another and then suppressing the latter to display the first. The palimpsest obstructs to make a view possible" (43–44). In classical Latin, *palimpsestus* denotes "paper or parchment that has been written on again" and in turn derives from an ancient Greek compound meaning "to sand again." Tracing the English etymology of *sand* reveals its origin in "the Old Teutonic *sandjan* (to send) . . . a message"; thus "'sand,' like 'palimpsest,' encompasses both the emission of a message and its omission." Furthermore, Dworkin notes that "[m]etonymically, 'sand' also denotes the bank of a river, or the seashore, the marge or margin," a sense that resonates with Bervin's project, as we will see (44).

The palimpsest, Dworkin concludes, "[b]ring[s] into view by erasing." This effect is precisely what Bervin's text accomplishes: by veiling the vast majority of Van Dyke's prose, Bervin renders the page a layered landscape. That is, instead of treating the page as a linear progression of lines to be read from left to right and top to bottom, she views it as a nonhierarchical whole whose parts can be associated in numerous ways. Bervin's sewing is thus a kind of seeing: it traces an intuitive rather than systematic movement through the text. A palimpsest implies a revision, literally "to look at or see again." As a result, Dworkin explains, "the palimpsest is a *parchemin ablué*: writing that has both a cleansing removal and a restoration." Moreover, erosion is the operative process in the creation of a palimpsest. Dworkin draws a line from "ablution" (*ablué*) to "ablation," which derives from the Latin *ablatio* and literally means "to carry away." While, as Dworkin notes, ablation "can of course denote any removal . . . it most commonly refers to removal of the surface layer of an object by sanding," again linking palimpsests to sand erosion (44). Ablation additionally denotes "the erosion of rock, typically by wind action" (*OED*). In other words, a palimpsest reproduces the action of erosion, effacing and revealing its texts much as wind and sand weather and rearrange rock.

Dworkin's argument carries us from "sand" to "ablution" through a fluid mixture of etymology and sound play—namely, the sonic and orthographic proximity of "ablation" to "ablution." As a version of Dworkin's parchemin ablué, Bervin's palimpsest similarly leads us to water, the final driver of erosion that *The Desert* enacts. Ablution derives from the Latin verb *ablutio*, "to wash away." Like *ablation*, *ablution* implies a process of removal but with the added sense of a cleansing or purification—the word was initially used in relation to alchemy and referred to "purification by using liquids" (*OED*). To adjust its meaning only slightly, the "cleansing removal" indicated by ablution is what Van Dyke sought by fleeing the industrialized east coast for the vast spaces of the American deserts. As Shelton, paraphrasing Blake, puts it in his introduction, "This man [Van Dyke] who rode through the desert" hoped "to cleanse and purify the doors of his perception" (xiii).

For Van Dyke, deserts represent a purer space separate from, and hostile to, human activity, and Van Dyke's desire in *The Desert* to remove himself from human society places him within the tradition of relinquishment that Lawrence Buell has identified as a frequent theme in what he calls ecocentric writing. To briefly recall his influential argument, Buell contends that in works such as Henry David Thoreau's *Walden* and Aldo Leopold's *Sand County Almanac*, the deliberate turn away from a social and into a natural realm responds to a need for "voluntary simplicity," a refreshing, if strenuous, shift from an "egocentric" to an "ecocentric" perspective. Van Dyke's disavowal of the east coast in favor of the desert certainly fits into this trope, and while, unlike Thoreau or Leopold, he maintains a nomadic itinerary rather than retreat to a Walden or a Sauk County, Van Dyke matches Buell's criteria that an "epic of voluntary simplicity" feature both the relinquishment of material goods and the relinquishment of the self (144). By his own account, at least, Van Dyke traveled light, slept rough, and rarely indulged in the comforts of civilization during his three years of wandering. More significantly, his writing about the desert displays a fairly ecocentric viewpoint focused on the details of slow geologic change. Paradoxically, one of the most important agents of that change in the desert is the element deserts should by definition lack: water.

Turning our attention to water, we can begin to see both Van Dyke's attempts to relinquish an anthropocentric stance and the real complexity of Bervin's intervention in his text. In chapter 3, "The Bottom of the Bowl," Van Dyke details the geologic history of the Salton Basin in south-central California. Water is central to this story, as the basin was once part of the Pacific Ocean floor and later the site of an inland lake that dried up when its connection to the Colorado River was cut off by deposits of sediment built up over centuries (46–47). Surprisingly, Bervin's alterations to this section tend to undercut rather than amplify Van Dyke's ecocentric angle. For example, on the second page of the chapter, Bervin's sewing creates the lines "Some / have / lost their identity" (45). However, Van Dyke has not been describing a Buellian experience of self-relinquishment but rather the persistence of the ancient seashore in the Colorado Desert: "The old bays and lagoons that led inland from the sea . . . the inlets and natural harbors are all in place. Some of them are drifted full of sand, but they have not lost their identity"—that is, their general outline and shape (45). Here, Bervin introduces a human perspective into the text even as she implies a loss of human identity in the midst of the desert's disorienting geography.

In another sense, however, Bervin makes present the absence of the human just as Van Dyke makes present the absence of water. One of the more notable features of Van Dyke's presentation of deserts is his awareness of the fundamental role of water in shaping desert topography: deserts are geographically defined by their relative lack of rainfall on the one hand and the action of water erosion (along with wind and sand) on the other. In chapters like "The Bottom of the Bowl," Van Dyke adopts the cliché of the desert as a "sea of sand" to emphasize that its basins and reefs and dunes were, in fact, once part of an ocean floor, or the result of erosion and sedimentation by rivers like the Colorado (45).

Bervin's sewing operates in a fashion similar to water in the desert. Like all palimpsests, it stages a tension between presence and absence, addition and subtraction. The question then becomes what Bervin brings into view by erasing. At times, as in the case above, Bervin troubles Van Dyke's emphasis on silence. For instance, next to the marginal gloss "The silences," Van Dyke exclaims, "Was there ever such a stillness as that which rests upon the desert at night! . . . You perhaps think to break the spell by raising your voice in a cry; but you will not do so again. The sound goes but a little way and then seems to come back to your ear with a suggestion of insanity about it" (107). Bervin keeps "Was there ever such a stillness as" a fragment that runs directly into the right margin and gloss, inviting us to read "Was there ever such a stillness as | The silences" as a complete phrase. This sentiment is immediately challenged, however, by what Bervin does with the rest of the passage. Bervin's version reads (sans marginal gloss): "Was there ever such a stillness as / raising your / voice / to come back to" (107). Whereas Van Dyke rejects the temptation of raising one's voice in the wilderness, Bervin, if not embracing the human cry, at least hints that noise and its reverberation bring the "silences" of the desert into relief.

Further down on the same page, next to the gloss "The cry of the human," Van Dyke declares that this cry "jars the harmonies! How it breaks in discord upon the unities of earth and air and sky! Century after century that cry has gone up, mobbing high heaven; and always insanity in the cry, insanity in the crier" (107–8). By contrast, Bervin's rendition is far more ambivalent: "it breaks in / Century after / century has gone up, / and always in the cry, / in the crier" (107–8). Bervin might offer a sort of commentary here, reminding us that the cry of the human is not so easy to erase, that "it breaks in" again and again in supposedly "empty" landscapes. Yet such a point is muddied by the very different ways these passages end. Van Dyke concludes with the strikingly nonanthropocentric assertion, "There is no appeal from the law of nature. It was made for beast and bird and creeping thing. Will the human never learn that in the eye of the law he is not different from the things that creep?" From this, Bervin maintains only "What / bird / is not different / ?" (108). If Van Dyke equates human and nonhuman,

Bervin seems to imply that the cries of the bird and the human are inherently "different," that nature does indeed distinguish between humans and other animals.

Bervin's insertion of noise into Van Dyke's desert wilderness calls to mind Leo Marx's famous argument in *The Machine in the Garden* that, from Virgil's *Ecologues* to the American transcendentalists and beyond, the busy world of civilization continually bursts into the silent solitude of pastoral retreats. Specifically, Marx takes as the paradigmatic American instance of this imposition a passage from Nathaniel Hawthorne's journal in which the writer is peacefully meditating in the woods near Concord, Massachusetts, when he is startled by a train's whistle (16). In other words, a piercing noise heralds the entry of the human into a natural landscape, thereby disturbing a clear separation of human and natural realms. Bervin's thread introduces such "noise" into Van Dyke's scene of material and self-relinquishment through a thematic amplifying of the human voice and, more fundamentally, through its material disruption of Van Dyke's signal. Following Michel Serres, we could view Bervin's thread as a kind of parasite that literally grabs hold of the text and redirects its semantic flow (5). More generally, Bervin's material intervention illustrates the core claim of information science that there is no signal, or communication, without noise.

Or, to put the matter slightly differently, Bervin's intervention uncovers, perhaps unwittingly, the noise of human industry that Van Dyke's text works so hard to conceal. While there is no scholarly agreement as to whether Van Dyke initially traveled to the Sonoran and Mojave Deserts at the behest of the steel baron Andrew Carnegie, it is true that Van Dyke and Carnegie maintained a longstanding friendship. As David Teague and Peter Wild detail in their introduction to Van Dyke's selected letters, Van Dyke often served as Carnegie's consultant on large art purchases and edited Carnegie's autobiography after the industrialist's death. According to Wild, Van Dyke may have even played a role in mending Carnegie's reputation following the 1892 massacre of twenty striking steel workers at a mill in Homestead, Pennsylvania. In his autobiography, Carnegie includes "an account written for the purpose by Van Dyke" in which the latter "recites a wonderful coincidence. In 1900, while traveling in Mexico as part of his trip to the Southwest, he chanced to meet . . . the poverty-stricken [John] McLuckie [one of the leaders of the strike]." The anecdote ends with the charitable Carnegie sending Van Dyke money to give to McLuckie (who, it would appear, lived up to his surname), and with Van Dyke landing the former striker a job "on the American-run railroad in northern Mexico" (*Secret Life* 20–21). Regardless of the veracity of this chance meeting in the desert, what is clear is that Van Dyke's account of his journeys in the west suppresses his deep involvement with the very industrial power he appears to disdain. Indeed, as Wild points out, *The Desert* is actually dedicated "not to some well-known nature lover and preservationist of the day such as John Muir, but—coyly using initials only—to nature-wrecking steel mogul Andrew Carnegie" (Van Dyke, *Secret Life* 6). Van Dyke's presentation of an ecocentric journey of relinquishment is, if not entirely false, a careful cultivation that crops out his broader pursuits in the service of empire. The machinations of industry, it seems, are never very far from *The Desert*.

While Bervin never alludes to this background, her intervention does posit that no desert is truly silent. This Cagean assertion destabilizes Van Dyke's idealized view of nature as necessarily separate from human activity and, in the very same gesture, points to the overlapping roles of water and human industry in the deserts of the western United States. Let me take each of these points in turn, focusing first on how Bervin's sewing unleashes a sort of fluid dynamics before moving to the way the project implicates irrigation and industry. The most obvious way that the thread resembles water is through a visual pun. If, on the recto, the thread amplifies the sound of *air* in "narrator," then on the verso the *tails* of thread, which Bervin has purposely left uncut, "trail their lengths" across the tan paper to simulate small desert streams. Moreover, the thread-as-water picks up on the abaca paper's characteristic porosity; it literally permeates, or passes through, the material support of the printed text. In this way, the thread both depicts and enacts a kind of fluidity that slyly erodes Van Dyke's authority.

For instance, when, in the midst of reporting on the prevailing winds in the Mojave, Van Dyke rather vaguely claims, "I am not prepared to point out the exact spot on the desert that the winds choose as a target" (30)—whether he simply cannot or does not want to say is unclear—Bervin adjusts the passage to state: "through loop holes / I am prepared to point out / you feel them softly / Yet about you / they cut" (30). "Loop holes" is Van Dyke's fanciful phrase for the mountain passes that funnel wind to and from the desert, but in the context of Bervin's revision they cannot help but imply the perforations made by her needles. Additionally, as *loophole* suggests the *eye* of a needle, Bervin creates a pun on the "I" that would "point out." Indeed, unlike Van Dyke, Bervin's I/eye of the needle is "prepared to point out" the erosional activity transfiguring his prose.

By co-opting Van Dyke's pronouns in this way, Bervin shifts the meaning and tone of the original passage. Crucially, her thread veils Van Dyke's "not," lending the retooled statement a certain edge of assurance: "I am prepared to point out." If Van Dyke strikes an oddly uncertain note here, Bervin's narrator sounds confident and composed. Similarly, Bervin adopts the second-person pronoun "you," deflecting it back onto the author. It seems as though Bervin is taking a jab at Van Dyke: while the needles that transform his prose are quiet and unassuming ("you feel them softly"), nonetheless "about you / they cut." At moments like this, Bervin literally undermines Van Dyke's rhetoric, her needle and thread "cutting" (in all senses) as they disarticulate his assertions and erode a stable sense of reference.

Bervin's disarticulation and transfer of Van Dyke's prose through thread that simulates both air and water deploy what has recently been called "liquid intelligence." Originating in an essay by the photographer Jeff Wall, the term "liquid intelligence" broadly refers to the capacity for liquids to carry and circulate information and thus to play a crucial role in the material production of photography, printing, painting, sculpture, architecture, and any number of other art forms (90). In Bervin's case, a kind of liquidity is present not in the thread itself but rather in the abaca paper's famous combination of toughness and porosity, which allows water to permeate, without dissolving, its fibers. In fact, this concomitance of liquid and solid structures reveals, according to art historian Jennifer Roberts, a critical insight of liquid intelligence. Roberts, in an essay on early nature printing, submits that we should "recognize the liquid-solid boundary as a boundary not of categories but of states. There are no such things as 'liquids' and 'solids'; there are only materials that exist variously in liquid and solid states"—that is, liquids require phase transitions to solids, and solids to liquids, in order to be able to transfer or reproduce any information at all ("Veins of Pennsylvania" 70).

While her work has not been cited in relation to liquid intelligence, the concept (and Bervin's project) has a precursor in Luce Irigaray's explanation of fluid dynamics. In the chapter of her 1977 book *This Sex Which Is Not One* titled "The 'Mechanics' of Fluids," Irigaray sketches a theory of fluidity that aims to correct the "historical lag in elaborating of 'theory' of fluids" as compared to the scientific fascination with solids (106). Irigaray is highly skeptical of the ability of scientific discourses to arrive at universal or mathematical truths. Indeed, she is skeptical of discourse writ large, as discourse for Irigaray is precisely the space wherein "truth" has been created and passed down by men ever since the master-disciple model initiated by Socratic thought. In short, "Solid mechanics and rationality have maintained a relationship of very long standing, one against which fluids have never stopped arguing" (113). Fluid defies rationality because it is irregular, fluctuating. Therefore, scientific discourse has not proposed a theory of fluids because the mechanics of fluids resist adequate symbolization. For example, Irigaray notes, "[I]t mixes with bodies of a like state . . . which makes the distinction between the one and the other problematical"; therefore, fluids reveal how a given solid "is already diffuse 'in itself,' which disconcerts any attempt at static identification" (111). Just as a small amount of water can be surprisingly effective at reducing seemingly solid rock to sediment, Bervin's sewing mixes with Van Dyke's text to weaken its conception of "nature."

Moreover, according to Irigaray, women similarly resist static identification: "women diffuse themselves according to modalities scarcely compatible with the framework of the ruling symbolics" (106). In its "fluid character," then, "*le sexe féminin*" is that which is "in excess with respect to form" (108). The very concept of woman in western thought exists only as a kind of gap or sieve. Irigaray terms this gap "L'afemme," a neologism that is meant to mark the unnamable excess of a system purporting to account for "all" that is (108).

Irigaray's point here is not to essentialize all women as somehow "fluid" but rather to show that idealism—and its insistence upon the male perspective as a default position—pervades language itself (a point that is even more literal in French, with its gendered nouns). She argues that we cannot think outside of a language that is based upon the strictures of rationalism and their phallocentric orientation toward clearly defined forms (that is, solids). Notably, the failure of language to articulate a mechanics of fluids showcases "the powerlessness of logic to incorporate in its writing all the characteristic features of nature," and because the subject is thoroughly embedded in language, for Irigaray the subject's utterances are "already repeating normative 'judgments' on a nature that is resistant to such a transcription" (106–7). In other words, the realm we refer to as nature exceeds our ideas about it; indeed, "nature" *is* a human concept and thus a product of the logical system it is supposed to transcend. Perhaps Gertrude Stein put it best: "Nature is not natural and that is natural enough" (141).

An idealized and gendered vision of capital-N Nature is precisely what Bervin's project complicates. For in Van Dyke, Nature is by default feminine. In *The Desert* he depicts "Mother Nature" as a figure who "intended that each [landscape] should remain as she made it" (62). Just as Bervin earlier reframed the pronoun "you" to point back to Van Dyke, Bervin's rendition of this passage both adopts and displaces the reference of the pronoun "she": "Nature goes calmly / on with her projects. She works / for her own satisfaction // and with no less care she made the des- / ert" (62). Given the project's continual allusions to its own compositional process, it is hard not to see these lines both as Bervin's assertion of her presence in Van Dyke's text and her rebuff of Van Dyke's "normative judgments" regarding Mother Nature. Furthermore, it is telling that Bervin actually reproduces a nonanthropocentric stance (that is, nature doesn't care about human projects) at the moment she comes closest to equating her artistic practice with a personified Nature. Like her zigzag stitch, it seems that Bervin often zigs when Van Dyke zags— that she prioritizes the human where Van Dyke emphasizes nonhuman forces, and the autonomy of nature where Van Dyke succumbs to anthropocentric tropes.

The unpredictability of Bervin's approach points to a key feature of fluids according to Irigaray: they operate obliquely, diffusely, and not in a proper fashion. By "proper," I mean in the sense of "a manner that is one's own, or self-same" (*OED*). Bervin's words are not her own; her thread uses Van Dyke's text to construct a found poem. Similarly, Irigaray asserts that L'afemme is not "proper" (*propre*)—that is, L'afemme poses a challenge to the integrated systems of capitalism and patriarchy; "she" is a figure that exceeds attempts to capture, or appropriate, property. Most important for my argument, L'afemme indicates a "zone of silence" within discourse; and yet, "that woman-thing speaks. But not 'like,' not 'the *same*,' not 'identical with itself'" (111). This in-between, improper, fluid-dynamic mode of utterance means that "sound is propagated in her at an astonishing rate" (112). Here we might recall that "dynamics" also refers to contrasting volumes of sound in music, and that water is an excellent conductor of sound. And while I do not want to conflate sound with noise, Irigaray's insistence on the propagation of sound echoes Bervin's characterization of her work in a conversation with fellow book artist Dianna Frid: "I'm trying to make poetry that points to the fact that many voices can be present in a text." The proliferation and amplification of these voices constitutes the core of Irigaray's ethics, which, as in the work of the philosopher Emmanuel Levinas, maintain the complexity and integrity of the other. Moreover, as Amanda Boetzkes observes, "in Irigaray's work ethics is coded as fluid and elemental." Recapitulating the claim that fluid dynamics undermines the science of solids, "the ethical," Boetzkes argues, "appears as a surprising flow of emotion in contrast to the solidity of reason's instrumental principles." Crucially, the ethical relation in Irigaray "is negotiated through a mode of corporeal interaction. This relation caresses and embraces, but never grasps or envelops, the other" (57). If Bervin pierces Van Dyke's pages, she does so to make them resound with the voice(s) of the other, and her palimpsest, which she creates by literally grasping, though never completely enveloping, Van Dyke's pages in a curious operation of addition by subtraction, enacts the ethical excess of fluid dynamics that makes a "zone of silence" reverberate with sound.

We might even say that fluid dynamics brings marginal(ized) features into view. As we have seen, Bervin uses Van Dyke's marginal glosses to help construct her poem, which unsettles the margin's supplemental relationship to the main body of the text. In her composition, the body of the text is as dependent upon its marginal glosses as those glosses are upon the body of the text. Center and margin constitute each other; there cannot be one without the other. Bervin links margins and water near the end of her book (the end of chapter 7 in Van Dyke) when, adjacent to the marginal gloss "water-mirage," Bervin proposes, "There are those / with / more lively imagination / drinking / along the margin" (123). Again, in its sly way the text seems to comment on its own process of composition: Bervin's sewing threads its way along the edges of Van Dyke's text, reimagining the structure of its relations.

At the same time, by presenting the margin as a place of sustenance, the passage recalls the etymological link between *margin* and *sand*, in which the latter metonymically denotes the bank of a river. Bervin, in other words, "channels" Van Dyke: her text not only reproduces Van Dyke's but also redirects it, flooding it with unforeseen sounds ("channel" and "canal" share the same Latin root, *canalis* (pipe or groove), from *canna* (reed) (*OED*). "Pipe," "groove," and "reed" each reinforce the link between channels and the production of sound (for example, the pipes of Pan of Greek myth, both the track cut in a record that the stylus follows and a rhythmic pattern in music, and reed instruments, respectively). "Channel," moreover, also designates a band of frequency used for broadcasting a signal. This overlap of *margin* and *channel* again points to the way Bervin underscores the insight from information theory that there is always noise in the channel.

In these senses, the margin(al) is bound up with the various resonances of irrigation. Put another way, the word *irrigation* itself alludes to Irigaray's ethical approach to the marginal. For in a wonderful instance of linguistic excess, the verb *irrigate*, from the Latin *irrigare*, literally means to "moisten into" or "make wet" (*OED*). Given Irigaray's signature insistence on the vaginal lips as the figure for that which cannot be reduced to binary constructions—and thus for what is marginalized in discourse—this definition is highly suggestive to say the least. Furthermore, recalling her claim that L'afemme exceeds "the proper," we might notice that such "irrigation" is almost literally Irigaray's signature: in French, the pronunciation of the infinitive *irriguer* (to irrigate) is strikingly close to that of "Irigaray." This near confluence of proper name and verb, a product of sheer chance and linguistic contingency, exemplifies the very mixture of proper and improper utterance that Irigaray seeks to describe in her theory of fluid dynamics and demonstrates the amplification of noise over signal she is trying to introduce into the rational bedrock of Western metaphysics.[6]

The place of the margin as an irrigation channel conducting the echo of *irriguer* in Irigaray directs us to the act of reclamation and its relevance to both Van Dyke's central ecological argument and its complicated refashioning in Bervin's book. In the context of land use in the American West, "reclamation" refers, of course, to the policy—under the direction of the United States Bureau of Reclamation—of rendering alleged "wastelands" or desert regions agriculturally and industrially productive through the damming and diversion of massive amounts of water from rivers like the Colorado. By redeeming (with its biblical implication) this dry land through irrigation, the project of reclamation aimed to make the desert bloom. However, the verb *to reclaim* derives from the Latin *reclamare*, "to cry out against" or "to shout back" (*OED*). Reclamation, in other words, also bears the trace of a sound, more specifically an echoing multiplication of sound that is consonant with both Irigaray's nonproper propagation of sound and Bervin's amplification of "the cry of the human" in Van Dyke's silent desert.

Each of reclamation's seemingly disparate meanings—as the cultivation of wasteland and as a shouting-back—are operative when Bervin engages with Van Dyke's theory of deserts. I have already shown how Bervin's text at times appears to recenter a human perspective even while at other times challenging Van Dyke's rhetorical authority. These tendencies are not mutually exclusive, however, as in both cases Bervin is interested in blurring the original text's strict separation of human and natural realms. While it is true that Van Dyke's orientation is quite ecocentric, he is nevertheless prone to essentializing nature as by definition free of human defilement. Likewise, he demonstrates a developed understanding of geologic and other nonhuman forces even as he views the desert primarily in terms of a landscape painting. Indeed, like the art historian that he is, Van Dyke calls deserts "[d]ecorative landscapes" and writes, "The landscape that is the simplest in form and the finest in color is by all odds the most beautiful" (*The Desert* 56). Crucially for Van Dyke, humans must not creep into this picture. The most attractive feature of deserts is that they are unscathed by human settlement: "There are no towns or roads or people . . . there are no dust and smoke of factories . . . and the white man is coming but has not yet arrived" (75–76). This lack of infrastructure and pollution is part of what makes deserts "breathing spaces"; however, as that final acknowledgment suggests, Van Dyke feared the expansion of Anglo-European settlement and industry into areas like the Colorado Desert of California.

The primary driver of such industrial expansion is, once again, water. Van Dyke laments this situation in "The Bottom of the Bowl" when he writes of "[c]hanging the desert": "But not even the spot deserted by reptiles shall escape the industry or the avarice (as you please) of man. A great company has been formed to turn the Colorado River into the sands, to reclaim the desert basin, and make it blossom as the rose" (57). In Van Dyke's view, industrial-scale irrigation is a bad idea because the desert is "the greatest dry-heat generator in the world. . . . To turn this desert into an agricultural tract would be to increase humidity, and that would be practically to nullify the finest air on the continent" (58). Deserts are not simply breathing spaces for humans, it seems, but breathing spaces for the entire planet. According to Van Dyke, "The deserts are not worthless wastes. You cannot crop all creation with wheat and alfalfa. Some sections must lie fallow that other sections may produce. Who shall say that the preternatural productiveness of California is not due to the warm air of its surrounding deserts?" (59). Van Dyke's plea is prescient and provocative, but it is also preservationist: it accepts that as long as certain places are maintained in their supposedly pristine state, certain others can be sacrificed for the sake of productivity.

In Bervin's version, this passage, which occurs between the marginal glosses "Value of the air supply" and "Value of the deserts," reads as follows: "Why is / this being done? Ostensibly / to keep heads pure / You cannot crop all creation with / preternatural productiveness" (59). The ambiguity of these lines hinges on the referent of the pronoun "this." In Van Dyke, "this" refers to preservation (specifically, the contemporaneous proliferation of National parks). In Bervin, "this" could point to preservation, but it also seems to indicate Bervin's act of sewing. Adding to the complexity is the adverb "ostensibly." Deriving from the Latin *ob + tendere*, or "stretched out to view," "ostensibly" implies that a truer motive is being concealed (*OED*). Does Bervin mean to suggest that preservation can only purport to maintain nature in a state of purity? Or that her treatment only appears to be concerned with maintaining "breathing spaces" that would "keep heads pure?" Or, from another perspective, might Bervin be punning on the way she has *not* concealed the traces of the book's production? After all, the extra lengths of thread are "stretched out to view" on each verso. Answering these questions only gets trickier once we realize that Bervin's material practice has in a sense been *cropping* Van Dyke's desert all along: her sewing has "cut" and rearranged the original text into found poems. The logic of cropping is operative in yet another sense if we take *to crop* as "to sow or plant (land) with plants that will produce food or fodder, especially on a large commercial scale" (*OED*). In other words, *to crop* implies the very system of industrial agriculture Van Dyke warns against, and Bervin's *sewing* becomes a kind of homophonic substitute for *sowing*. Her blue thread irrigates *The Desert*, resulting in porosity and suggesting a kind of leakiness in the text's material support. This leakiness extends to the thematic level, in which the seemingly stable distinctions between categories like "human" and "nature" are undermined and made to flow.

Bervin excavates what Ovidiu Anemtoaicei and Yvette Russell, in an essay on Irigaray, identify as "a culture of being-with" (779). Anemtoaicei and Russell, quoting from Irigaray's book *In the Beginning She Was*, explain that "man has searched for his becoming in objects, things, representations, or mental reduplications," and therefore "displays 'a culture of performance, of know-how, of mastery'" (778). This is because Western culture constructs "man" as the default, universal subject through the narrative of the imperial male journey. Van Dyke, for all of his anti-industrial stances and obvious love of desert landscapes, reveals traces of such an attitude through his approach to nature as an aesthetic object able to be appreciated by, while ultimately separate from, humans.

If, as Anemtoaicei and Russell conclude, the "journeys made by men in and through the world have to be rethought," Bervin's text offers one such rethinking (778). By appropriating Van Dyke's text and redirecting its flows, Bervin produces a "strange" reading: on the first page of Chapter 2 appear the unsewn lines, "The / reality shows / the idea / reading strange / 'seas'" (23). In the cliché of the desert as a "sea of sand," Bervin glimpses an analogue of her method: seeing the desert as a sea of sand is "reading [a] strange / [sea]" in a place where water is supposed to be absent. Bervin foregrounds the physical act of reading through the line break between "strange" and "seas," which isolates the concept of "reading strange." "Seas," which Bervin leaves ensconced in Van Dyke's scare quotes, functions as a homonym of the verb *to see*. Bervin's book is a visual record of her "strange" reading, where in "strange" we might hear a faint echo of *queer* in its contemporary sense. And while it may be going too far to assert that Bervin queers Van Dyke, her palimpsest does hybridize authorship and thus implies "the finitude of

[male] gendered embodied presence in the world . . . that [the male subject is] *not all*, i.e. the universal and the world" (Anemtoaicei and Russell 778).

In a further erosion of Van Dyke's androcentrism—once again involving water—Bervin rewrites a description of the Colorado River. Van Dyke characterizes the Colorado as a symbol of the "un-known and the undiscovered. . . . The lonely stream that so shunned contact with man," and portrays its arrival at the Gulf of California as a kind of funeral: "The river is no more. It has gone down to its blue tomb in the Gulf—the fairest tomb that ever river knew" (75). In contrast to Van Dyke's melodrama, Bervin's rendition of this passage emphasizes the river's own existence beyond human categories: "Something of serenity / something of the monumental / something of the un- / lonely stream / that dug its bed thousands of feet in / depth / and trailed its length / across / mountains" (75). In addition to foregrounding the river's geologic force, Bervin cleverly unhooks the prefix *un* from Van Dyke's "unknown" and reattaches it to "lonely," thus revising Van Dyke's romantic conceit (which Bervin has sewn over) that the river has "shunned contact with man." In a similar fashion, Bervin undercuts the earlier gloss "Sense of beauty" and instead suggests, "It is not likely that / sound, or form, or color, / belong to / man" (13). Bervin's adjustments here register how even as Van Dyke laments human incursions into the desert, he cannot help but describe the desert in human terms.

The question of what "belong[s] to / man" is a concern for both ecopoetic and feminist criticism—in fact, it could be argued that this is where these two theories overlap as ecofeminism most clearly. One way of approaching this question is to return to the idea of the "proper," in the sense of both property and name. Of course, the most basic method humans have devised in order to claim something as his property is naming. Bervin points to the arbitrary character of this practice when, next to the gloss "The river's name," Bervin's text reads, "River / was / the name that finally clung." In Van Dyke's footnote detailing the Spanish origin of the name *Colorado*, Bervin simply leaves the lines, "the word was so obviously / superfluous" (65). Strictly speaking, Bervin is right: "superfluous" means literally "to flow over." Thus, the names humans impart to rivers (not to mention the term "river" itself) are "superfluous" because superfluity is precisely what a river does. Bervin's depiction of the Colorado indicates a dynamic very much like Wall's liquid intelligence or Irigaray's hydrology. The river, though vulnerable to human influence in the form of dams and other reclamation projects, manifests properties and dynamics that are not reducible to anthropocentric narratives.

Indeed, the very method of production Bervin employs to sew her edition deconstructs Van Dyke's strict separation of industry and the natural world and calls attention to the central role of women's labor in the project. In the colophon, Bervin discloses the curious fact that for the edition of forty books "[e]very page was machine sewn by the author and a very dedicated team of seamstresses in Seattle." To be sure, practical considerations—such as the massive amount of labor hours it would have taken Bervin to complete the entire edition of forty books herself—may have driven her thinking. But all the same, a group of women sitting at sewing machines evokes a kind of micro–textile factory—that is, the airless industrial setting Van Dyke sought to escape. This method of assembly, then, recapitulates Marx's trope of the machine in the garden, or the appearance of "a premonitory sign of industrial power" at "the center of primal nature": "Art and nature," Marx asserts, "are inextricably tangled at the center. Hence there is no way to apprehend the absolute meaning of a natural fact" (171–72). Boetzkes, likewise, extends this argument to the realm of ecology, which, while it "implies an ethical commitment to preserve or reestablish the balance of ecosystems" is nonetheless "inextricable from technology and industry" (2). In this light, Bervin's production appears as an ironic commentary on Van Dyke's own hopes to find in the desert an unspoiled space free from the contamination of industry. What seems to be a purified artifact, a handcrafted artist book on the themes of silence and light in the desert, is also a noisy space of overlapping texts—one that is, moreover, assembled by laborers using machines. And yet, these very same circumstances render Bervin's book a collective creation, these anonymous seamstresses becoming an instance of Irigaray's nonsingular L'afemme.

As I have argued in this chapter, Bervin's project is significant precisely because it manifests this tension between an idealized depiction of deserts and the human activity occurring both in and around them. In this sense, it is Van Dyke who produces an erasure, not Bervin. His text obscures the industrial power that either directly or indirectly informed his journeys through the Southwest, even as he makes an earnest and influential case for the preservation of desert lands. Regardless of whether Bervin actually intended to insert human industry into Van Dyke's undefiled desert, her specific material intervention forms an integral part of her book's subject matter, as it dramatizes the inescapable entanglement of human and environment, nature and culture.

CHAPTER 6

Crystal Gazing

> The text of crystal might / reveal everything but itself
> —*Clark Coolidge*

If the works I have examined in the last two chapters have each been singular efforts to enact geologic processes, in this coda I offer a brief reading of several texts that function as a sort of collective composition, an accreting series of reflections of and on crystals. I want to look at this set of "crystal texts" to show North American poetry's ongoing fascination with geologic processes and how this interest is shifting to a more explicitly political concern about ecology and human impacts on the environment. Robert Smithson's entropic vision of crystallization and enantiomorphism is again the catalyst for works by Christian Bök, Clark Coolidge, and Craig Dworkin. With Coolidge, a close study of a quartz crystal opens onto an unexpected mediation on writing and subjectivity, while Bök and Dworkin—despite the latter's direct citation of Coolidge—undertake attempts to literalize a crystal language. Melissa Mack's *The Next Crystal Text*, by contrast, foregrounds the political stakes—and ambivalences—of a geologic text in a warming, postindustrial world. I propose that what draws these lucid and ludic crystal texts together, beyond the obvious similarity of subject matter, is their conflation of crystals and mirrors through a focus on symmetrical, or mirroring, structures. The association of crystals with mirrors marks a tension in these texts between opacity and transparency, between what gets obscured and what gets reflected. In fusing language and crystalline structures, the texts together form their own crystal lattice, an overlapping set of compositional methods and concerns that leads to replication, as if once they have started growing they will not stop.

The trajectory I track here begins with Smithson's brief essay "The Crystal Land," first published in *Harper's Bazaar* in 1966. The piece recounts Smithson's day trip from Manhattan to New Jersey to go mineral hunting in the company of his wife and fellow artist Nancy Holt, the artist Donald Judd, and Judd's wife Louisa. Specifically, the purpose of this double date (which includes a detour to a kitschy diner to share a milkshake confection known as an "Awful-Awful") is to visit the Upper Montclair and Great Notch quarries in the industrial and (at the time) rapidly suburbanizing New Jersey meadowlands. Descending from the homogenous surfaces of the suburbs into the maw of the mines, Smithson experiences an acute sense of dislocation that anticipates his hallucinatory experience a few years later at the site of the *Spiral Jetty*:

> Fragmentation, corrosion, decomposition, disintegration, rock creep, debris slides, mud flow, avalanche were everywhere in evidence. The gray sky seemed to swallow up the heaps around us. Fractures and faults spilled forth sediment, crushed conglomerates, eroded debris and sandstone. It was an arid region, bleached and dry. An infinity of surfaces spread in every direction. A chaos of cracks surrounded us. (8)

This veritable word-slide of geologic terms anticipates his subsequent remarks about the ruptures and fissures in words as well as his invocation of another desert in a suburban sandbox detailed in chapter 1. This journey to the suburbs becomes literally a descent into the *sub-urb*, the chthonic realm beneath the city in which the rational order of the sectioned, striated landscape above is undermined by the quarry's entropic geology. Time, movement, and space are both frozen and disordered; different temporal strata from the deep time of geology to the acceleration of human time under industrial (and postindustrial) capitalism occur simultaneously. This conflation of time scales is a key feature of crystals for Smithson. As Hikmet Sidney Loe explains, "Although crystals are inorganic, they expand and multiply—often in spiraling shapes—lending the idea and appearance of growth to static objects" (83–84). In the quarry, the results of both geologic processes and human extractive industry also serve to shatter spatial contiguity, much as Chris Marker's film *La Jetée* fragments spatiotemporal movement. And as in Smithson's homage to Marker in the film *Spiral Jetty*, "The Crystal Land" turns on the conflation of topography and text: in the former, scattered pages of a geology textbook cover the cracked desert ground; in the latter, a newspaper "folded over" the laps of Smithson's passengers forms "temporary geographies of paper. A valley of print or a ridge of photographs would come and go in an instant" (9). Like his later "Spiral Jetty" essay, Smithson's account of the trip is less a linear narrative than a collection of superimposed snapshots—reverse Polaroids that fade as soon as they are seen.

Or perhaps, to appropriate Smithson's own description, the essay is a series of "reflections," a term that, unlike Polaroids, suggests an overlap of crystal and glass (7). These "reflections" emphasize the alien, extraterrestrial qualities of the mineral, making this sojourn to the industrialized wilds of New Jersey an early example of his use of tropes from science (and science fiction) to describe the entropic exurban landscape. Smithson prefaces the text with an epigraph from P. A. Shumskii's *Principles of Structural Glaciology*, which asserts that "[i]ce is the medium most alien to organic life," and he writes in the opening sentence that Judd's "pink plexiglass box" sculpture, which Smithson had recently seen and which prompted him to get in touch with the artist, "suggested a giant crystal from another planet" (7). The quarry they visit "resembles the moon" while the New Jersey swamps present "a good location for a movie about life on Mars" (9). Smithson's sci-fi stylings in this short piece evoke a world that has been mineralized through an icy, inorganic takeover, with the chilly "medium" of ice intimating the gradual loss of thermal energy through entropy.

Indeed, for Smithson crystallization is a sort of metonym for entropy. In his vision of New Jersey, "the entire landscape has a mineral presence. From the shiny chrome diners to glass windows of shopping centers, a sense of the crystalline prevails" (8). Likewise, with the "infinity of surfaces spread in every direction," we begin to witness the state of dedifferentiation, the frozen crystalline sameness that for Smithson signals the endpoint of entropy. To illustrate this state Smithson turns to shiny, glassy images: "My eyes glanced over the dashboard, it became a complex of chrome fixed into an embankment of steel. A glass disk covered the clock. The speedometer was broken.

... The rearview mirror dislocated the road behind us" (8–9). The rearview mirror reflects but, in reflecting, distorts, leaving the viewer without a clear perspective.

The use of mirrors and mirror images were central to this early period of Smithson's sculptural work. In 1966, the same year "The Crystal Land" was published, Smithson displayed two sculptures exploring visually the kinds of perceptual dislocations that Smithson's later Nonsites and site-specific sculptures would investigate spatially.[1] For *The Cryosphere*, the title of which refers to the realm of frozen water on Earth, Smithson mounted "six solid hexagonal modules," each consisting of twelve mirrors in a row on the gallery wall. Their proliferating reflections create an excess not of visibility but of frustrated vision, as the mirrors on each module are positioned so that they fail to reflect the other modules (38). Similarly, *Enantiomorphic Chambers* pairs two sets of mirrors in such a way that, as Ann Reynolds explains, "[t]he exchange of reflections and counter-reflections generated . . . would cancel out the central illusionistic plane of focus" and "create a blind spot at the center of vision" (138). Thus, "When observers stand in front of" the chambers, Reynolds continues, "their gaze is not met by the expected set of reflections. They do not see reflected images of themselves in the mirrors" but rather the failure of the stereoscopic format of vision (138–39).[2] The displacement at the center of vision in each of these examples is replicated, for Smithson, in the enantiomorphic structure of crystal growth. *Enantiomorph* refers to two crystalline structures that together form a mirror image, though, as Thomas Crow details, Smithson "came upon a phenomenon in the deposition of crystals in which the original symmetry of the process is displaced by a single step" (54). As we saw in chapter 1, this "screw dislocation," in which the molecules of the crystal accumulate in a spiral around "the original point of reflection," motivates the form of the *Spiral Jetty* and its reproduction, at a larger scale, of the process of crystal growth. Moreover, as Crow observes, this type of crystal structure is itself a figure for entropy in Smithson's artistic cosmos: "In this variant of enantiomorphism, a single dislocation generates both perpetual change and ultimate stasis" as "the spiral or screw form . . . never ceases its arching backwards in perpetually frustrated attraction" in the direction of its unreachable center (54). This helical deposition of salt crystals obscures vision in a way analogous to the occlusion of reflection in *Enantiomorphic Chambers*. As Jennifer Roberts notices, the salt crystals that accumulate over time on the basalt rocks of *Spiral Jetty* obstruct a view of history as "retrospective" and instead "remove history from its perspective envelope and place it under the rhetoric of burial" ("Taste" 99). Smithson's engagement with the enantiomorphic logic of crystals and mirrors produces faults and cracks rather than glassy transparency.

In Christian Bök's *Crystallography* (first published in 1994, with a revised and reformatted edition appearing in 2003), the conflation of crystals and mirrors is achieved through etymology. As Bök details in a brief essay that closes the book, "*Crystallography* is a pataphysical encyclopedia that misreads the language of poetics through the conceits of geology." The primary catalyst for this misreading, Bök elaborates, comes from the literal denotation of the term for the scientific study of crystal structures: "the word 'crystallography' quite literally means 'lucid writing'" (156). A "crystal writing," then, mixes the geologic and literary senses of *crystalline* —as, on the one hand, having the structure and form of a crystal and, on the other, being exceedingly clear. Ironically, however, the pellucid glass of mirrors is not a crystalized substance. As opposed to crystalline or polycrystalline solids such as ice and rocks, glass is a noncrystalline, amorphous solid and does not have the periodic arrangement of molecules characteristic of crystal lattices. Glass and crystals are two different materials that are being pressed together through Bök's etymological reading of the word "crystallography."

If Smithson's use of crystals and mirrors emphasizes the flaw that spawns a spiral, Bök seems to insist on strict symmetry, claiming that his "work predicates itself upon an aesthetics of structural perfection." Mirrors are doubly important in Bök's demonstration of crystal science: they not only figure the enantiomorphic growth of crystals but also "have historically provided a mathematical means for identifying a crystalline structure." As Bök explains, "A scientist determines the class of symmetry to which a crystal belongs by slicing the crystal along diverse axes with a mirrored blade. The reflections in the blade define the degree to which the crystal is symmetrical with itself" (156). Bök applies the symmetrical structure of crystals to language in a quite literal manner, presenting the shapes of letters and their arrangement in words as themselves enantiomorphic. Defining enantiomers as "[c]rystalline forms that mirror each other through an axis of symmetry," Bök observes, by way of example, that "a vertical axis makes enantiomers not only of *b* and *p*, but also of *d* and *q*." By the same token, "Enantiomers can also occur when two crystals undergo the process of interpenetrant twinning; for example, *w* takes shape at the moment when *v* twins with its enantiomer through a vertical axis, just as *X* takes shape at the moment when *v* twins with its enantiomer through a horizontal axis." If individual letters can be read as enantiomorphic crystal structures, so can entire words and phrases, though "only when one translates into the other through reflection." One such example would be a palindrome, as in Bök's example "*mirror rim*," which "reveals sequential symmetry" when read backward. In this particular phrase, symmetry even holds at the level of the letter, with "the doubled *r*, doubled," and "the letters *m*, *i* and *o*, each symmetrical through a vertical axis" (150). As Bök states early in the work, "A word is a bit of crystal in formation" (12). In short, in place of a conventional use of words as vehicles of "information," this text treats words and letters *as* molecular, crystalline structure.

In a pattern we have seen throughout this study, Bök's material approach to language—his attention to the shapes of letters and words outside of their potential to mean—resists the lucidity of transparent communication. Thus "lucid writing," while conflating crystal structure with crystalline clarity, "does not," Bök cautions, "concern itself with the transparent transmission of a message (so that, ironically, much of the poetry may seem 'opaque'); instead, the book concerns itself with the reflexive operation of its own process" (156). As with Bervin's *The Desert* and O'Sullivan's *A Natural History*, Bök's emphasis on the process and materiality of composition aligns *Crystallography* with artists' books. The book is meticulously arranged using Bök's own design and features typographic and visual experiments that nod to everything from cabinets of curiosity to concrete poetry. Specific varieties of crystals such as amethyst are depicted in poems that imitate their elemental makeup through interlocking arrangements of the names of their component chemicals. In similar fashion, another visual poem organizes the words "crystal lattice" into a repeating, interconnecting structure that resembles a crystal lattice. These literal transpositions of words and crystals are epitomized by Bök's fractal poems, which suggest another kind of "reflexive operation": reflexive symmetry. Bök enlarges and transforms individual letters such as *A*, *Y*, and *S* into fractal repetitions. In "Trigon Mirror," for instance, a *transparency* (a page printed on transparent plastic) interpolated between two pages that are mirror images of each other creates an overlay of a "photomicrograph of the letter Y magnified 25x to reveal its innate crystalline structure" (104–5). The title of the poem suggests a triangular mirror; however, since "trigon" is also an archaic term for a triangular lyre or harp, this visual sequence may be read as Bök's ironic literalization of the "lyric" poem. Like the spiral salt crystals coating Smithson's *Spiral Jetty*, Bök's fractal poems are recursive, revealing the same formal pattern at different scales. But as with Smithson's recursive use of crystals and mirrors, Bök's formal experiments in magnification and reflection produce opacities rather than transparencies.

This failure of reflection is all to the point. In a humorous and Borgesian section titled "Enantiomorphosis," Bök writes about several real and apocryphal examples of "mirror-writing" in which reflection implies a crisis of representation, including Jacques Lacan's famous essay "The Mirror Stage as Formative of the Function of the I." As Bök summarizes this treatise, "Lacan upheld the idea that an infant in the first months of its life could only apprehend the experience of both self and other via *méconnaisance*" (148). This méconnaisance (misrecognition) by which the child "misconstru[es] itself as other when seeing itself in a mirror for the first time" creates a "crisis of alienation" and leads the infant to "not only [admire] its own image for providing a coherent representation of the self, but also [despise] its own image for withholding a representation congruent with the self" (148–49). The space between the self and its reflection is indicative of, in Bök's words, "the transition . . . from a state of lack to a state of desire" (149). For Lacan, this state of desire also marks the child's entrance into the symbolic, the realm of language, thus foreclosing a presymbolic illusion of completion and integration. Words, like the child's reflection, similarly promise coherent (or transparent) representation while somehow exceeding singular meaning. Bök suggests this further connection between words and enantiomers when, regarding the palindrome *mirror rim*, he brands "the gap between the two words a flaw in the gem." Further emphasizing the misrecognition of mirror images, directly below this appears a sentence written backwards (as if seen in a mirror): "MIRRORS INDUCE DYSLEXIA" (150).

Such "flaws" or impurities form the core of Bök's many lettristic poems in *Crystallography*, in which letters and phonemes undergo subtle shifts and displacements that disrupt perfect symmetry. For example, in "Fractal Geometry" Bök observes, "Fractals are haphazard maps / that entrap entropy in tropes" (20). Fractals freeze entropic disorder in repeating patterns, but the more salient effect here is that of the *near* repetition of phonemes and words-within-words: *hap-map*; *trap-trope*. What is more, the very *trope* applied here is that of the chance sonic and orthographic similarities between words, one of the *ha*z*ards* of language use (from the French *hasard*, or "chance"). Entropy is temporarily entrapped but not permanently defeated.

Like "impurities" in crystal growth, which develop due to numerous variables such as spatial constraints, temperature, pressure, and the addition or subtraction of molecules, the not-quite-symmetrical images of etymologically unrelated words may be random, but they are not unstructured. "Grain Boundaries" spirals around a sequence of orthographic faults, continuously accreting and losing letters. The poem is arranged into two columns with five words running down the gap in the middle. It begins:

rim			rime
	emery		
memory		remora	
memoir			
	moiré		
	mirror (134)		

Instead of perfect symmetry, the words on the left and right margins display a slight difference, an added vowel or consonant, so that the *e* added to *rim* to make *rime* gets reflected in the *em* of *emery*, which in turn gets sandwiched by another *m* to make *memory* and so on. In fact, the "grain boundary" of the title designates the interface between two individual crystals that forms a defect in a larger polycrystalline structure. Facing each other at a diagonal across this boundary, "rim" and "mirror" repeat, in reverse, the *mirror rim* palindrome discussed above. In addition to being a homophone of *rhyme*, "rime" denotes a kind of ice or frost and thus a kind of crystal growth, and "emery" is a rock used as an abrasive for polishing or grinding surfaces, for instance in the manufacture of mirrors. "[R]emora" denotes a type of fish, but the *OED* notes that the word literally means a hindrance or *delay*, thus making it a possible allusion to Marcel Duchamp's *The Bride Stripped Bare by Her Bachelors, Even (The Large Glass)* which the artist famously referred to as "a delay in glass." Once again, crystals and mirrors are conflated through a "misrecognition" of crystals as glassy surfaces. Finally, "moiré" refers to a silken fabric rippled by the application of heat and pressure and derives from a term for "a watered appearance," tying it both sonically and semantically to the motif of mirrors. Through these lettristic shifts, the poem approximates a crystal lattice wherein the "elegant / element / letter" undergoes a series of displacements.

In *Polaroid*, as Michael Golston has argued, Clark Coolidge crosses language with crystallography in order to produce a linguistic equivalent to the chemical apparatus of photography: "After precipitating poetic crystals from the solution of the dictionary . . . Coolidge will want next to reorient the unordered crystals into 'a single big crystal' that will once again act as a medium for producing images" (91–92). And as Coolidge himself explains in *Smithsonian Depositions*, "The process by which Polaroid [the photographic sheet] is manufactured turns all the crystals the same way, so that the film is much like a broad, thin, single crystal plate of tourmaline" (26). In other words, Coolidge's aim across works from the 1970s and 1980s such as *The Maintains*, *Quartz Hearts*, and *Polaroid* is to simulate the material, chemical process of developing film. While Golston focuses on Coolidge's debt to Surrealist techniques, I maintain that Coolidge develops another, simultaneous strand in his voluminous output — the so-called "Longprose"— that experiments with the sedimentation (that is, the *deposition*) of words across a cycle of texts including *A Geology*.

Given this detailed involvement with crystal and geologic processes, one might expect Coolidge's *The Crystal Text* (which Golston doesn't address in his study) to extend the experiments of *Polaroid*. Coolidge, however, has something very different in mind. The ostensible subject in this book-length poem is a clear quartz crystal that accosts the writer from his desk. Functioning as if it were a mirror, the quartz seems to require its witness to make an inward turn; as Coolidge promises at the outset, "No, nothing but what comes from the inside this time" (7). As in his previous works, Coolidge still wants "[t]o grasp the relation of words to matter" but proposes to do so in a more confessional mode (8). For Coolidge, this shift to the self is appropriate to the quartz's composition. Colorless and "almost invisible in taking on and in / the tones of everything else in the room," the crystal suggests an odd combination of transparency and opacity (27). The more Coolidge contemplates it, the more he sees his own face staring back: "I reflect myself in the darkness / the world has made of me" (10). The crystal provides Coolidge the opportunity, then, "[t]o write / a long book of nothing 'but looking deeply into oneself'" (12). Coolidge provides a brief note at the end of the text listing sources for the numerous quotations that appear in the text, but it does not include a citation for the line "but looking deeply into oneself." It is thus tempting to read this as less a quotation than an ironic statement regarding the popular perception of lyric poetry as a meditative exploration of the self.

To be sure, Coolidge's unexpected pivot to a poetics of self-reflection may not be as straightforward as it seems. Coolidge's fixation on the reflection of his face could be motivated not by introspection but rather a pun on the *facets* of the quartz crystal—that is, its sides, or faces. In this light, the poem's promised depth transforms into a play of surfaces—or, recalling Coolidge's fondness for spelunking, perhaps this dive into the depths only reveals more surface to explore.[3] After all, what Coolidge locates on the inside is a tissue of quotations from other texts and not some sort of sui generis essence of self. Although, as Coolidge insists, "I have limited myself / here to the crystal, to everything / among the missing," the transparent quartz functions more as a sort of mystic writing pad by means of which Coolidge contemplates a characteristically eccentric range of topics: jazz (specifically Dave Brubeck and Thelonius Monk), Nikola Tesla, Jack Kerouac, Samuel Beckett, Yukio Mishima, Akira Kurosawa, and flying saucers, to name but a few. Coolidge's crystal gazing activates a linguistic flow redolent of Denise Riley's description of inner speech. For Riley, inner speech is always already both inside and outside the self, confusing the topography of surface and depth: "The outer world, dense with signs, is soaked up inside the head already sign-stuffed. . . . The sign trespasses all the boundaries of inner and outer" (Lecercle and Riley 27). Just as the crystal adopts "the tones of everything else in the room," the writer's mind reflects all that it has read, watched, witnessed, remembered, and forgotten at any given moment. While Riley rejects an image of inner speech as a "limpid stream of consciousness, crystalline from its uncontaminated source in Mind," her enumeration of its "sludgy" morass could work as an account of Coolidge's style: "thickened with reiterated quotation, choked with the rubble of the overheard, the strenuously sifted and hoarded . . . crammed with slogans and jingles . . . irrepressible puns" and "the embarrassing detritus of advertising" (20–21). Coolidge's meditation on the crystal demonstrates that the depths of the inside are, as Riley says of the psyche, "outside from the start" (27).

In its attempt to register language passing through the mind, *The Crystal Text* articulates a theory of writing expressed through the epigraph to this chapter. Like Smithson's screw dislocations, Coolidge's crystal acts as an absent center around which the text accretes. Moreover, this movement posits a theory of the autograph (literally "self-writing") that doubles as Coolidge's authorial signature. Near the end of the text, Coolidge confesses, "I read all the words of the novels too and remove them and write them. / Write with them." This method recalls the model of reading and writing as a dual process of erosion and deposition that I trace in terms of *Book Beginning What*. As Coolidge further admits, "I perhaps / do not intend this but it is the draw of the process. / Words pulled into sentences and away from me" (150). To use Riley's terms, in place of "the stamp of authorial authenticity," Coolidge's method comprises "both a response to and a compendium of all the voices" he has encountered (Lecercle and Riley 26). Coolidge echoes this explanation early in *The Crystal Text*, offering a surprisingly straightforward statement of his poetics: "The line is an assemblage of broken smaller pieces" (25). Paradoxically, when compared to the disruption of syntax and fracturing of individual words in many of his works, this line does not itself appear to be the result of disintegration and deposition. And yet, the unusual lucidity is the point. Nowhere in his poetry is Coolidge more *transparent* regarding his writing process than in this sustained exercise in reflection.

Coolidge's *The Crystal Text* would itself be subjected to this process of deposition in 2012 with Craig Dworkin's *The Crystal Text (After Clark Coolidge)*. Printed and hand-bound with rose-red covers in a small edition by Compline, the chapbook, as its subtitle indicates, adopts Coolidge's assemblage method to address a quartz crystal stationed on the writer's desk. From the start, however, there is a key difference: Dworkin's crystal is rose, not clear quartz. The color variation arises from impurities in the molecular structure; or, as Dworkin's text has it, "Impurities in the massive material fibre the fleshy hue." The adjective "massive" is used here in its geologic sense to refer to a rock or mineral that has no obvious structure or is "not visibly crystalline." Appearing in its British spelling, "fibre" seems to be employed as an unconventional verb, perhaps suggesting the mineral's filamentous texture. At the same time, as *fiber* derives from a Latin word for "entrails," it accentuates the humanlike "fleshy hue" Dworkin ascribes to the crystal. Indeed, earlier on the same page, Dworkin describes the rose quartz as "expressive, biomorphic and easily anthropomorphized, and yet, at the same time, the most remote and indifferent to human wishes . . . the most like a body the least like an organism." Recalling the allusion to alien ice in Smithson's epigraph to "The Crystal Land," this passage points to two crucial facets of Dworkin's *Crystal Text*: the agency of the mineral and the nonhuman accumulation of words.

The ellipsis in the second half of the above passage marks it as a quotation. Flipping to the end of this twelve-page prose poem, we find, as in Coolidge's text, a set of notes listing the various sources (including Coolidge's *The Crystal Text* and *Smithsonian Depositions*) Dworkin has quoted from in his composition. As a composition—an assemblage, a tissue of other texts—Dworkin's *Crystal Text* doubles down on Coolidge's method while attempting to (re)center the crystal itself. Dworkin manages this through a close, precise attention to the crystal's fleshlike "body" which, in his account, is eerily both organic and inorganic. Specifically, in describing the crystal as "the most like a body the least like an organism," Dworkin is quoting the art historian T. J. Clark's discussion of Paul Cézanne's paintings of Mont Sainte-Victoire. In his essay on Cézanne, Clark calls the painter's color in *Mont Sainte-Victoire Seen from the Bibémus Quarry* "crystalline" and declares that Cézanne's "color and texture will make the mountain a mountain again—make it an object that in its whole structure and materiality, as opposed to mere accidents of surface, has nothing to do with us and our scripts" (96–97). In Cézanne's doubly geologic painting (a mountain viewed from a quarry) and his brushstrokes that collectively lend the mountain a vaguely feminine form, Clark sees a tension between "the least habitable, the most anthropomorphized" (98). Dworkin, likewise, is trying to make the crystal a crystal again, to render it in all its materiality.

Of course, to do this Dworkin uses language, and—to bring my argument back to mirrors and mirroring—his attempts to *reflect* the crystal in prose inevitably both anthropomorphizes the crystal and produces signifiers that point beyond the crystal even as they are the most precise terms imaginable. Unlike Coolidge's crystal, which seems to only mirror the writer back to himself, Dworkin's crystal gazes back: "The crystal winks and lustres" and "glaces glare." And yet, the very terms used to suggest this return of the author's gaze can also operate as apt descriptions of the crystal's motiveless physical qualities. "Wink" and "lustres" could both describe the crystal's mineral sheen. "Glaces" intimates ice, although, placed next to "glare," which could function as either a noun or a verb, it also conjures a glossy, polished surface.

Dworkin repeatedly refers to the crystal in terms that appear to give it humanlike motives or agency but are themselves reliant on the nonhuman and excessive material components of language. For instance, the poem begins: "The rose quartz quarters on my desk. It obligates. It obliquates" (*Crystal Text*). To "quarter" is to lodge, or be lodged somewhere, though there is also a possible secondary suggestion of sight as quartering can also mean to look over or "survey." But "quarters" operates, most immediately, as a play on the sound and spelling of "quartz"; "quartz" leads to "quarters" through simple sonic and orthographic association. Continuing with just this opening line, to *obliquate* is an archaic way of saying "to bend . . . to one side," reflecting not only what happens when light strikes the crystal's facets but also the refraction of language here: the g of "obligate" is bent into a q to form a near homophone. A similar operation occurs later in the poem with the sentence "The opalescence spreads with the color's obsolescence." The p in "opalescence" rotates to form the b in "obsolescence." Slightly more obscure is the phrase "Sincipital wedges brow the crown," where "sincipital" denotes "the front of the skull from the forehead to the crown," so that this is both a description of the cranium and a pleonastic pile-up of synonyms for the human skull––recalling, additionally, Prynne's conflation of glacial moraines and brows discussed in chapter 3 (*OED*). The more humanlike the crystal, the more nonhuman, or resistantly material and opaque, the language.

This paradoxical situation encapsulates a broader paradox in "the relation of words to matter" (to use Coolidge's phrase) that I have been tracking throughout this study. Dworkin alerts us to this paradox with another quotation from Clark, this time as the epigraph to the text:

> The moment at which a text or depiction reaches out most irresistibly to a thing seen or expressed is also the moment at which it mobilizes the accidents and duplicities of markmaking most flagrantly, most outlandishly—all in the service of pointing through them, and somehow with them, to another body that is their guarantor.

Clark recognizes that in trying to accurately represent an object, the artist (or writer) must utilize the very system—"markmaking"—that such a representation hopes to transcend or make transparent. Thus Cézanne, Clark argues, reaches for a kind of zero mark that would complete the aesthetic impulse, collapsing phenomenon and sign. However, instead of this transcendent moment, Clark writes that any system of signs must leave us with "the vividness of procedure," in which "the accidents of process . . . [set] off an unstoppable automatism whereby accidents become what the process is directed to as well as by" (108, 110). Indeed, Dworkin's writing even takes its cue from the "accidents" of the crystal's own inscriptions: "Edges distress the desk. The crystal scrawls where the base has scraped the laminate. The rose leaves lesions along the plastic." Dworkin's crystal not only gazes back but also creates its own writing. Much as Smithson's crystals accumulate perpetually around an initial fault, Dworkin's text accretes around such faults, or accidents, of language. The more intently one reaches for the mineral or bedrock layer, the more one encounters the excesses of markmaking.

Near the top of the final page, Dworkin writes that the crystal "remains a gift"—that is, seemingly outside of an exchange economy—and yet the poem's last two lines suggest a debt: "The crystal was beheld. The crystal is beholden." Echoing this economic note on the final page is the phrase "The bank, in cycles, rents." While, as always, the field of potential meanings exceeds any single explanation—for example, "bank" could refer to the sides of the "stream" that is mentioned in the following sentence, and the action of renting could portend a tearing or opening, perhaps the cyclical destruction of "the bank" in fluvial flooding—the sentence nonetheless stands out as one of the few in the text that points away from technical, geologic language and towards a broader social and political context. Dworkin's intimation here of the potential economic value of the crystal becomes the explicit theme of the most recent entry in this genre, Melissa Mack's *The Next Crystal Text* (2017). Mack uses the same appropriative collage structure as Coolidge and Dworkin do in their crystal texts, but if Coolidge insists on the crystal as a kind of translucent blank slate reflecting the author's thoughts and Dworkin enacts the material effects of inscription, then Mack considers the material economic effects of "the other end of the production chain" where gems are cut, refined, and set in order to create expensive jewelry and other luxury goods (131).

In other words, Mack centers what is *not* reflected in previous crystal texts: "the actual work of mining" and the violent, exploitative practices that underpin the trade in precious minerals (20). Foregrounding the crystal as commodity, Mack's text reframes the tension in this chapter between crystals and mirrors, between opacity and transparency, as a struggle of omission and recognition. Many of the pages in *The Next Crystal Text* feature a large blank space in the center of the page. These large gaps between lines of text at the top and bottom of the page index the erasure of violence and exploitation at the heart of extractive practices such as rare earth mineral mining. While the language in the poems draws from a wide range of sources and registers, from colloquial, diaristic reflection to song lyrics and Frankfurt School theory, they also speak directly to the social, economic, and ecological costs of extractive industries. For example, Mack observes how "[i]n Myanmar, indigenous Kachin day laborers extract jade and the cost to them is a terrible rate of heroin addiction. You don't see that in the ad." At the bottom of the page, after a long gap, Mack notes that "[a]t the Smithsonian Museum of Natural History in Washington, DC, the crystal and mineral collection is enormous" (38). The large blank space between these statements asks the reader to fill in the excised connections between capitalism, colonialism, and the acquisitions of museums such as the Smithsonian. And, while Robert Smithson is not directly named in Mack's text, one senses that Mack may be playfully alluding to his crystal fascination (and his enthusiasm for natural history museums) by choosing to focus on this particular collection.

Mack's critique of museums informs several such pages, which are phrased like museum title cards and placed below absent photographs of artefacts: for example, "Gold body chain set with amethyst and garnets" or "Pendant in the form of a ship in gold, silver, opal, tourmaline, small diamonds, and enamel" (43, 77). Here, the blank expanse at the center of the page suggests the museum's role in the expropriation of colonized societies through the theft of cultural objects. Articulating this decolonial critique, at the top of the page that follows the reference to the Smithsonian, Mack writes, "The valuing of minerals as pristine pieces of the earth presumes a system of global relationships in which value is extracted from all over, but only recognized—and thus realized—by those in the United States and Europe" (39). This recognition of value by the West must conceal that it is only arrived at through appropriation. Indeed, in Mack's text, the use of textual appropriation not only calls back to the method used by Coolidge and Dworkin but is also tied thematically to a broader network of economic and political connotations like the extraction of mineral wealth from the Global South and the transformation of that wealth into capital (both monetary and cultural) in the West. While all three writers include a section of notes at the end of the text listing sources—thus distancing them somewhat from a kind of hard-core conceptualism that playfully employs plagiarism—Mack's project offers, if not an outright criticism of appropriative poetics, then at least a skeptical appraisal of the similarities between textual and colonialist modes of appropriation.[4]

Mack's commentary on the extraction and appropriation of mineral wealth resonates as well with Yusoff's argument that geology has never been a neutral science, entangled as it is with the advent and "weaponization of extraction as a motivation and mode of dispossession" (*Billion Black Anthropocenes* 103). For Yusoff, "Deep-time and near-time geologic questions are entangled with hard political questions about decolonizing and the possibility of futures," and, she argues, there is no getting away from the radical presencing of geology in our lives, as energy, sensibility, storm, rift, and a growing awareness of what that energy costs across corporeal and planetary bodies." Mack makes a similar point about the destruction extraction has wrought in an acrostic poem that loosely recalls some of Bök's molecular typographic experiments. The poem's first two stanzas list different gems such as "Diamond / Emerald / Amethyst / Ruby," while its third and fourth stanzas shift to a blunt declaration of the "Terrible / Human / Exploitation" when "Capital / Overburden / Slickens / Travesty (what the waste became)"; ultimately, the acrostic spells out the phrase "dear regard the cost" (86). Coolidge's regard of the crystal and its reflection of his face here becomes a request to look at the occluded costs of mining and capitalism more broadly.

The act of regarding these costs, whether hidden or, more often, in plain sight, broaches the issue of complicity. Through her text's post-Internet, post–social media self-awareness about potential complicity and privilege, Mack repeatedly compares her situation as a white woman in the West to that of poor laborers in the Global South who are forced to mine and process rare earth minerals. For instance, Mack recalls a time when she walked barefoot across a lacustrine shoreline of "slag, which . . . cut my feet all up" as well as "a youth program summer job at the post office on the military base unloading bags of mail from the trucks," both of which she immediately disqualifies as adequate analogues with the exclamation "God, this is embarrassing" (49). But despite the necessary failure of comparing her own relatively comfortable existence to that of people living in dire poverty, on the very next page she admits, "If I feel / I have to make an offering" (50).

In an allusion to an affective undercurrent and the imperative to reveal it, Mack uses a fragment of a phrase from critic Siane Ngai's book *Ugly Feelings*: "belated and dysphoric disclosures of complicity" (16). In the passage Mack excerpts, Ngai is speaking about a mode of writing (specifically: feminist, avant-garde poetry) "that insistently foregrounds the subject's inscription within the system she opposes" (331). Coming at the end of the chapter "Paranoia," Ngai's explication of poetry that stages its own complicity with the prevailing economic order—and thus its failure to escape the systems it critiques—captures the anxiety suffusing Mack's project. Ngai's argument in her analysis of affects like anxiety, envy, and irritation is that these "minor" feelings, unlike the more familiar emotions of anger or sadness, harbor an inherent ambiguity, an uncertainty or unease surrounding both their origin and their utility. This sense of frustration and discontent with both the current political order and one's own unavoidable (but somehow no less incriminating) complicity makes *The Next Crystal Text* very much of its early twenty-first-century moment, in which there is a growing awareness in the West or "Global North" of intransigent systems of racial oppression, massive wealth inequality, and ecological destruction—paired with the increasingly apparent fact that growing awareness does not necessarily translate into systemic change. But Mack's work, and these crystal texts taken collectively, also hints at a different, less negatively coded, take on complicity. *Complicity* is derived from Latin *complic* (allied) and *complicare* (folded together) (*OED*). Complicity is complicated; it is a process of folding together—like the leaves of a book or the replication of a spiral crystal lattice—that brings individuals into relation. Taken together, these crystal texts perform a similarly plicate arrangement. Reflecting each other's citational method, mirroring the opacities of language and matter, of money and molecules, these crystal texts constitute a quietly growing subgenre of contemporary poetics.

Extractive industries, like the continuing colonialist dispossession of land and cultural artifacts Mack laments or the rapid growth of suburban and exurban sprawl documented in Smithson's New Jersey drives, are some of the prime movers of the global ecological disruption and environmental crisis humans have precipitated, the drastic consequences of which are becoming ever clearer for those who care to look. In fact, the changes wrought by climate change and ecological destruction could come to intervene in geopoetic works. For example, the Great Salt Lake, site of Smithson's basalt spiral, is currently at one of its lowest levels historically, and prolonged drought combined with a wasteful state water policy means the lake is likely to dry up entirely in the coming decades, if not sooner. If the lake does disappear, or even if it simply remains at very low levels, *Spiral Jetty* will no longer be periodically submerged beneath saline waters, which means, in turn, that salt crystals and their spiral lattices will no longer precipitate on its basalt boulders, removing one of the primary ways the sculpture articulates scale and symmetry. To be sure, the effects of the lake level on Smithson's sculpture are hardly important compared to the dust storms carrying toxic heavy metals (mainly from agricultural run-off precipitated on the lakebed) that Utah's densely populated Wasatch Front faces once the lake is no more. The disappearance of the lake would not necessarily trouble Smithson either; *Spiral Jetty* is meant to be subject to the elements, whatever they might be. Toxic dust storms stemming from an evaporated salt lake sounds like a scenario out of the science fictions of J. G. Ballard, one of Smithson's favorite authors. All the same, we might consider the enormity of the ecological and environmental changes human activity is in the process of creating. Mack's emphasis on complicity, with its suggestion of connection and folding together, exemplifies the geopoetic projects I have looked at in this book, which entwine language and geology, shifting our relation to the earth from one of separation and domination to one of interconnection. Such works, whether or not they explicitly thematize geology and ecology, return the world to us by deploying the materiality of language. Their attempts to establish a nonarbitrary relation of word and thing or to enact geologic processes may not succeed literally, but such endeavors to demonstrate the world's material interrelatedness are ever more pivotal if we are to imagine a way to live on the earth that is not possessive and environmentally ruinous.

Notes

Introduction

1. For example, Diana Coole and Samantha Frost find in "the dominant constructivist orientation to social analysis" an "allergy to 'the real' that is characteristic of its more linguistic or discursive forms—whereby overtures to material reality are dismissed as an insidious foundationalism." See their "Introducing the New Materialisms" in *New Materialisms* 6.
2. Billitteri defines the Cratylic as "an archaic understanding of language as a natural phenomenon, of words as emanating from or belonging to things and so as univocal in their reference" (4). Discussing primarily the work of Whitman, Laura (Riding) Jackson, and Charles Olson, Billitteri argues that these poets' desire to "[make] language one with things" indicates their broader, utopian projects of societal transformation, of which finding a "perfect language" is a central part (5–6). I share Billitteri's interest in the dream of a natural language, though instead of social transformation, I focus more narrowly in this study on works that propose, without necessarily thematizing explicitly, a transformed sense of how the human and nonhuman are entangled.
3. The English poet and critic—and undergraduate mentor of Jeremy Prynne—Donald Davie makes this connection between Fenollosa and Olson in a letter to Prynne. See Latter 53.
4. The many-layered situation of Fenollosa's understanding of Chinese grammar and poetry—and Pound's subsequent appropriation of Fenollosa's argument for his own polemical purposes—is, as Haun Saussy has explained, far more complicated than my description in this introduction. My interest here is limited to how Fenollosa's geologic language has been taken up by Prynne and Olson, among others. For a detailed account of Pound's editing and interpretation of Fenollosa's philology in relation to both Pound's modernism and the skepticism of various sinologists, see Saussy's "Fenollosa Compounded: A Discrimination" in *Fenollosa and Pound* 1–40.
5. Zukofsky wrote the sections in 1928 and 1970–1973, respectively.
6. Lytle Shaw has written at length about this specific connection between Williams and Smithson, as well as what he calls the "overdetermined" relationship between Smithson and the poetic interests of his childhood doctor. Shaw documents the links between *Paterson* and Smithson's deadpan "Tour of the Monuments of

Passaic, New Jersey" and the "proto-conceptual art" of Williams's geological bore samples. As Shaw notes, however, "Where Williams mines, Smithson strip-mines" (*Fieldworks* 17). In other words, if Williams's project is ultimately about uncovering layers of difference beneath the surface of an American city, Smithson's goal is to discover an entropic sameness, a crystalized world. See *Fieldworks* 15–44 for his full discussion.

7. Such an understanding of matter, mind, and language echoes Jussi Parikka's argument that signification is materially bound to geophysical processes, from the minerals that make up computers to the metallic and mineral sediment in "our brains, bones, and bodies" (79).

8. As Halpern elaborates, Oppen was writing, in the early 1960s, in the context of the imminent destruction of human time by nuclear war. If poetry, for Oppen, should "represent the truth of things out there where i [sic] have never been and can never be," this does not render poetry ahistorical. *Pace* "object-oriented-ontologists" such as Quentin Meillassoux—who imagines an ahistorical apocalyptic scenario in which humans no longer exist on earth—Halpern argues that historically situated work such as Oppen's is more relevant for ecopoetics because it takes up the ecocritical call to respond to the specific, concrete conditions (whether nuclear missiles or carbon emissions) that threaten human and planetary life.

9. Craig Dworkin links Oppen's lament to Paul de Man's practically despondent recognition of a "nonhuman aspect of language" that operates "independently of any intent or any drive or any wish or any desire we might have"; such language, for de Man, "does things which are so radically out of our control that they cannot be assimilated to the human at all" (qtd. in *Radium* 13).

10. Such a sentiment is summed up by Sianne Ngai's response, in *Ugly Feelings*, to critics focusing on the materiality of language and the continual deferral of meaning in signification: "Tell me something I don't already know" (309). For Ngai, there exists "a certain redundancy or obviousness" in the pairing of twentieth-century avant-garde writing and poststructuralist language theory, and "most attempts to articulate a poetics based on foregrounding connections between the literary text and poststructuralist theory will end up seeming, well, predictable or descriptive," a result that actually counteracts the emphasis on defamiliarization so fundamental to both practices (308). While, as I say above, my aim in this book is, in fact, for the readings to be more descriptive than hermeneutical, Ngai's argument, coming in a chapter titled "Paranoia," does pinpoint the potential (in a theorist like de Man, say) for a kind of poststructuralist psychosis—or, at least, an impasse in which it's just language all the way down. However, while I take Ngai's point that the instability of signification and the materiality of language have become familiar conceits in literary studies, in this book I am bringing linguistic materiality and nonhuman language into contact with the ecocritical position that decenters human agency. It is somewhat surprising, in fact, that this link between nonhuman language and

nonhuman agency has not been made more explicitly in ecocriticism up to this point.
11. For Riley's own take on the "disinterested machinations of language" see Lecercle and Riley 62.
12. See Iijima.
13. McGurl's claim here echoes and builds on the historian Dipesh Chakrabarty's much-cited essay "The Climate of History: Four Theses," in which Chakrabarty maintains that "the human being has become something much larger than the simple biological agent that he or she has always been. Humans now wield a geological force." See Chakrabarty 206.
14. To take only the most obvious example, Yusoff reminds us that Sir Charles Lyell, the author of *The Principles of Geology* (1830), melded geologic and racial theories. In his writings on slavery—which are integrated into his speculations on geologic formations—Lyell discusses the "Negro" in the same way he discusses fossils, asserting that the "White" and "Black" races are distinct species inhabiting different temporalities, "so Blackness is always belated in time and never fully now and human." As Yusoff explains, Lyell's paternalist and essentialist views on race not only parallel the models of gradual change and temporal progression central to his understanding of geologic time but also serve as a justification for the "subjection and material dispossession (from intimate kin and sexual relations to the ownership of land)" that forms the core of modern liberalism and its colonial offshoots. See Yusoff, *Billion Black Anthropocenes*.
15. Yusoff labels this failure and its attendant erasures of dispossession and colonization "White Geology" (*Billion Black Anthropocenes* xi). My study does not, in the main, address the problematics of race or gender as they relate to the presentation of language as geologic. One could argue that an inorganic model points the texts under consideration here away from humanist hierarchies and thus posits the potential for a nonhierarchical politics. I have engaged with such questions at moments when they provide traction on our understanding of a text—as, for instance, in chapter five on Bervin's *The Desert*, which, I think, rewards a feminist reading with specific interpretive payoffs. For a wider perspective on these issues, I can only point readers to Yusoff's crucial work unpacking the colonialist legacies of dehumanization and violence in the Anthropocene.
16. For instance, in a 1973 interview with the art historian Moira Roth, Smithson spoke about his recent interest in repurposing abandoned strip mines and the project's difference from a more activist, ecological perspective: "The idea in mining is that a lot of people would like to put the landscape back together again the way it was, back in the nineteenth century. And of course that won't happen. But you will be able to perhaps confer a different kind of value through a different kind of cultivation. . . . But a good deal of ecology strikes me as nostalgia, as I said, for a view of the landscape that at one time existed. It's like yearning for the unspoiled paradise garden, the Eden." See Roth 93–94.

17. From "Frederick Law Olmsted and the Dialectical Landscape." See especially Smithson 159–61.

Chapter 1

1. While an account of the full range of Smithson's artistic output is outside the scope of this chapter, the studies of Christ's passion in early paintings such as *Feet of Christ* and *Man of Sorrow (The Forsaken)* may suggest that Smithson considered deposition in its religious and art-historical aspects as well, i.e., the Deposition, or the taking down of Christ's body from the Cross. On the Christian imagery in Smithson's work and its links to later projects, see Crow 33–56.
2. On Smithson's reading, see Alberro; Tatransky.
3. For more on the influence of science fiction writers such as J. G. Ballard on Smithson, see Shaw, "Smithson, Writer."
4. See Loe.

Chapter 2

1. All citations to this text refer to the edition published by Duke University Press in 1989.
2. Both Michael Davidson's important early essay on the poem and Marjorie Perloff's introduction to the Duke UP version view the Projector as an unimportant, if amusing, aside in the poem. Perloff dismisses the Projector as "the ultimate useless technological tool, the emblem of the signifier tied narrowly to a single transcendental signified" (Dorn, *Gunslinger* xv).
3. One piece of evidence, while anecdotal and failing to establish a clear chronology of Dorn's encounter with Baudrillard's work, comes from Tom Clark's biography of Dorn, which quotes Dorn's widow Jennifer Dunbar's recollection of a 1968 sojourn to Paris: "We did attend lectures at the Sorbonne . . . going from room to room to catch the range of polemic from structuralists to situationists. Jean Baudrillard, *par exemple*, whose work Ed always admired" (39). There is another clue that is tempting but far from definitive: In Universe City the Slinger meets a Dr. Jean Flamboyant, Dorn's caricature of a twentieth-century French intellectual, to whom an advanced degree is denied because "[t]hey couldnt find the . . . / the Object of my dissertation" (82). Baudrillard's dissertation (which became his first book) is titled "Le systéme des objects" (The system of objects).
4. Deleuze and Guattari's depiction of the smooth space of nomads resonates, as well, with the Slinger's ability to exist in several times and spaces simultaneously. In the poem, such simultaneity appears to the mortal I as the Slinger's "unmatchable speed." As Davidson explains, the Slinger exceeds the proverbial "fastest gun

in the west" moniker as he is able to "eliminate the draw" entirely (129). The Slinger collapses time and space, intention and act, into a single, instantaneous gesture. Like Deleuze and Guattari's nomad, the Slinger eschews models of linear causality, insisting "[s]peed is not necessarily fast." The Slinger's "self-contained... act" renders measurement obsolete (Dorn, *Gunslinger* 30).

5. While its connections to geology are ultimately too minimal to be within the scope of this study, Ishmael Reed's 1969 novel *Yellow Back Radio Broke-Down* holds some rather uncanny—and instructive, from the perspective of literary history—similarities with *Gunslinger*. As an elaboration of a period style it shares with Dorn's poem, Reed's novel uses the setting and archetypes of the genre Western to critique internal and external American imperialism. The novel opens with its protagonist, the Loop Garoo Kid, traveling with a carnival to perform at the town of Yellow Back Radio. When they arrive, the circus discovers that the town's "children" have driven all the adults out of town and taken over. The circus, it turns out, has been hired by the leader of the "adults," Drag Gibson, to distract the children so Gibson and his posse can retake the town and, more importantly, steal its land so Gibson can expand his ranching operation. The "adults" are victorious, slaughtering the children and most of the carnies in a fiery ambush that explicitly recalls American massacres in Vietnam. The Loop Garoo Kid, "[a] cowboy so bad he made a working posse of spells phone in sick," vows revenge on Drag Gibson, and invokes his command of HooDoo *Loa* (spirits), which he claims to have learned in New Orleans, to destroy, through a series of ingenious spells and slapstick scenarios, Gibson and his band of hired guns. As this brief synopsis suggests, the novel not only exhibits the same collision of ersatz Wild West and 1960s pop culture as *Gunslinger* but also features HooDoo(s) (in Reed's spelling), albeit of the ritual rather than geologic variety. While Reed does not make much of the geologic connection, and while an etymological link between ritual HooDoo and geologic hoodoos can only be speculative, the convergences are nonetheless intriguing, and a different study might make much of these texts as expressive of a particular moment in the American cultural zeitgeist.

6. See Fredman and Jenkins 84, 133; Elmborg 98–99.

7. The town has since reinvented itself as a small artist community and trendy stop along the touristy Turquoise Trail (NM Highway 14) between Albuquerque and Santa Fe.

8. Placitas is a small village nestled in the Sandia Mountains a twenty-minute drive northeast of Albuquerque, which for a period running from roughly the late 1950s to the early 1970s boasted a poetry community consisting of Dorn, Robert Grenier, Bobbie Louise Hawkins, Larry Goodell, Joanne Kyger, Ken Irby, and Dorn's friend and fellow Black Mountain traveler Robert Creeley.

9. This essay informs *Gunslinger* as well. The Slinger's mescaline-aided act of becoming-desert in which he "turn[s] his eyes into the landscape" is a

proprioceptive activity. For Olson, "the soul is proprioceptive. . . . the 'body' itself as, by movement of its own tissues [gives] the data of depth," and thus "one's life is informed from and by one's own literal body" (*Collected Prose* 182). Similarly, in his essay "Human Universe" Olson insists that the human must "comprehend his own process as intact, from outside, by way of his skin, in, and by his own powers of conversion, out again" (61). Proprioception, in other words, refers to stimuli that are internal to the body yet provide information about the position and movement of that body in physical space. Proprioception, then, melds inner and outer states much as the Slinger melds "the inside real and the outsidereal."

10. See Phil Maillard's introduction to *The Magic Door* (15).
11. Miriam Nichols cites Jung's etymology in relation to Olson and typewriter, explaining that "with this device it is possible to score the lines of the poem as if one were scoring music. With typos, Olson addresses the durables of the human universe—the pattern, the musical score that binds the dancing atoms into shapes" (46).
12. Cath Palug was a legendary monstrous cat and merciless slaughterer of soldiers in Welsh mythology, a bit like Grendel in *Beowulf*.
13. Torrance's mixing of Jung and geology may also be an instance of Thomas Moynihan's claim that Steno's law of superposition, which states that lower geologic strata are older, finds a psychological analogue in our presumption that repressed memories, or unconscious urges, exist somehow "deeper" in the brain. Such an analogy is certainly implied by Maillard's "psychogeology." See Moynihan 85–88.

Chapter 3

1. All underlining, capitalization, and unconventional spellings and usages by Prynne and Olson are in the original correspondence unless otherwise noted.
2. For technical details on glacial geology, I have referred to Richard Foster Flint's *Glacial and Pleistocene Geology* (1957). While some of the science Flint presents is no doubt out of date, the general terminology still holds, and as one of Prynne's cited sources, the book allows us to see how Prynne was making use of these concepts as they were presented at the time.
3. My argument in this chapter is greatly indebted to Roebuck and Sperling's incredibly close, word-by-word and line-by-line dissection of the first half of Prynne's poem, in particular its attention to geologic and etymological vectors.
4. Prynne's "we," as well as his and Olson's equation of physiognomy and landscape discussed later in this chapter, raises the issue of just how far in the direction of nationalism and conservative ideologies that identify soil with "folk" or race Prynne's theory of language goes. As David W. Anthony has shown, linguistic and archaeological speculations about proto-Indo-European languages need not veer

toward racist, nationalist politics. Writing of the development of romantic theories of "folk" and authentic language and/or homelands in nineteenth century German philology and its ideological legacy in the twentieth century, Anthony states, "The mistakes that led an obscure linguistic mystery to erupt into racial genocide were distressingly simple and can be avoided by anyone who cares to avoid them. They were the equation of race with language, and the assignment of superiority to some language-and-race groups." And Anthony continues: "Anyone who *assumes* a simple connection between language and genes, without citing geographic isolation or other special circumstances, is wrong at the outset" (10–11). However, in their correspondence, Prynne and Olson do, at times, appear to hold to essentialist notions about language and landscape determining cultural identity. They are somewhat less clear about how their theories relate to race; while Olson does assert a deeply problematic aesthetic preference for one supposed ancient skull type over another, his mythological and archaeological notions, like Prynne's, and like Torrance's in the previous section, are syncretic, incorporating not only "proto-European" cultures but also Sumerian and Indigenous New World creation myths. These ideas are further complicated by the tension between bedrock and drift that is one of the central topics of this chapter. As Latter puts it, "Prynne's description of language 'resting' on the earth implies something impermanent, delicate, or fragile . . . a process, of something not fixed but in flux" (69). For Latter, at least, rather than cultural nostalgia, "[t]he ultimate object of [the recovery of ancient cultures] lay in the revitalization of poetic form and language" (77). At the same time, however, we should be mindful of Mellors's reminder that "late modernist" poets like Olson and Prynne "continue to affirm," in the 1950s and 1960s, "a redemptive aesthetic that links *poesis* with occult power while disowning the reactionary politics of high modernists such as Yeats, Eliot, and Pound" (42).

5. Prynne sent Olson a typescript of the poem on May 27, 1966. See Olson and Prynne 188.
6. See note above for a discussion of the inherent problems in Olson's swerve into this pseudoscientific, physiognomic territory.
7. See Ryan Dobran's introduction to Olson and Prynne (10). Rachel Blau DuPlessis, writing in the context of the Olson's correspondence with Robert Creeley and Frances Boldereff, makes a similar claim about the import of letters in *Purple Passages* (138–40).
8. In his "Editor's Afterward" to Olson, *Maximus Poems*, Butterick specifically notes that on "June 11, 1966," Olson was "laboring over proofs set from a typescript prepared by Jeremy Prynne for a proposed but never published Corinth Books edition of *Maximus Poems IV, V, VI*" (638).
9. Prynne was obviously taken with this line, as he uses it for the title of another poem in *The White Stones*. See "Frost and Snow Falling" in *Poems* 70–71.
10. All quotations from this work refer to the black-and-white version reprinted in *Body of Work* unless otherwise noted. Elaborating on the production process,

O'Sullivan recalls that she and Cobbing "constructed the entire book going from xeroxing my original pages, collating, binding, glueing, trimming the A5 pages, etc." finishing, over the course of just five days ("working intensively from 10 til 5 every day"), some 80 editions" (qtd. in Manson 71)..

11. Excepting, perhaps, some of Prynne's later work. I'm thinking in particular of his chapbook *Red D Gypsum* (1998), a work whose similarities to O'Sullivan's poetry include, but are not limited to, its deployment of the *red/read* pun; an incredibly dense, wide-ranging, though also seemingly restricted, vocabulary; radical parataxis; and a complicated use of the natural sciences to indicate topological and agricultural processes. See *Poems* 433–49.
12. A list of acknowledgements printed at the end of the original chapbook version tags this image as Degas's *Old Roman Beggarwoman*.
13. For more on the Peace Camp, see Hipperson; Moore, et al.
14. See "The RUC: Lauded and Condemned."
15. Notably, this image is one of several in *A Natural History* that O'Sullivan also uses in a 1984 visual work that takes the form of a series of disjunct film strips titled "POINT.BLANK.RANGE." This work might be another reference to Chris Marker, this time his film *La Jetée*, which is composed of a series of snapshots. As I mention below, O'Sullivan at this time was working as a researcher for the BBC program *Arena* and may have been thinking of these images in terms of the physical process of cutting and splicing film strips in the editing room. See *Body of Work* 223–60. Also see my discussion of *La Jetée* in relation to Smithson's work in chapter 1.
16. For this general overview I have relied on South Wales Coalfield Collection Staff.
17. Luke Roberts points out this connection to Orgreave, although he discusses it in terms of O'Sullivan's allusions to violence in Northern Ireland. See Roberts 156.
18. For an in-depth recounting of the police tactics and systematic coverup at Orgreave, see Conn. For more on Orgreave and how it has reverberated in British art and society, see Buck.
19. It's worth adding that combining red and blue creates the color *magenta*, the name of O'Sullivan's press under which *A Natural History* originally appeared.

Chapter 4

1. Poets and critics such as Bernstein, Michael Golston, Alan Halsey, Bernadette Mayer, and Barrett Watten have noted the prevalence of geologic terminology in Coolidge's writing and, at times, even proposed that the work itself resembles geologic features. For example, Mayer, in a review of Coolidge's 1982 book *Mine: The One That Enters the Stories*, writes, "I've heard it mentioned this is Coolidge's most accessible work; it is no more accessible than some rock cliff, easy enough to reach, climbable by all."
2. Michael Golston provides perhaps the most sustained treatment of Coolidge and geology. Citing Craig Owens's coinage "earthwords," which we encountered in

chapter 1, Golston contends that if "Smithson's works signaled the 'catastrophe' of postmodernism in the visual arts by being consciously constructed as texts," then Coolidge's work "operates precisely as literature into which language has *erupted*"—that is, Coolidge makes language visible, not reducible to a transparent channel of communication. "Like Robert Smithson," Golston continues, "Coolidge exploits a network of intersections and parallels between the scientific discourses and crystallography, on the one hand, and the aesthetic mediums of film and language on the other." Ultimately, Golston focuses on the latter components—film and language—because he wants to argue that Coolidge borrows compositional concepts from Surrealism (particularly surrealist painting) in order to create "an allegorical writing of photography"(82). That is, Golston reads the set of Coolidge's (not necessarily chronological) writings stretching from *The Maintains* (1974) to *Smithsonian Depositions & Subject to a Film* (1980) as stages in an allegory that transcodes "the photographic process of image making" into language. Crucially, in Golston's argument Coolidge begins the process at the point "*prior* to the taking of the photograph" and thus "enacts filmic *emulsion*, that layer of silver halide crystals that coats film before it has been exposed (94). Golston's study is excellent at uncovering the formal structure of Coolidge's poetry and opens up the work in numerous, highly useful ways. And yet, the way geology fades from its purview is somewhat curious, given that geologic concepts inform the structure of a piece like *Smithsonian Depositions*. For one thing, Golston emphasizes the role of "filmic *emulsion*" but does not connect this insight to the emulsionlike composition of the very work in which Coolidge explains the Polaroid process.
3. References to *A Geology* use the text as it appears in *Book Beginning What and Ending Away*.
4. In the latter quotation, Halsey is borrowing a line from Coolidge's book *American Ones*, published in 1981.

Chapter 5

1. See Richard Shelton's introduction to Van Dyke, *The Desert* (xiv).
2. See the colophon in Bervin, *The Desert*. The book was produced in an edition of forty. For this essay, I consulted number 34/40, housed in special collections at the University of Utah's Marriott Library.
3. Poetry featuring nonaleatory erasure procedures has become more prevalent recently. Examples include Mary Ruefle's *A Little White Shadow*, Hugo Garcia Manríquez's *Anti-Humboldt*, and M. NourbeSe Philip's *Zong!* among many others. The artist Basia Irland's series *River Books* recalls Bervin's engagement with water, rivers, and a kind of erosional damage. Irland discovered a pile of library books disposed of on the banks of the Rio Grande in New Mexico and recovered them, preserving their water-damaged pages in cord, wire, and beeswax. On this project, see Boetzkes 194–96.

4. While her understanding of the topography of the page might be similar to Bervin's, Drucker may not agree that *The Desert* is an artist's book. An "artist's book," Drucker has argued, "is a book created as an original work of art, rather than a reproduction of a pre-existing work." Bervin's *Desert* is an interesting test case of this definition, as one would be hard pressed to deny that it is an original work of art, and yet, it is also a reproduction of (part of) Van Dyke's original book. More importantly—and however one defines it— the book does "[integrate] the formal means of its realization and production with its thematic or aesthetic issues" and is "[s]elf-conscious about the structure and meaning of the book as a form." See Drucker, *The Century of Artists' Books* 2.
5. For more on abaca and Manila hemp see Food and Agriculture Organization.
6. Craig Dworkin, whose ear is keener than mine and to whom I owe this observation regarding the material similarities of Irigaray and *irriguer*, has developed a theory of "The Onomastic Imagination," or the dissemination of proper names and authorial signatures in certain avant-garde texts. While some of Dworkin's examples do indeed suggest at least some authorial intentionality, his broader point—and my point regarding Irigaray—is that such encryptions "can be at once encoded and unintended," the outcome of reading language as material and not simply a clear channel of communication. See Dworkin, *Radium* 65.

Chapter 6

1. Of course, my separation of the visual and spatial here is reductive: as Thomas Crow has observed, "Not enough has been made of the obvious pun in these pieces: 'nonsight,' that is, 'nothing to see'" (53).
2. Smithson would go on to do more experiments with mirrors in such site-specific (again noting the pun on "sight") works as the "Mirror Displacements" in various locations in Yucatán, México, in 1969. For more detailed discussions of the prevalence of mirrors in Smithson's work, see especially J. Roberts, *Mirror-Travels* and Boettger.
3. As Deleuze puts it, "Everything that happens and everything that is said happens or is said at the surface. The surface is no less explorable and unknown than depth" (qtd. in Lecercle and Riley 38).
4. On the politics of appropriation and the recent controversies regarding conceptual writing, see Rivera Garza, who argues for a communalist vision of disappropriative writing, that is, writing that foregrounds writing as a collection of communal labor practices; writing that draws on and acknowledges its debt to a broader community that makes the writing possible. Notably, Rivera Garza calls disappropriative writings "geological" as they "[produce] layers upon layers of connection to language as mediated by others' bodies and experiences" (65).

Works Cited

Ades, Dawn, and Michael R. Taylor. *Dalí*. Rizzoli / Philadelphia Museum of Art, 2004.
Alberro, Alexander. "The Catalogue of Robert Smithson's Library." *Robert Smithson*, pp. 244–48.
Anemtoaicei, Ovidiu, and Yvette Russell. "Luce Irigaray: Back to the Beginning." *International Journal of Philosophical Studies*, vol. 21, no. 5, Dec. 2013, pp. 773–86.
Anthony, David W. *The Horse, the Wheel, and Language: How Bronze-Age Riders from the Eurasian Steppes Shaped the Modern World*. Princeton UP, 2007.
Barthes, Roland. "The Death of the Author." *Image–Music–Text*, edited and translated by Stephen Heath, Hill and Wang, 1977, pp. 142–48.
Baudrillard, Jean. *America*. Translated by Chris Turner, Verso, 1988.
Bernstein, Charles. "Maintaining Space: Clark Coolidge's Early Work." 1978. *Electronic Poetry Center*, U of Pennsylvania, 2001, writing.upenn.edu/epc/authors/coolidge/bernstein.html.
Bervin, Jen. *The Desert*. Granary Books, 2008.
Billitteri, Carla. *Language and the Renewal of Society in Walt Whitman, Laura (Riding) Jackson, and Charles Olson: The American Cratylus*. Palgrave Macmillan, 2009.
Bloomfield, Mandy. "Maggie O'Sullivan's Material Poetics of Salvaging in *red shifts* and *murmur*." *Salt Companion*, pp. 10–35.
Boettger, Suzaan. "In the Yucatán: Mirroring Presence and Absence." *Robert Smithson*, pp. 200–205.
Boetzkes, Amanda. *The Ethics of Earth Art*. U of Minnesota P, 2010.
Bök, Christian. *Crystallography*. 2nd ed., Coach House, 2003.
———. *'Pataphysics: The Poetics of an Imaginary Science*. Northwestern UP, 2002.
Braidotti, Rosi. *The Posthuman*. Polity Press, 2013.
Brandt, Joan Elizabeth. *Geopoetics: The Politics of Mimesis in Poststructuralist French Poetry and Thought*. Stanford UP, 1997.
Brinton, Ian. "Black Mountain in England (2): Chris Torrance." *PN Review* 163, vol. 31, no. 5, May–June 2005, www.pnreview.co.uk/cgi-bin/scribe?item_id=2470.
Buck, Louisa. "Mike Figgis's *The Battle of Orgreave*." *Artforum*, Jan. 2002, www.artforum.com/print/200201/mike-figgis-s-battle-of-orgreave-2063.
Buell, Lawrence. *The Environmental Imagination: Thoreau, Nature Writing, and the Formation of American Culture*. Belknap Press of Harvard UP, 1995.

Chakrabarty, Dipesh. "The Climate of History: Four Theses." *Critical Inquiry*, vol. 35, no. 2, winter 2009, pp. 197–222.

Clark, T. J. "Phenomenality and Materiality in Cézanne." *Material Events: Paul de Man and the Afterlife of Theory*. U of Minnesota P, 2001, pp. 93–113.

Conn, David. "The Scandal of Orgreave." *The Guardian*, 18 May 2017, www.theguardian.com/politics/2017/may/18/scandal-of-orgreave-miners-strike-hillsborough-theresa-may.

Coole, Diana, and Samantha Frost. "Introducing the New Materialisms." *New Materialisms: Ontology, Agency, and Politics*, Duke UP, 2010, pp. 1–43.

Coolidge, Clark. "Arrangement." 1977. *Electronic Poetry Center*, U of Pennsylvania, 2011, writing.upenn.edu/epc/authors/coolidge/naropa.html.

———. *A Book Beginning What and Ending Away*. Fence Books, 2012.

———. *The Crystal Text*. The Figures, 1986.

———. *A Geology*. Potes & Poets Press, 1988.

———. "Notebooks (1976–1982)." *Code of Signals: Recent Writings in Poetics*, edited by Michael Palmer, North Atlantic Books, 1983, pp. 43–56.

———. *Smithsonian Depositions/Subject to a Film*. Vehicle Editions, 1980.

———. *Space*. Harper & Row, 1970.

Crow, Thomas. "Cosmic Exile: Prophetic Turns in the Life and Art of Robert Smithson." *Robert Smithson*, pp. 32–56.

Dalí, Salvador. *The Secret Life of Salvador Dalí*. Translated by Haakon Chevalier, Dial, 1942.

———. *The Collected Writings of Salvador Dalí*. Edited and translated by Haim Finkelstein, Cambridge UP, 1998.

Davidson, Michael. "To Eliminate the Draw: Narrative and Language in *Slinger*." *Internal Resistances*, edited by Donald Wesling, U of California P, 1985, pp. 113–49.

Deleuze, Gilles, and Félix Guattari. *A Thousand Plateaus*. Translated by Brian Massumi, U of Minnesota P, 1984.

Dorn, Edward. *Gunslinger*. Duke UP, 1989.

———. *Geography*. Fulcrum Press, 1965.

Drucker, Johanna. *The Century of Artists' Books*. Granary Books, 1995.

———. "Un-Visual and Conceptual." *UbuWeb*, 2005, www.ubu.com/papers/kg_ol_drucker.html.

DuPlessis, Rachel Blau. *Purple Passages: Pound, Eliot, Zukofsky, Olson, Creeley, and the Ends of Patriarchal Poetry*. U of Iowa P, 2012.

Dworkin, Craig. *No Medium*. MIT Press, 2013.

———. *Radium of the Word: A Poetics of Materiality*. U of Chicago P, 2020.

———. *The Crystal Text (After Clark Coolidge)*. Compline, 2012.

Dworkin, Craig, and Kenneth Goldsmith, editors. *Against Expression: An Anthology of Conceptual Writing*. Northwestern UP, 2011.

Elmborg, James K. *A Pageant of Its Time: Edward Dorn's* Slinger *and the Sixties*. Peter Lang, 1998.

Fenollosa, Ernest, and Ezra Pound. *The Chinese Written Character as a Medium for Poetry: A Critical Edition*. Edited by Haun Saussy et al, Fordham UP, 2008.

Flint, Richard Foster. *Glacial and Pleistocene Geology*. John Wiley & Sons, 1957.

Food and Agriculture Organization of the United Nations. "Abaca." *Future Fibres*, www.fao.org/economic/futurefibres/fibres/abacao/en/.

Fredman, Stephen, and Grant Jenkins. "First Annotations to Edward Dorn's *Gunslinger*." *Sagetrieb*, vol. 15, no. 3, winter 1996, pp. 57–176.

Frid, Dianna, and Jen Bervin. "Interview." *Bomb Magazine*, 2016, bombmagazine.org/article/668198/jen-bervin-and-dianna-frid.

Golston, Michael. *Poetic Machinations: Allegory, Surrealism, and Postmodern Poetic Form*. Columbia UP, 2015.

Halpern, Rob. "'The Idiot Stone': George Oppen's Geological Imagination; or, Objectivist Realism as Ecopoetics." *Ecopoetics: Essays in the Field*, edited by Angela Hume and Gillian Osborne, U of Iowa P, 2018.

Halsey, Alan. "From a Diary of Reading Clark Coolidge." *Jacket*, vol. 13, Apr. 2001, jacketmagazine.com/13/coolidge-halsey.html.

Hawkes, C. F. C. *The Prehistoric Foundations of Europe to the Mycenean Age*. 1940. Routledge, 2015.

Hickman, Mary. "Defaced/refaced books: The Erasure Practices of Jen Bervin and Mary Ruefle." *Jacket2*, 2014, jacket2.org/article/defacedrefaced-books.

Hipperson, Sarah. "Greenham Common Women's Peace Camp 1981–2000." www.greenhamwpc.org.uk.

Iijima, Brenda, editor. *The Eco Language Reader*. Portable Press at Yo-Yo Labs, 2010.

Irigaray, Luce. *Ce sexe qui n'en est pas un*. Éditions de Minuit, 1977.

———. *This Sex Which Is Not One*. Translated by Catherine Porter and Carolyn Burke, Cornell UP, 1985.

Jung, C. G. *Psychology and Alchemy*. 1953. 1968. 2nd ed., Princeton UP, 1980. Vol. 12 of *The Collected Works of C.G. Jung*, edited by Herbert Read et al., translated by R. F. C. Hull. Bollingen Series XX.

Latter, Alex. *Late Modernism and* The English Intelligencer: *On the Poetics of Community*. Bloomsbury, 2017.

Lecercle, Jean-Jacques, and Denise Riley. *The Force of Language*. Palgrave Macmillan, 2004.

Loe, Hikmet Sidney. *The* Spiral Jetty *Encyclo: Exploring Robert Smithson's Earthwork Through Time and Place*. U of Utah P, 2017.

Lorange, Astrid. *How Reading Is Written: A Brief Index to Gertrude Stein*. Wesleyan UP, 2014.

MacDonald, Travis. "A Brief History of Erasure Poetics." *Jacket*, vol. 38, 2009, jacketmagazine.com/38/macdonald-erasure.shtml.

Mack, Melissa. *The Next Crystal Text*. Timeless, Infinite Light, 2017.

Manson, Peter. "A Natural History in 3 Incomplete Parts." *Salt Companion*, pp. 71–79.

Marsh, Nicky. "Agonal States: Maggie O'Sullivan and Feminist Politics of Visual Poetics." *Salt Companion*, pp. 80–96.

Marx, Leo. *The Machine in the Garden: Technology and the Pastoral Ideal in America*. Oxford UP, 1964.

Mayer, Bernadette. "Review of *Mine: The One that Enters the Stories* by Clark Coolidge." *Poetry Project Newsletter*, no. 100, Oct. 1983, web.archive.org/web/20060912070744/www.poetryproject.com/newsletter/mayerrev.html.

McCaffery, Steve. *Prior to Meaning: The Protosemantic and Poetics*. Northwestern UP, 2001.

———. *Theory of Sediment*. Talon Books, 1991.

McGurl, Mark. "The New Cultural Geology." *Twentieth Century Literature*, vol. 57, fall/winter 2011, pp. 380–91.

Meillassoux, Quentin. *After Finitude: An Essay on the Necessity of Contingency*. Translated by Ray Brassier, Bloomsbury, 2012.

Mellors, Anthony. *Late Modernist Poetics: From Pound to Prynne*. Manchester UP, 2005.

Middleton, Peter. "On Ice: Julia Kristeva, Susan Howe and Avant-Garde Poetics." *Contemporary Poetry Meets Modern Theory*, edited by Anthony Easthope and John O. Thompson, U of Toronto P, 1991, pp. 81–95.

Moore, Suzanne, et al. "How the Greenham Common Protest Changed Lives." *The Guardian*, 20 March 2017, www.theguardian.com/uk-news/2017/mar/20/greenham-common-nuclear-silos-women-protest-peace-camp.

Moynihan, Thomas. *Spinal Catastrophism: A Secret History*. MIT Press, 2019.

Nardelli, Matilde. "No to the End: The Desert as Eschatology in Late Modernity." *Tate Papers*, vol. 22, autumn 2014, www.tate.org.uk/research/tate-papers/22/no-end-to-the-end-the-desert-as-eschatology-in-late-modernity.

Ngai, Sianne. *Ugly Feelings*. Harvard UP, 2005.

Nichols, Miriam. *Radical Affections: Essays on the Poetics of Outside*. U of Alabama P, 2010.

OED Online: Oxford English Dictionary, Oxford UP, accessed 2018–2020, www.oed.com.

Olsen, Redell. "Writing / Conversation with Maggie O'Sullivan." *Salt Companion*, pp. 203–12.

Olson, Charles. *Collected Prose*. Edited by Donald Allen and Benjamin Friedlander, U of California P, 1997.

———. "Human Universe." *Selected Writings of Charles Olson*, edited by Robert Creeley. New Directions, 1967, pp. 53–66.

———. *The Maximus Poems*. Edited by George F. Butterick, U of California P, 1983.

Olson, Charles, and J. H. Prynne. *The Collected Letters of Charles Olson and J. H. Prynne*. Edited by Ryan Dobran, U of New Mexico P, 2017.

Oppen, George. "Of Being Numerous." *New Collected Poems*, edited by Michael Davidson, New Directions, 2002, pp. 163–208.

Orange, Tom. "Arrangement and Density: A Context for Early Clark Coolidge." *Jacket*, vol. 13, April 2001, jacketmagazine.com/13/coolidge-o-a.html.

O'Sullivan, Maggie. *Body of Work*. Reality Street Editions, 2006.

———. *A Natural History in 3 Incomplete Parts*. Magenta, 1985, eclipsearchive.org/projects/naturalhistory/.

Owens, Craig. "Earthwords." *October*, vol. 10, autumn 1979, pp. 120–30.

Parikka, Jussi. *A Geology of Media*. U of Minnesota P, 2015.

Perloff, Marjorie. "'The Saturated Language of Red': Maggie O'Sullivan and the Artist's Book." *Salt Companion*, pp. 123–35.

Pizza, Joseph. "Continental Drift: Charles Olson and the *English Intelligencer*." *Contemporary Literature*, vol. 59, no. 3, 2018, pp. 277–307.

Prynne, J. H. *Poems*. Bloodaxe Books, 2005.

Rasula, Jed. *This Compost: Ecological Imperatives in American Poetry*. 2002. U of Georgia P, 2012.

Rasula, Jed, and Steve McCaffery, editors. *Imagining Language: An Anthology*. MIT Press, 1998.

Reed, Ishmael. *Yellow Back Radio Broke-Down*. Doubleday, 1969.

Reeve, N. H., and Richard Kerridge. *Nearly Too Much: The Poetry of J. H. Prynne*. Liverpool UP, 1995.

Reynolds, Ann. "Enantiomorphic Models." *Robert Smithson*, pp. 136–40.

Rivera Garza, Cristina. *The Restless Dead: Necrowriting & Disappropriation*. Translated by Robin Myers, Vanderbilt UP, 2020.

Roberts, Jennifer L. *Mirror Travels: Robert Smithson and History*. Yale UP, 2004.

———. "The Taste of Time: Salt and *Spiral Jetty*." *Robert Smithson*, pp. 96–103.

———. "The Veins of Pennsylvania: Benjamin Franklin's Nature-Print Currency." *Grey Room*, vol. 69, fall 2017, pp. 50–79.

Roberts, Luke. *Barry MacSweeney and the Politics of Postwar British Poetry: Seditious Things*. Palgrave Macmillan, 2017.

Robert Smithson. Organized by Eugenie Tsai with Cornelia Butler for the Museum of Contemporary Art, Los Angeles, U of California P, 2004.

Roebuck, Thomas, and Matthew Sperling. "'The Glacial Question, Unsolved': A Specimen Commentary on Lines 1–31." *Glossator: Theory and Practice of the Commentary*, vol. 2, 2010, pp. 39–78.

Roth, Moira. "An Interview with Robert Smithson (1973)." Edited by Naomi Sawelson-Gorse. *Robert Smithson*, pp. 80–95.

"The RUC: Lauded and Condemned." *BBC News*, 31 October 2001, news.bbc.co.uk/2/hi/in_depth/uk/2000/ruc_reform/780311.stm.

The Salt Companion to Maggie O'Sullivan. Salt Publishing, 2011.

Serres, Michel. *The Parasite*. Translated by Lawrence R. Schehr, U of Minnesota P, 2007.

Shaw, Lytle. *Fieldworks: From Place to Site in Postwar Poetics*. U of Alabama P, 2013.

———. "Smithson, Writer." *Robert Smithson: Spiral Jetty: True Fictions, False Realities*, edited by Lynne Cooke and Karen Kelly, U of California P, 2005, pp. 115–27.

Sheppard, Robert. "Talk: The Poetics of Maggie O'Sullivan." *Salt Companion*, pp. 154–78.

Shklovsky, Victor. "Art as Technique." *Russian Formalist Criticism: Four Essays*, translated by Lee T. Lemon and Marion J. Reis, U of Nebraska P, 1965, pp. 3–24.

Sieburth, Richard. "*A Heap of Language*: Robert Smithson and American Hieroglyphics." *Robert Smithson*, pp. 218–23.

Skystone Foundation. "About." *Roden Crater*, rodencrater.com/about/.

Smithson, Robert. *The Collected Writings*. Edited by Jack Flam, U of California P, 1996.

South Wales Coalfield Collection Staff, "Introduction: Miners' Strike 1984–85." *Archives Hub*, Jisc, archiveshub.jisc.ac.uk/features/mar04.shtml.

Stein, Gertrude. *Ida: A Novel*. Cooper Union, 1971.

Tatransky, Valentin. "Catalogue of Robert Smithson's Library: Books, Magazines, and Records." *Robert Smithson*, pp. 249–63.

Torrance, Chris. *The Magic Door*. Test Centre, 2017.

Uroskie, Andrew V. "La Jetée en Spirale: Robert Smithson's Stratigraphic Cinema." *Grey Room*, vol. 19, spring 2005, pp. 54–79.

Van Dyke, John C. *The Desert: Further Studies in Natural Appearances*. 1901. Peregrine Smith, 1980.

———. *The Secret Life of John C. Van Dyke: Letters*. Edited by David Teague and Peter Wild, U of Nevada P, 1997.

Wall, Jeff. "Photography and Liquid Intelligence." *Jeff Wall*, edited by Thierry de Duve, Arielle Pelenc, and Boris Groys, Phaidon, 1996, pp. 90–93.

White, Kenneth. "Elements of Geopoetics." *Edinburgh Review*, no. 88, 1992, pp. 163–78.

Williams, William Carlos. *Paterson*. 1963. Penguin, 1983.

Wilson, Rachael M. "Clark Coolidge's Cave Art." *Jacket2*, Oct. 2015, jacket2.org/article/clark-coolidges-cave-art.

Yusoff, Kathryn. *A Billion Black Anthropocenes or None*. U of Minnesota P, 2018.

———. "Geologic Subjects: Nonhuman Origins, Geomorphic Aesthetics, and the Art of Becoming Inhuman." *Cultural Geographies*, vol. 22, July 2015, pp. 383–407.

———. "Politics of the Anthropocene: Formation of the Commons as a Geologic Process." *Antipode*, vol. 50, Jan. 2018, pp. 255–76.

Zukofsky, Louis. *"A."* New Directions, 2011.

Index

ablution, 128
abstract geology, 116
abstraction, 86
Acconci, Vito, 10, 28
"Addition" (Smithson), 29
adéquation, 19
Ades, Dawn, 109
L'afemme, 134–35, 137, 142
agency, 164n10
alchemy, 58, 63–64
allegorical language, 26
American Desert Southwest, 3, 31, 39–41, 47
American Museum of Natural History, 22, 115
American Wild West, 47
Andrews, Roy Chapman, 102
androcentrism, 141
Anemtoaicei, Ovidiu, 140
L'Angélus (Millet), 109
Anisimov, A. F., 78
anteriority, time as, 118
Anthony, David W., 168n4
Anthony d'Offay Gallery, 95
Anthropocene, 15, 17–18, 36
Apollinaire, Guillaume, 27
arche-fossil, 118
archetypes, 60–67
"Arcospirical Meanderings in a Tongue of the Time" (Torrance), 64
Arena (documentary), 95
Ark of the Covenant, 8

"Arrangement" (talk by Coolidge), 100–102
"An Array of Matter" (Smithson), 29
Asphalt Rundown (Smithson), 28
Astral America, 48
Astronomicon (Manilius), 83
autograph, 154

bad word, 13
Bailey, D. R. Shackleton, 83
Ballard, J. G., 162
Barthes, Roland, 119–20
Bataille, Georges, 17
Battle of Orgreave, 95, 98
Baudrillard, Jean, 47–50, 75, 166n3
BBC, 95
Beckett, Samuel, 111, 153
bedrock, 3, 8–9, 11–12, 64, 70
Benjamin, Walter, 24–25, 29, 36
Bennett, Jane, 14
Beresford, M. W., 78
Bernstein, Charles, 87, 99–100
Berrigan, Ted, 102
Bervin, Jen, 1, 27, 131; Colorado River and, 141; *The Desert*, 4, 120, 122–24, 128, 140; Irigaray and, 136; on light, 124; liquid intelligence and, 133; materials of, 122; *Nets*, 123; palimpsest and, 127, 128, 130; sewing and, 4, 122–27, 129–30, 132, 134, 139–40; textual space and, 126
Beuys, Joseph, 95

A Bibliography on America for Ed Dorn (Torrance), 57, 75
A Billion Black Anthropocenes or None (Yusoff), 36
Billitteri, Carla, 6, 163n2
Black Mountain, 68, 70
"Black Mountain in England" (Torrance), 57
Blanchot, Maurice, 17, 127
Bloomfield, Mandy, 87, 89
bodily harm, 88
Body of Work (Coolidge), 87
Boetzkes, Amanda, 14–15, 20, 115, 136, 142
Bök, Christian, 4, 112, 117, 144, 148–51
A Book Beginning What and Ending Away (Coolidge), 104, 108, 110, 119, 154
The Book of Brychan (Torrance), 57, 61
"The Bottom of the Bowl" (Van Dyke), 129
Braidotti, Rosi, 16, 27
Brandt, Joan Elizabeth, 17
breathing spaces, deserts as, 122, 123, 125, 138–39
The Bride Stripped Bare by Her Bachelors, Even (The Large Glass) (Duchamp), 152
"A Brief History of Erasure Poetics" (MacDonald), 124
Brinton, Ian, 57
Britain, 6, 72, 86–87
brows, 69–86
Brubeck, Dave, 153
Buell, Lawrence, 14, 19, 128–29
Butterick, George, 79–80

Cage, John, 108, 123
Cape Goliard, 79
capitalism, 66, 145
carbon, 63–65
carbon cycle, 106–7
Carnegie, Andrew, 121, 131–32
Cath Palug, 168n12
The Cave (Coolidge and Mayer), 101
caving, 101, 105
Cézanne, 155, 157
Chakrabarty, Dipesh, 165n13
change, rates of, 113
Charters, Samuel, 65
Childe, V. Gordon, 76
The Chinese Written Character as a Medium for Poetry (Fenollosa), 6
Chomsky, Noam, 13
Cinema 2 (Deleuze), 33
cinematic time, 34
Citrinas (Torrance), 59–61
Clark, T. J., 5
Clark, Tom, 166n3
clastic arrangements, 4
clastic mates, 100–103
climate change, 77, 161
"The Climate of History" (Chakrabarty), 165n13
"Closed Limits" (Smithson), 29
coal, 64, 86, 94–95; industry, 4; mining, 51–52
Cobbing, Bob, 87
Cold War, 31
Colebrook, Claire, 17
Coleridge, Samuel Taylor, 5
The Collected Writings (Smithson), 115
collective contingency, 14
colloid, 100, 103, 110–12
colonialism, 158–59
colonial mining, 37
Colorado Desert, 123, 138
Colorado Plateau, 48, 50, 54
Colorado River, 129–30, 138, 141
communism, 17
complicity, 161, 162
Concrete Pour (Sieburth), 28
"Contained Information" (Smithson), 29
continental drift, 12, 68; grief, glazes,

graves, and gravel, 86–98; moraines, ridges, and brows, 69–86
Coole, Diana, 163n1
Coolidge, Clark, 1, 4, 7, 10, 19, 26–27, 68, 98, 144, 153; "Arrangement," 100–102; *A Book Beginning What and Ending Away*, 104, 108, 110, 119, 154; *The Cave*, 101; clastic mates and, 100–103; *The Crystal Text*, 152, 154; *A Geology*, 99–100, 104–10, 112; Longprose and, 103–11; *The Northeastern Caver*, 101; *The Secret Life of Salvador Dalí*, 108–9; *Smithsonian Depositions*, 103, 104, 112; *Space*, 99, 102–3
covenants, 82
Cratylic, 163n2
Crow, Thomas, 147, 172n1
Crozier, Andrew, 69
"The Crystal Land" (Smithson), 145, 147
Crystallography (Bök), 148–49, 151
crystals and crystal text, 4–5, 153–62; enantiomorphic structure of, 147, 149; entropy and, 146; fluid, 109; impurities in growth, 151; mirrors and, 144, 147–48, 150, 152; photographic film and, 103; reflections and, 146; salt, 2, 34–35; time and, 145
The Crystal Text (After Clark Coolidge) (Dworkin), 154–55
The Crystal Text (Coolidge), 152, 154
cycles, 56, 65–66; carbon, 106–7

Dalí, Salvador, 108–10
The Danube in Prehistory (Childe), 76
Davidson, Michael, 44–45
Death Valley, 47
dedifferentiation, 30
Degas, Edgar, 96
Deleuze, Gilles, 33–34, 48–49, 112–13;

166n4, 172n1
deposition, 2, 20, 23, 30
Derrida, Jacques, 96
The Desert (Bervin), 4, 120, 122–24, 128, 140
The Desert (Van Dyke), 121
desert of the real, 44–51
dialectical landscape, 18
"Dialectic of Site and Nonsite" (Smithson), 24, 29
The Diary of Palug's Cat (Torrance), 61
différance, 2
disappropriative writings, 172n4
Dogtown, 79–80
Dorn, Ed, 1, 2–3, 7, 10–11, 27, 39, 42, 52, 68; *A Bibliography on America*, 75; "West of Moab," 54. See also *Gunslinger*
drift, 3; linguistic, 11. See also continental drift
Drojarski, Jan, 122
Drucker, Johanna, 126, 172n4
Duchamp, Marcel, 152
Dunbar, Jennifer, 166n3
DuPlessis, Rachel Blau, 62
Dwan Gallery, 25, 28, 128
Dworkin, Craig, 4, 27, 127, 144, 154–57, 164n9, 172n6

earthwords, 170n2
"Earthwords" (Owens), 24–25
ecocriticism, 13–14, 16, 128
Ecologues (Virgil), 131
ecology, 142
ecopoetics, 164n8
ecopoetics (journal), 14
eggs, 109
Ehrenzweig, Anton, 30, 116
Eigner, Larry, 107
Eliade, Mircea, 78
embedded sediments, 4
embodied poetics, 87

Emerson, Ralph Waldo, 5, 53
emulsion, 103
Enantiomorphic Chambers, 147–48
England, 3–4, 70, 74
The English Intelligencer, 69
entropy, 28, 30, 65, 81, 146–47, 151
"Entropy and the New Monuments" (Smithson), 30
The Environmental Imagination (Buell), 19
environmentalism, "tree hugger," 52
Erased de Kooning Drawing (Rauschenberg), 127
erosion, 30, 122, 124, 126–27
estrangement, 16
ethics, recessive, 15
exomodern, 15
extractive industries, 161

Fence Books, 104
Fenollosa, Ernest, 6–7, 69, 86, 163n4
Flam, Jack, 115
Fletcher, Ray, 105
Flint, Richard Foster, 168n2
fluid crystals, 109
fluid dynamics, 134, 136
The Force of Language (Lecercle and Riley, D.), 13
forgetfulness, 31
fossil poetry, 5, 53
Foucault, Michel, 16
"The Fountain Monument" (Smithson), 30
Four Corners, 48, 50, 54
"Fractal Geometry" (Bök), 151
Frankfurt School, 158
Frid, Dianna, 136
Fried, Michael, 25
Fried Eggs on a Plate without the Plate (Dalí), 109–10
Frost, Samantha, 163n1
frozen water, 147

futures, remote, 29–32

gender roles, 62
genre Westerns, 47
geochronology, of strata, 82
Geography (collection), 54
geological imagination, 12
geologic boundaries, 71
geologic history, 22
geologic subjects, 17
geologic turn, 15–19
geology. *See specific topics*
A Geology (Coolidge), 99–100, 104–10, 112
geomorphology, 70
Glacial and Pleistocene Geology (Flint), 168n2
"The Glacial Question, Unsolved" (Prynne), 70–73, 75, 76–78, 80, 82, 84
glaciation, 70
glaciers, 74, 78
glazes, 86–98
Global North, 161
global slave trade, 37
Global South, 159–60
Global Standard Stratigraphic Age, 37
global warming, 15, 37, 67
Gloucester, 79
Gobi Desert, 102
Golden Spike National Monument, 35–36, 39
golden spikes, 17, 32–38
Golston, Michael, 152, 170n2
Graham, Dan, 114
gravel, 86–98
graves, 86–98
Great Salt Lake, 10, 18, 33–34, 161
Greenham Common Women's Peace Camp, 93
grief, 86–98
Guattari, Felix, 48–49, 112–13, 166n4

A Guide to the Maximus Poems (Butterick), 79
Gunslinger (Dorn), 2–3, 10–11, 39, 78, 167n5; archetypes and, 60–67; desert of the real and, 44–51; language contingencies in, 41; as Literate Projector, 40–45; narrative of, 40–41; Neath Valley and, 55–60; real of the desert and, 51–55

Halpern, Rob, 12, 164n8
Halsey, Alan, 104–5, 107
Harper's Bazaar, 145
hate speech, 13
Hawkes, C. F. C., 76–77
Hawthorne, Nathaniel, 131
A Heap of Language (Smithson), 2, 27–29
heaps, 21–29
Heidegger, Martin, 12
Heizer, Michael, 21, 31
Helderberg Escarpment, 106
Heraclitus, 21, 39
Hickman, Mary, 124–25
historical periods, 2–3
Holocene, 37
Holt, Nancy, 21, 145
hoodoos, 50
Howe, Susan, 81
human-imposed time, 32
human industry, 131–32
humanism, 16
human universe, 84

idealism, 134
identity, of structure, 7
Iijima, Brenda, 14
"I," lyrical, 44–45, 55–56
Imagining Language (Rasula and McCaffery), 5
individuation, 61, 62, 64
Indo-European etymology, 70

Indogermanisches etomologisches Wörterbuch (Pokorny), 81
industrial agriculture, 18
Industrial Revolution, 66
"Inner Coordinates" (Smithson), 29
inner speech, 13, 153–54
institutional critique, 21
instrumentalization, 86
interior reality, 48
In the Beginning She Was (Irigaray), 140
IRA. *See* Irish Republican Army
Irigaray, Luce, 4, 121, 135–37, 142, 172n6; *In the Beginning She Was*, 140; *This Sex Which Is Not One*, 134
Irish Republican Army (IRA), 93–94
irrigation, 137, 139
isothermic temperature, 80

La Jetée (film), 33, 146, 170n15
Judd, Donald, 21, 145, 146
Jung, Carl, 58, 60–62, 168n11

Kerouac, Jack, 153
Kerridge, Richard, 72, 81
King, W. B. R., 71, 73
Koch, Kenneth, 102
Kurosawa, Akira, 153

Labour government, 85
Lacan, Jacques, 150
lamé, 92, 97
land use, 137
language. *See specific topics*
language-as-nature, 5
language-as-thing, 44
Language To Be Looked At and/or Things To Be Read (press release), 25
lapis philosophorum (philosopher's stone), 63
"Lastworda" (McCaffery), 29, 111–13
latent violence, 89
Latter, Alex, 7, 69–70, 86

Lecercle, Jean-Jacques, 1, 13–14
Leopold, Aldo, 128
Levinas, Emmanuel, 136
Lévi-Strauss, Claude, 20, 41
LeWitt, Sol, 24
light, 106, 109, 123–24
linguistic drift, 11
linguistic tropes, 53
linguistic turn, 2
liquid intelligence, 133, 141–42
Literate Projector, 40–45, 54
lithic detritus, 25
A Little White Shadow (Ruefle), 124
Loe, Hikmet Sidney, 145
Longprose, 103–11, 152
Lorange, Astrid, 19
Lyell, Charles, 165n14
lyrical "I," 44–45, 55–56

MacDonald, Travis, 124, 125
The Machine in the Garden (Marx), 131
Mack, Melissa, 4, 144, 158–62
Mac Low, Jackson, 27, 108, 123
"Maen Madoc" (Torrance), 59
The Magic Door (Torrance), 2–3, 11, 40, 54, 55–57, 59, 61–63
Maillard, Phil, 55
Mallarmé, Stéphane, 5, 27
Man, Paul de, 5, 164n9
manifest destiny, 37
Manila hemp, 126
Manilius, Marcus, 83–84
Maria, Walter de, 21
Marker, Chris, 33, 92, 146, 170n15
markmaking, 157
Marsh, Nicky, 89, 94–95
Marx, Leo, 131, 142
Marxism, 47
masculine/feminine archetypes, 60, 62
masculine/feminine duality, 58
material embeddedness, 2
materiality, 15, 21, 25, 27, 44, 53; of thought, 10
matrix, 54, 60; of Neath Valley, 55–60; place as, 3
matter, 53; printed, 2, 25–26, 29
Mauss, Marcel, 8
The Maximus Poems (Olson), 10, 65, 76, 79
The Maximus Poems IV, V, VI (Olson), 57
Mayer, Bernadette, 10, 101
McCaffery, Steve, 4, 7, 27, 82, 98, 100; *Imagining Language*, 5; "Lastworda," 29, 111–13; *Prior to Meaning*, 114; *Theory of Sediment*, 111, 119; "Theory of Sediment," 119; word strata and, 111–20
McGurl, Mark, 15, 16, 165n13
McLuckie, John, 131–32
Meillassoux, Quentin, 118, 164n8
mental mud, 21
metamorphic engagement, with geology, 1
metaphors: geologic, 6–7; mining as, 63
micropolitical incitement, 17
Middle English, 85
Middleton, Peter, 81–82
Millet, Jean-François, 109
mineral fact, 12
mineral wealth, 158–59
miners' strikes, 18
mining: coal, 51–52; colonial, 37; as metaphor, 63
"Mirages" (Torrance), 61
mirrors, 144, 147–48, 150, 152
"The Mirror Stage as Formative of the Function of the I" (Lacan), 150
Mishima, Yukio, 153
misrecognition, of mirror images, 150
modernism, geologic, 5–12
Mojave Desert, 47, 123
Monk, Thelonius, 153
Mont Sainte-Victoire Seen from the Bibémus Quarry (Cézanne), 155
monuments, 30

moraines, 69–86
Mother Earth, 54
Mother Nature, 135
Moynihan, Thomas, 168n12
Muir, John, 132
"A Museum of Language in the Vicinity of Art" (Smithson), 10, 27
Museum of Natural History, 32, 109

Nardelli, Matilde, 31, 32
National Coal Board, 94
National Union of Mineworkers (NUM), 94, 96
natural history, 98
A Natural History in 3 Incomplete Parts (O'Sullivan), 3, 86–88, 90, 92, 94, 96, 100
natural language, 11, 69
Neath Disturbance, 58, 63
Neath Valley, 55–60
Nets (Bervin), 123
Nevada Test Site, 31
"New Cultural Geology" (McGurl), 15
new materialism, 14
New River Project, 87
The Next Crystal Text (Mack), 4, 144, 158, 160
Ngai, Siane, 160, 164n10
Nichols, Miriam, 57–58, 79, 168n11
nomadic ethos, 48
nomadology, 49
nomads, 166n4
nonaleatory erasure procedures, 171n3
nonarbitrary material language, 46
nonhuman language, 5, 12–15
Nonsites, 2, 21–29, 31, 33, 45
The Northeastern Caver (Coolidge), 101
Northern Ireland, 93–94
Novalis, 5
NUM. *See* National Union of Mineworkers
Of Being Numerous (Oppen), 13

Old English, 92
Old French, 85
Old Roman Beggarwoman (Degas), 96
Olsen, Redell, 89
Olson, Charles, 3, 7, 11, 12, 40, 52, 62, 68, 69–86; *The Maximus Poems*, 10, 65, 76, 79; *The Maximus Poems IV, V, VI*, 57; "Projective Verse," 6, 60; "Proprioception," 56
"On Ice" (Middleton), 81
open-field poetics, 78, 91
Oppen, George, 12–13, 164n8
Orange, Tom, 102, 107, 108
The Order of Things (Foucault), 16
Orgreave Coking Plant, 97, 170n17
Orgreave Coking Works, 95, 96
O'Sullivan, Maggie, 1, 26, 40, 67, 68, 86–98; *Body of Work*, 87; *A Natural History in 3 Incomplete Parts*, 3, 86–88, 90, 92, 94, 96, 100; *States of Emergency*, 94–95
Owens, Craig, 23, 24–27, 33, 36, 170n2
Oxford English Dictionary, 28–29

Painted Desert, 123
palimpsest, 127–28, 130
Pangea, 57, 69, 84
pansemiosis, 5
Parikka, Jussi, 22–23, 164n7
particle poetics, 114
Passaic River, 9
pasts, remote, 29–32
Paterson (Williams), 9
patriarchal poetry, 62
Perloff, Marjorie, 43, 45, 51, 89, 166n2
The Persistence of Memory (Ades and Taylor), 109
Phillips, Tom, 27
philosopher's stone (lapis philosophorum), 63
phonemic mutations, 93
photographic film, 103

photography, 152
physiognomy, 3
Pizza, Joseph, 69
plate tectonics, 68
Plato, 6
Pleistocene, 70–71, 73, 75, 77, 80, 84–85
"The Pleistocene Epoch in England" (King), 71, 73
poetic principle, 26
Pokorny, Julius, 81
Polaroid (Golston), 152
Polaroid film, 103, 146
police riot, 96
police violence, 18
Ponge, Francis, 19
postglacial topography, 79
posthumanism, 16
poststructuralism, 14
Potes & Poets Press, 104
Pound, Ezra, 6, 7, 111, 163n4
Předmost, 76
prehistoric civilizations, 70, 76
The Prehistoric Foundations of Europe (Hawkes), 76–77
"pre-semantic" qualities of words, 114
The Principles of Geology (Lyell), 165n14
Principles of Structural Glaciology (Shumskii), 146
printed matter, 2, 25–26, 29
Prior to Meaning (McCaffery), 114
"Projective Verse" (Olson), 6, 60
property, 49
"Proprioception" (Olson), 56
proto-European cultures, 77
"proto" qualities of words, 114
protosemantic language, 4
Prynne, J. H., 1, 3, 7, 11–12, 52, 67–68, 69–86, 156; "The Glacial Question, Unsolved," 70–73, 75, 76–78, 80, 82, 84; *Red D Gypsum*, 170n11; *The White Stones*, 65, 85; "The Wound, Day and Night," 82, 84
psychogeology, 55–56
Psychology and Alchemy (Jung), 58

quantum physics, 21

radical formalism, 98
railroads, 18, 37
rare earth minerals, 19
Rasula, Jed, 5, 10
rationalism, 134
Rauschenberg, Robert, 127
Reagan, Ronald, 48
realism, speculative, 118
real of the desert, 51–55
recessive ethics, 15
Red D Gypsum (Prynne), 170n11
Reed, Ishmael, 167n5
Reeve, N. H., 72, 81
reflections, 146
reflexive symmetry, 149–50
relative point, 72
remote futures and pasts, 29–32
Renaissance, 22
Reynolds, Ann, 147
ridges, 69–86
Riley, Denise, 13, 14, 153, 154
Riley, Peter, 69
Rivera Garza, Cristina, 172n4
Roberts, Jennifer, 34–36, 38, 133–34
Roberts, Luke, 170n17
Rodefer, Stephen, 99
Roden Crater, 123
Roebuck, Thomas, 72, 80
Roget's Thesaurus, 28
Roth, Moira, 165n16
Royal Society, 68
Royal Ulster Constabulary (RUC), 93–94
Rozel Point, 35, 36
RUC. *See* Royal Ulster Constabulary
Ruefle, Mary, 124

Ruskin, John, 32
Russell, Yvette, 140
Russian futurists, 27
Rutgers College, 121

salt crystals, 2, 34–35
Salton Basin, 129
sandbox, 30–31
Sand County Almanac (Leopold), 128
Saroyan, Aram, 101
Saussure, Ferdinand de, 43–44
Saussy, Haun, 163n4
Scargill, Arthur, 95
science, 17
The Secret Life of Salvador Dalí, 108–9
sedimentation, 30, 66, 82, 119, 120, 127
"A Sedimentation of the Mind" (Smithson), 21, 25, 103, 116–18
self-presence, 26
self-reflection, 153
self-writing, 154
Serres, Michel, 131
sewing, 4, 122–27, 129–30, 132, 134, 139–40
Shakespeare, William, 44, 75
shamanism, 78–79
Shaw, Lytle, 24, 163n6
Shelton, Richard, 121–23, 128
Shklovsky, Viktor, 16
Shumskii, P. A., 146
Sieburth, Richard, 24, 27–28
signification, 11, 164n7, 164n10
silence, 130
Skinner, Jonathan, 14
skull shapes, 77
Skystone Foundation, 123
Smithson, Robert, 1, 4, 7, 14, 18, 20, 68; "Addition," 29; American Museum of Natural History and, 22; "An Array of Matter," 29; "Closed Limits," 29; *The Collected Writings*, 115; "Contained Information," 29; "The Crystal Land," 145, 147; "Dialectic of Site and Nonsite," 24, 29; entropy and, 30, 81, 146; "Entropy and the New Monuments," 30; "The Fountain Monument," 30; *A Heap of Language*, 2, 27–29; "Inner Coordinates," 29; "A Museum of Language in the Vicinity of Art," 10, 27; Nonsites and, 23; The Second Law of Thermodynamics and, 30; "A Sedimentation of the Mind," 21, 25, 103, 116–18; "Spiral Jetty," 9, 24, 35, 146; "Strata," 114–15; "Tour of the Monuments of Passaic, New Jersey," 30
Smithsonian Depositions (Coolidge), 103, 104, 112
Smithsonian Museum of Natural History, 158–59
sociopolitical issues, 3–4
soft-structures, 109
solids, 26
sonic mutations, 93
Sonnet 60 (Shakespeare), 44
sound-image, 43
South Wales, 3, 54, 64
South Yorkshire Police, 96
space, 49, 51
Space (Coolidge), 99, 102–3
speculative realism, 118
speech: hate, 13; inner, 13, 153–54
Sperling, Matthew, 72, 80
Spiral Jetty (film), 2, 18, 20, 31, 32, 38, 145
"Spiral Jetty" (Smithson), 9, 24, 35, 146
spirals, 32–38
standing stones, 3, 54, 58–61
"Star Wars" missile defense system, 48
States of Emergency (O'Sullivan), 94–95
Stein, Gertrude, 135
strata, 20, 24; geochronology of, 82; word, 111–20

"Strata" (Smithson), 114–15
stratigraphy, 10; of language, 4
subsidence, 66
Surrealism, 152
A Symposium on Continental Drift, 68, 70

Tanguy, Yves, 109
Tatransky, Valentin, 21
Taylor, Michael R., 109
Teague, David, 131
temporal boundaries, 71
temporal layering, 34
"Terrain" (Torrance), 67
Tesla, Nikola, 153
textual artworks, 115–16
Thacher, Emma Treadwell, 106
Thacher, John Boyd, 106
Thacher Park, 105–6
Thatcher, Margaret, 4, 87, 94
Theory of Sediment (McCaffery), 111, 119
"Theory of Sediment" (McCaffery), 119
This Sex Which Is Not One (Irigaray), 134
Thoreau, Henry David, 128
A Thousand Plateaus (Deleuze and Guattari), 48
time: as anteriority, 118; cinematic, 34; crystalline structure of, 35; crystals and, 145; geologic, 10; human-imposed, 32
time-image, 33
topography, 126, 172n4
topology (*topos*), 40, 53, 54–58, 64
Torrance, Chris, 1, 39; "Arcospirical Meanderings in a Tongue of the Time," 64; *A Bibliography on America for Ed Dorn*, 57; "Black Mountain in England," 57; *The Book of Brychan*, 57, 61; *Citrinas*, 59–61; *The Diary of Palug's Cat*, 61; "Maen Madoc," 59; *The Magic Door*, 2–3, 11, 40, 54, 55–57, 59, 61–63; "Mirages," 61; "Terrain," 67; tropes and, 58–59

"Tour of the Monuments of Passaic, New Jersey" (Smithson), 30
transcendentalists, 131
Transcontinental Railroad, 37
transferences of force, 6
transparency, 150
"tree hugger" environmentalism, 52
trees, 53
Trinity Site detonation, 37
tropes, 58–59; linguistic, 53
Turquoise Trail, 51, 167n7
Turrell, James, 123, 124
Twinrocker Handmade Papers, 122
typology, 105

Uccello, Paolo, 110
Ugly Feelings (Ngai), 160, 164n10
United Kingdom, 40, 55
unknowing, 116
"Un-Visual and Conceptual" (Drucker), 126
Uroskie, Andrew, 33, 34, 38

Van Dyke, John C., 4, 124, 126–32; deserts as breathing spaces and, 122, 123, 125, 138–39; Shelton and, 121–22
Vicuña, Cecilia, 89
Vietnam War, 42
violence, 88, 90, 94; latent, 89; police, 18
Virgil, 131
visual poetics, 27

Walden (Thoreau), 128
Wall, Jeff, 133, 141
"The Wanderer," 81
Wasatch Front, 161
water: Colorado River, 129–30, 138, 141; frozen, 147; Passaic River, 9; reclamation, 18, 137–38
weather, 65

Wegener, Alfred, 57, 68–69, 84
Westerns, genre, 47
"West of Moab" (Dorn), 54
White, Kenneth, 16
"White Geology" (Yusoff), 165n15
Whitehead, Alfred North, 19
The White Stones (Prynne), 65, 85
Wild, Peter, 131
Williams, William Carlos, 9–10, 40, 55
Wilson, Harold, 85
Wilson, Rachel M., 101
women, 61, 62, 134
words: earthwords, 170n2; material qualities of, 18; "pre-semantic" qualities of, 114; "proto" qualities of, 114

word strata, 111–20
"The Wound, Day and Night" (Prynne), 82, 84
writerly text, 119

Yellow Back Radio Broke-Down (Reed), 167n5
Yusoff, Kathryn, 17–18, 23, 27, 36–37, 159, 165nn14–15

0 to 9 (journal), 10
Zukofksy, Louis, 8–10

www.ingramcontent.com/pod-product-compliance
Lightning Source LLC
Chambersburg PA
CBHW020934230426
43666CB00008B/1677